TEACHING FRENCH CIVILISATION

IN BRITAIN, THE UNITED STATES AND AUSTRALIA

*Proceedings of the Anglo-American Seminar
held at Portsmouth Polytechnic,
18th–20th September 1987*

edited by Eric Cahm

**ASSOCIATION FOR THE STUDY OF
MODERN AND CONTEMPORARY FRANCE**

First published in Great Britain in 1988 by
Association for the Study of Modern and Contemporary France
London

Printed in Great Britain by the Trent Print Unit
University of Nottingham

ISBN 0 947791 02 7

CONTENTS

Introduction
6

INTRODUCTION

The Anglo-American seminar on which the present publication is based, and which was held at Portsmouth Polytechnic in September 1987, arose out of a suggestion made to me by Professor Nicholas Wahl, of the Institute of French Studies, New York University. In view of the growing student demand for and the growing provision of courses on French Civilisation in American universities, it seemed to Professor Wahl that it would be useful to arrange an Anglo-American meeting of academics practising in this field, so that experience in teaching the subject on both sides of the Atlantic could be compared, particularly in the light of the well-established, varied and extensive British provision in universities, polytechnics and colleges. At the same point in time and quite independently, surveys of French Civilisation teaching in universities had been initiated in Britain by Geoffrey Hare and John Roach, and in Australia by Karis Muller, while Joe Coutts had been involved in two research projects on the year abroad.

The seminar therefore had the great good fortune to be at the point of junction of several convergent research initiatives, and it acquired not only an Anglo-American but even a Pacific dimension, as Theda Shapiro from Riverside California, exchanged notes in Portsmouth with her "neighbour" Karis Muller from Canberra.

Portsmouth was selected as the venue, and participation was by invitation. The seminar eventually brought together 35 academics, of whom nine were from the US, one from Australia, and the rest from various British institutions. The US delegation was the largest that could be brought to Portsmouth, and included some of the most distinguished US teachers of French Civilisation: their doyen Laurence Wylie (Harvard), Jean Carduner (Michigan), Edward Knox (Middlebury), and Nicholas Wahl himself. The British contingent was made up of as strong a group as could be constituted, so as to be at once properly representative of the broad range of institutions involved, from the older universities to the newest polytechnics and colleges, and also capable severally of covering the various topics selected for the papers.   For a full list of the participants, *see* below.

Each participant was asked to provide in advance current French Civilisation syllabuses from his or her own institution, relevant booklists and a list of staff concerned with French Civilisation.   The syllabus information has been reproduced here as fully as possible: it should be noted that it refers to the session 1986-1987.

The venture received from the outset most generous support from the Association for the Study of Modern and Contemporary France, from its secretary Brian Darling, and, through the Association, from Gilles Chouraqui, of the French cultural service in London, which was represented at the seminar by Jean-Michel Mullon.   The School of Languages and Area Studies at Portsmouth Polytechnic, and in particular its Head, Bob French, also provided material and moral support.   Without the assistance received from these quarters, the seminar would not have been possible, and our warmest thanks are due to them.

Participants spent a congenial week-end at Rees Hall in Portsmouth, overlooking Southsea Common and the Solent, and it is a pleasure to thank the staff at Rees Hall for providing a comfortable and nourishing context for discussion, also Celia Clark, a local history expert, who guided the participants round Old Portsmouth and reminded them of Portsmouth's many (warlike) French connections.

From the outset, Joy Harwood has provided, as secretary to the seminar, and later as word-processor operator for the book-text, invaluable support and help and this has extended to help in editing the text.

The seminar finally owed its academic success to Nicholas Wahl's idea of a trans-Atlantic meeting of minds, to the liveliness and thoroughness of the papers given, to the research findings generously made available thereby, and to the wide-ranging discussions on the papers.   I hope readers of the book will be as grateful as I am to participants from both sides of the Atlantic, and to a former Portsmouth colleague, Karis Muller, who came all the way from Australia to join us, for the hard work they put in both before and after the seminar.   It has resulted in a fascinating overview in the pages below of the growing educational field of French Civilisation teaching in three countries.   As organiser of the seminar, I owe all who took part a personal word of thanks for the seriousness with which they approached their task.   The book now contains the author's definitive version of each of the papers given at Portsmouth.   Most of the discussions, which were very full and enjoyable, were also recorded - with, alas ! some omissions - and, after being ably transcribed by Liz Entwistle, have been shortened and re-structured, so as to offer the reader, with the papers and syllabus material, as coherent a picture as possible of what was said at Portsmouth, or in my case what I would have like to have said, if I had been less pre-occupied with running the seminar itself !   Having now had the opportunity to study the papers and discussions in their final form, I have taken the liberty of writing a brief historical introduction to the section on the British experience, and of fleshing out the somewhat breathless conclusions I was prevailed upon to draw at the end of the week-end.

It was my hope initially that the proceedings of the seminar would be available very quickly for the benefit of those who were not present at Portsmouth.   I hope they and others will accept my apologies for the fact that pressure of work made it impossible to produce them before now.

Eric Cahm

Tours, July 1988

LIST OF PARTICIPANTS

Mr Laurence Bell
University of Surrey

Professor Eric Cahm
Université de Tours

Dr Tony Callen
Portsmouth Polytechnic

Professor Jean Carduner
University of Michigan

Dr Martyn Cornick
University of Loughborough

Mr Joe Coutts
Buckinghamshire College of Higher
  Education

Mr Brian Darling
North East London Polytechnic

Dr Claire Duchen
Oxford Polytechnic

Dr Peter Findlay
Portsmouth Polytechnic

Dr Jill Forbes
Polytechnic of the South Bank

Mr Bob French
Portsmouth Polytechnic

Dr Linda Hantrais
University of Aston

Mr Tony Harding
Oxford Polytechnic

Dr Geoffrey Hare
University of Newcastle-upon-Tyne

Mr John Harris
Cambridgeshire College of Arts
  and Technology

Professor Micheline Herz
Douglass College
Rutgers University

Dr Nicholas Hewitt
University of Warwick

Professor Jolyon Howorth
University of Bath

Dr Brian Jenkins
Portsmouth Polytechnic

Professor Alice Kaplan
Duke University

Professor Michael Kelly
University of Southampton

Professor Edward Knox
Middlebury College

Dr Karis Muller
The Australian National
  University

M Jean-Michel Mullon,
Ambassade de France, London

Professor Christopher Pinet
Montana State University

Dr Siân Reynolds
University of Sussex

Dr Adrian Rifkin
Portsmouth Polytechnic

Dr John Roach
University of Aberdeen

Mr Vaughan Rogers
University of Edinburgh

Professor Theda Shapiro
University of California,
  Riverside

Professor Homer Sutton,
Davidson College, North Carolina

Professor Nicholas Wahl
New York University

Dr Neville Waites
University of Reading

Mr Stuart Williams
Wolverhampton Polytechnic

Professor Laurence Wylie
University of Harvard

9

THE AMERICAN EXPERIENCE

HOW WE STARTED TO TEACH THE *COURS DE CIVILISATION* IN THE UNITED STATES
by Laurence Wylie, Harvard University

In the Fall of 1918 when it became obvious that the Germans would soon be forced to surrender, the French and American authorities became more and more concerned about a social problem - possibly an international crisis - that might face them. It had taken 19 months to transport the more than two million young Americans to France, and it would take at least that long to return them all home. These boisterous Americans, whom the French found to be just *grands enfants*, relieved of the anxiety of combat, would be left with nothing to do. Frustrated in their longing to return home at once, they were capable of massive and serious childish mischief. They would no longer be satisfied with singing, as they did as they marched up to the front, of a Mademoiselle d'Armentières who might be willing to "to wash a soldier's underwear". To avoid serious damage, creative diversions had to be invented!

No doubt there were many discussions between the French government and the American military leaders to seek solutions. Historians have apparently been uninterested in this problem, or at least I have found no reference to any account except one. Charles Guignebert, a young professor of History who was to become over the years one of the favourite teachers of foreign students in the Sorbonne's *Cours de Civilisation*, wrote in 1929 a brief article in which he described a discussion he had attended ten years before:

> *En ce temps-là - c'était, si je ne me trompe, un soir de décembre 1918 - mon collègue et ami Legouis, qui se trouvait, par ses fonctions mêmes, l'intermédiaire naturel entre les Professeurs américains mobilisés et l'Université de Paris, me demanda d'assister à une petite assemblée qui allait se tenir à la Salle des Actes de la Faculté des Lettres. Nous nous trouvâmes une douzaine autour de la table et M. Legouis nous tint à peu près ce langage: "Jusqu'à la paix, qui sera peut-être longue à débattre, le gros de l'armée américaine va rester en France. Son état-major militaire et aussi son état-major universitaire ont pensé que cette obligation leur offrait une occasion*

unique d'initier aux choses de France un grand nombre de jeunes gens
qui, sans elle, n'auraient jamais connu l'Ancien Continent que par oui-
dire.   Ils nous préparent une belle équipe de ces braves garçons,
choisie bien entendu, parmi ceux qui ont du français une connaissance
suffisante pour suivre nos enseignements: qu'est-ce que nous allons
faire pour eux ? "   La discussion qui suivit, dans l'enthousiasme,
s'inspira du désir de présenter à nos futurs auditeurs les divers
aspects de la vie française dans le passé et dans le présent, dans le
passé pour faire comprendre le présent.   Et il en sortit un plan
d'études qui, amputé d'un prolongement scientifique reconnu à
l'empirisme médiocrement utile, est, à peu près celui que nous
appliquons encore aujourd'hui.

Je ne pensais pas avoir à me mêler de son exécution; mais, sur
cette considération que nos collègues américains souhaitaient que le
professeur d'Histoire générale eût enseigné dans un lycée, qu'il fût
habitué à manier les jeunes gens et eût la réputation de parler son
cours, les membres de la section d'histoire me firent l'honneur de
croire que je répondais aux conditions requises et ils me désignèrent.
Je ne leur en eus, sur le moment, qu'une gratitude sans élan: je
m'étais enquis de mes obligations et je les trouvais fort lourdes.   Je
devais, m'assurait-on, exposer à ces guerriers toute l'histoire de
France en trente leçons.   Après une soirée passée à réfléchir, à
combiner, à ébaucher divers projets, je me décidai à essayer et
aujourd'hui je me félicite grandement de n'avoir pas cédé à mon premier
effroi.

There had been discussion as early as 1904 of establishing special courses
for foreigners at the Université de Paris, but the proposal had always been
rejected because it was assumed that foreign students would not be able to
survive in the French university atmosphere: *L'étranger, dans ces cours de*
Faculté, qui ne présentent que des aspects fragmentaires de notre évolution
historique, alors qu'il ignore les faits les plus élémentaires et les noms
les plus indispensables, est perdu dès l'abord. (Henri Goy, Directeur des
Cours de Civilisation, ibid, p.7).   Now the urgency of the situation
overcame such scepticism.   Bureaucratic red tape was pushed aside.   On the
first of January 1919, it was announced to the Université de Paris that it
was soon to receive a thousand or so American students, *officiers et*
soldats en congé temporaire, détachés du front pendant que dure l'occupation
américaine après l'armistice (*ibid*).   At the same time, orders were issued
from the American General Headquarters to various Army units in France,
instructing the commanders to select promising American college men for a
four months' sojourn in French universities.   Guignebert reports: *Je fis*
donc ma première leçon le 6 mars 1919, devant 84 officiers et soldats, dont
les uniformes kakis remplissaient l'hémisphère de l'amphithéâtre Richelieu.
Leur nombre s'accrut quelque peu dans les jours qui suivirent. (*op.cit.* p.11).
So far as I have been able to learn, this was the beginning of the first
cours de civilisation.

Of course, it was not just the Université de Paris which was involved. Without understanding the implications I see now, I learned this fact years ago from a colleague at Haverford College who had been in the American Army in France in 1918. He said he had been chosen by his officer to study in a French university and had been assigned to the Université de Cannes. He took the train down to the Côte d'Azur only to learn that there was no Université de Cannes. A city official kindly made inquiry for him and learned that his assignment was to the Université de Caen ! We may hope that he eventualyly learned the difference in pronunciation between Caen and Cannes, but for us French teachers it is reassuring to note that he became not a teacher of French but of Classics.

Apparently, American soldiers were assigned to all French universities, and the success of these courses had an impressive influence on French studies in the United States. One young man, Raymond Kirkbride, was assigned to the Université de Grenoble, which was to become the favourite French university for Americans during the next twenty years. He returned to the United States determined to share his wonderful experience with many American students. He persuaded the University of Delaware to start a Junior Year in France Group which, with financial aid from the Du Pont family, recruited students from many American universities to spend a year studying in France, the summer in Nancy and the following winter in Paris. These Delaware Groups, with their 100-odd students (four-fifths of them women) were continued until the outbreak of the Second World War. (Indeed, the reason I found the obscure periodical, *Foreign Study Notes*, was that it was published by the Delaware Foreign Study Group of which I was a member in 1929-30, and I happen to have saved these old copies!).

The students were joined in the *cours de civilisation* by students from many countries as well as by students from other American groups, for more and more colleges, especially women's colleges, adopted the idea of sending groups of students to France. After World War Two Sweet Briar College took over the erstwhile Delaware Group. When I was serving as Cultural Counsellor at the American Embassy in 1967, there were 65 of these foreign study groups. Eventually, American colleges accepted the idea of granting individual students a year's leave of absence to study in a foreign country. It is safe to assume that thousands of young Americans eventually had the experience of studying in the *cours de civilisation* of French universities. Some of the students became French teachers and undoubtedly tried to adapt the *cours* to their own particular teaching situation.

However, the experience of the *cours de civilisation* had little immediate effect on American Departments of French. After all, American university departments, like university departments everywhere, did not offer courses concentrating on a single modern culture. If a student wanted to learn about France, he studied French history in the History Department, French Government in the Political Science Department, Art in the Art Department, etc. The French Department was devoted uniquely to the study of language and literature. Each French professor was a specialist in the literature of a century or a *genre*. Only the underlings were relegated to the teachingh of language and composition. They could aspire to teaching a literature course only when they got their doctorate and had served their apprenticeship.

Traditionally, very few men studied French. It was a woman's subject. Men studied Latin to prepare themselves for Medicine or Law or the Ministry, or German to prepare them for research in Science. Spanish, which was supposed to be easy, was for college athletes. French was for women and aesthetes. Over the course of centuries, the French had persuaded the rest of the world that they had a monopoly on Culture. The unappreciated sociologist, Thorstein Veblen (*The Theory of the Leisure Class*, New York, MacMillan, 1899), pointed out in 1899 that in the capitalist system the function of men was to acquire a fortune, and the function of their wives was, besides having babies, to become cultivated and acquire works of art in order to demonstrate their husband's success in amassing a fortune. So a woman seeking culture had to learn French and French Art. Consequently women's colleges had big French departments, men's colleges modest ones.

World War I changed this stereotype. Two million American men experienced contact with French people. Some of them hated it, of course, but some of them loved the experience. When the college men returned home they often wanted to study French and learn more about France to understand their experience. Some even married French women and wanted to understand their predicament! Men invaded French Departments. In the mid-1920s, the enrolment in Romance Languages at Harvard College was third in size in the curriculum, surpassed only by English and Economics. Today it is about 30th ! In our Library, the section on French literature has been moved from the main floor down to the darkest basement.

Another curious factor came into play during World War One. Most colleges introduced a programme of ROTC (Reserve Officers Training Corps) to prepare their men for military service. Military personnel invaded the

13

campuses to teach, but they had little experience in actual warfare. Harvard, and perhaps other universities I do not know about, invited the French Government to detach wounded officers of the French Army, in good shape but not fit for service, and send them to teach Trench Warfare to American ROTC students. Among those sent to Harvard were two young *agrégés*, who were billeted together at the Harvard Club, Jean Giraudoux and André Morize, who became lifelong friends. (This explains why Giraudoux, when he became French Minister of Information in World War Two, appointed Morize as his Director). After the Armistice, when Morize was preparing to return home, President Lowell invited him to his office and asked him to remain to become a fully-fledged member of the French Department. Morize had always wanted to teach in the United States. In fact, he had come over to teach at the Johns Hopkins University just before the war began and had had to return home because of his military obligations. Now *"le beau André"*, as the students called him, was to settle in Cambridge and remain there, except for the World War Two years in France, until his retirement in 1951. Known as "the other French Ambassador", he was extremely popular as a public speaker throughout the country.

In 1925, a small but highly respected college in Vermont, Middlebury College, asked him to reorganise its summer school which it had established in 1915 to offer foreign language training. Without leaving his post at Harvard, Morize accepted the summer position. He took with him his favourite graduate student, Stephen Freeman, who remained to become Chairman of the Foreign Language Department for the rest of his professional career. It was assumed that students enrolling in the summer school had already studied French, and they were forbidden to speak English while they were in residence. In those days, when going to France meant a long ocean trip, language teachers who needed experience in a French atmosphere considered that a summer in Middlebury was the next best experience. Perhaps it was even better since the emphasis was on learning rather than on adventure ! Morize recruited professors from France to teach the courses, and their teaching was strongly slanted toward the holistic approach embodied in the new *cours de civilisation*. Soon the school included other languages and cultures in its curriculum, and Middlebury became and still is an essential language centre in the United States.

In the winter at Harvard, Morize taught only courses in Literature, heading a team that developed the basic course called *General View of French*

Literature. More and more, he came to the conclusion that American students could never fully appreciate French literature unless they learned something about the history and present state of the society that produced it. A younger colleague, Louis Mercier, taught a course called *Social Background of French Literature*, the nature of which I have been unable to learn, but apparently Morize found it insufficient, although it was popular with the students. With a teaching Assistant and imbued with the principles underlying the Sorbonne's *Cours de Civilisation*, he began to offer a new course called *Introduction to France: A Survey of French History and Civilisation*. With Morize's load of charisma this course was bound to be a success. In 1938, Howard Rice and he turned it into a book, *Introduction to France: An Outline for Study and Reference*, published by MacMillan and adopted by many colleges. Its best feature consisted of an extensive and well-chosen bibliography and lists of "key words" essential to any understanding of French life. It also contained significant passages from books to be analysed with the characteristic French method of *explication de texte*. This book became a model for civilisation courses in many colleges.

The emphasis I place on Harvard in this statement reflects, of course, my proximity to the Harvard Archives. There were other universities who were even more open to the new ideas implicit in the *cours de civilisation*. Columbia University had long had more than scholarly relations with France. Early in the century, a beautiful house on the rue de Chevreuse, Reid Hall, had been bequeathed to Columbia so that young women from Columbia-Barnard might study in Paris and yet live in this virtuous and well-protected atmosphere. This property has ever since served as a focus for American foreign study groups, special courses and lectures on France and French-American relations. Also at Columbia, The Teachers College inaugurated a project to send graduate students to study at the Ecole de Préparation de professeurs de français à l'étranger. Many other such projects could be mentioned. Most of the students involved in such projects came home to teach French and often started a *cours de civilisation* in the colleges where they taught.

When I speak of "many" colleges teaching a *cours de civilisation*, I may give an exaggerated impression. As I have said, French departments concentrated on teaching Language and Literature, and they were completely dominated by professors of Literature who were more and more defensively adamant that the Social Sciences must not take over their domain. *Cours de civilisation*

15

were dismissed as the speciality of deviant professors who were not convinced that Gustave Lanson had written the ultimate judgement of French literature. It was true that the Social Sciences had made tremendous advances and were assuming preponderance in curricula. Younger scholars were becoming convinced that the new findings of the Social sciences might help them in their vocation to teach students to understand themselves, their relationship to their own cultures, and the conflicts that arise among people of different cultures. The problems that the French people had had with American soldiers, who in turn were confused by French behaviour, seemed more important to understand than, say, la bataille d'Hernani. Why did the French find that so important, anyway ?!

The growing relevance of the Social Sciences in the 1930s was strengthened by two basic developments: the acceptance of psychoanalysis and the birth of cultural anthropology. Anthropology had been dominated until then by archaeology and physical anthropology – or stones and bones, as the students said. The nearest anthropologists came to studying actual human behaviour was in the dubious area of racial differences. The younger generation of anthropologists became interested in psychoanalysis and the light it might shed on the differences in cultures and in human bewhaviour. Emphasis came to be placed more on childhood and family relationships. The Polish-British anthropologist Malinowski made extremely influential cultural studies of peoples in the south-east Pacific. Margaret Mead studied the relationship of child-bearing, adolescence and family life to cultural patterns in New Guinea and Samoa. Ruth Benedict used psychoanalytic concepts to study the basic differences in the psychology of different American Indian tribes. The trend was intensified by the migration of refugee European scholars to the United States, many of them heavily involved in psychoanalysis and interested in cultural differences because of their sudden immersion in American culture.

These differences were naturally of great relevance at that point in history. The Nazis claimed their natural racial superiority and proclaimed the necessity of destroying the semitic "race", which they said was polluting civilisation. Then, as war approached and allied countries were trying to draw together to annihilate a common enemy, these cultural differences became a practical problem of the utmost importance. It was essential for allies to overcome their cultural differences in order to co-operate, and it was equally essential to understand the mentality of the enemies in order to do them in more effectively. There had been plenty of

propaganda and psychological warfare in World War One, and now the new
Social Sciences with their more subtle, it seemed then, psychoanalytical
undertones came into their own. The armed forces tried to find ways of
preparing soldiers to face the inevitable culture shock from contact with
foreign cultures. But what were the basic cultural differences which they
should be prepared to face ? The United States government offered huge
sums ("huge", at least, in the eyes of academic people) for social
scientists to mobilise to seek answers to such questions.

The Navy gave Columbia University funds for Ruth Benedict to organise a
project that was known as the Columbia Research in Contemporary Cultures.
Scores of social scientists and psychoanalysts were enlisted to organise
teams to study the cultures with which the United States forces would have
serious contact   -   Russia, Poland, Germany, Italy, France, Great Britain,
Japan and others. Even literary experts were hired to analyse the themes
of foreign literature and movies. Foreigners in New York were interviewed
intensively and given projective tests. Cora Du Bois had shown in her
studies of the people of Alor, for instance, that the Rorschach tests could
reveal a great deal about the psychology not only of individuals but of
whole cultures. Other anthropologists used the Thematic Apperception Test,
the Draw-a-Man Test etc. The psychiatrist Kardiner and the anthropologist
Linton used whole batteries of tests and statistical information to draw up
the "Model Personality Profile" of different cultures. At Harvard , Florence
Kluckhohn and her staff of young anthropologists were identifying different
cultures through a set of "Basic Value Orientations". I know about these
trends because it was at this time that I began to study anthropology, and
before I made my village study in the Vaucluse, I spent a year studying
projective techniques and a summer at the Klopfer Summer Rorschach School.

In the Columbia University project, two sets of investigating committees
were organised: one group of teams was to concentrate on specific cultures,
the other was to compare "themes" cross-culturally. Themes were denoted as
"the family", "child-rearing", "the stranger", "friendship", etc. The point of
departure was a set of hypotheses, generalisations about each theme or
culture, to be tested and evaluated by the study groups. The chairmen of
the group studying French culture were the the American anthropologist
Rhoda Métraux and the British anthropologist Geoffrey Gorer. Gorer had
started out as a French teacher but had switched to anthropology and made
a study of a village in the Himalayas before coming to the United States.
It was Gorer who formulated the forty hypotheses concerning French culture.

The protopsychoanalytic flavour of the hypotheses can be tasted by the first one, which, if I recall correctly, was something like this: "The French child considers his excrement a love-offering to his mother". French teachers enlisted, to seek themes in French literature were shocked. Analysts were critical: "That's not just French. It's true of all cultures !" When the hypotheses were presented, the teams endeavoured to test them through analysis of all evidence available to them in the libraries and personal experience of people they could find in New York. Later, Margaret Mead and Rhoda Métraux explained the system in a book entitled *The Study of Culture at a Distance* (Chicago, Chicago University Press, 1953). Eventually, they published *Themes in French Culture*, amplified and corrected by the teams' discussion and research (Stanford, Stanford University, 1954). In the French translation, which was later published, the title was corrected with quotation marks around the word "culture": *Thèmes de la "culture" française*.

Most of the tremendous quantity of material gathered by this project has never been published and is stored in the Library of Congress. The research inspired the publication of many articles and books – most of it appearing after the war when the original motivation had passed. There was a famous, often quoted and misquoted, article by Geoffrey Gorer on the effect of swaddling on Russian character, (*see* Gorer and Rickman, *People of Great Russia*, London, Cresset, 1949). To mention a few other books that emerged from this project: Margaret Mead,, *And Keep Your Powder Dry: An Author Looks at America* (New York, Morrow, 1942). Ralph Linton's *The Cultural Basis of Personality* was published by Appleton-Century in 1945. Ruth Benedict's book on Japan, *The Chrysanthemum and the Sword*, was published by Houghton-Mifflin in 1946. Gorer's book on the Americans, *The American People: A Study of Americans* (New York, Norton, 1948). These are examples. To provide an extensive bibliography here would be superfluous.

What effect did all this activity have on the teaching of *cours de civilisation* ? It certainly had an influence on many of us younger professors who were essentially interested in understanding and teaching about cultural differences, although I myself knew too little about psychoanalysis to try to utilise its terms and concepts consciously. My emphasis on child-training, education and the family in what I have written and taught certainly derives from that source. But no one, certainly not psychoanalysts nor anthropologists, would make the claims today that many people, especially the more amateurish social scientists, were making in the

1940s and 1950s. The area of cultural anthropology is no longer of interest. Lévi-Strauss and the French structuralists, Evans-Pritchard and the British social anthropologists have taken the place of students of *personality and culture*, which once seemed to be a coming field.

The failure of cultural anthropological studies of the 1940s and 1950s does not mean, however, that the traditional *cours de civilisation* has prevailed, with heavy emphasis on history, art and philosophy. In fact, the word *civilisation* has little meaning to Americans except as it reminds us of what our old history books called its "cradle", between the Tigris and the Euphrates – and that area bears quite different implications today. In fact, *Culture* with a capital *C*, meaning, as Matthew Arnold wrote a century ago, "the acquainting ourselves with the best that has been known and said in the world", provokes yawns amongst most students, who *can* become interested in lower-case *c culture* meaning "the total way of life of a people". All through the above I have persisted in using the French *cours de civilisation* because a *civilisation course* has no meaning except in a French context or in referring to old Near Eastern cultures. I did call my own course *French Civilisation*, but then I used most of my first lecture time to explain that I really meant *An Anthropological approach to the Study of Culture in France*, that is, "the total way of life of the French people".

One of the most successful new educational institutions in the United States is the Institute of French Studies, at New York University, created through the efforts of Professor Thomas Bishop and the direction of the Political Science professor Nicholas Wahl. It answers the needs which gave rise to the *cours de civilisation* but in American terms and with American structure. It is interdisciplinary, with emphasis on the Social Sciences. It resembles other institutes, common in our universities, devoted to specific cultures or groups of cultures – Russian, Scandinavian, African, Near Eastern., Japanese, etc.. It is not overwhelmed by the defensive *littérateurs*.

But even traditional French Departments, or at least the heirs of the traditionalists, are forced to come out of their Ivory Tower of aesthetics to exist, especially since French literature has become too esoteric for popular consumption. French Departments nowadays often give lip service to the possibility of a Civilisation concentration. They emphasise learning French for commercial purposes. They "modernise" learning with audiovisual and computer equipment. They offer courses on Francophone cultures. They provide "French Oral Survival" courses for students to revive their earlier French learning in preparation for a trip to France. They even give courses on French literature in translation. They may even give a *cours de civilisation*.

TEACHING FRENCH CIVILISATION IN THE AMERICAN CULTURAL CONTEXT
by Homer Sutton, Davidson College, North Carolina

How does one begin to address such an imposing topic? My first impulse is
to use Jim and Tammy Bakker, Fawn Hall, or Vanna White to illustrate, in a
Bakhtinian fashion, the carnival aspect of American culture. Yet it would
be difficult to relate the topic of French civilisation to these wholly
domestic phenomena. Instead, I would like to share with you a few brief
thoughts on some recent legislative developments related to the study of
foreign cultures and languages in the US, and also on the current situation
of French civilisation in our small colleges.

One legislative development of the past few months is disturbing for those
who teach foreign language, literature, and civilisation in the US. As you
may know, about nine state governments have recently passed legislation
making English the "official language" in those states, thereby catering to
a certain xenophobic provincialism found in the electorate of those states.
A possible influence of this legislation will be to relegate foreign
languages and literature to "alien" status, thereby telling our students that
to speak French or German is somehow a vice, an "anti-American" action that
should be repressed. This legislation could harm our efforts in
international education.

At the same time, there is a realisation in Washington that the teaching of
foreign languages and cultures is vital for the competitivity of the US in
the world economy, and there will probably be additional funds available
for foreign language programmes; the American Council of Education has
been surveying selected colleges and universities to lay the framework for
a national endowment for Foreign Languages and Area Studies. There were
protests in the beginning of the study when major academic organisations
were not consulted, but one can hope that they will be intimately involved
in the planning and implementation of such an endowment. Early indications
are that such an endowment would centralise the granting of funds available
for international area studies, and that departments of Social Science may
profit more than departments of Language. It may be true as well that the

traditional languages (French, German and Spanish) may not benefit as much as the more exotic, more geopolitically "important" languages such as Russian or Arabic. It is too early to make definitive statements on the eventual impact that these two legislative actions could have on our educational efforts.

The teaching of French social and cultural issues is a recent pedagogical development in the US. Many departments of French still operate under the model inherited from the past, where students took enough grammar until they could be admitted into literary studies. Many students today would prefer courses in French on French politics, history, economics and social studies, and the requests of these students have often been the reason why departments have established courses in those areas, as a means of retaining majors in French. In general, however, literary history and analysis seem to remain the primary pedagogical objectives of most departments, which should not surprise us, given the training found in most graduate departments of French.

In most small colleges, it is rare to find more than one course in French Social and Cultural studies; faculty are burdened by the heavy number of language courses that they must teach in order that students fulfil the language requirements, and there are generally no graduate assistants to teach these courses. Moreover, even the "specialist" in cultural studies will be asked to teach literature courses (in addition to those in language), as the major requirements generally require a heavy dose of literary studies.

When one speaks of the American cultural context and the teaching of French Civilisation, one should not forget our continental insularity. In a study several years ago by the OECD, the US had the distinction of having the smallest percentage of articles devoted to international affairs in a sample of major newspapers of all OECD member states. Our commercial television networks do a dismal job in the coverage of overseas developments, and their recent budget cuts (particularly at CBS) do not bode well for improvements. Also, some students entering our universities are unprepared to undertake Social Studies even in English; a recent study by the National Endowment for the Humanities showed that 68% of 8,000 17-year-old students could not place the American Civil War in the correct half century and nearly one third placed the date of Columbus' first landing after 1750. Finally, outside Manhattan, Chicago, Boston, Los Angeles, San Francisco and Washington, the French "presence" is invisible. In Charlotte, NC, with a population of 300,000, possibilities for daily contact with France are virtually non-existent. How do we afford a "window" onto France in such conditions?

Recent developments in video technology (satellite, cable, tri-standard TV and VCR) have permitted us to inundate the students with documentaries and films, yet also lead to the problems related to choice of material and pedagogical application. We use French exchange students, visiting professors and guest lecturers to quench our thirst for updates on recent events; a new wave of French introspection allows us to *déguster la France* through statistics (Mermet, *Francoscopie*), through comparative analysis (*La France paresseuse*), or through study of social anachronism in French society (de Closets).

France remains distant for our students, particularly given the decline of the dollar. Our major tool in educating students to the reality that is France will most likely remain the Junior Year Abroad. Of course, only a small percentage of all students are able to participate, but the experience is required of majors at many colleges. Moreover, long-standing problems in the *premier cycle* in the French university system, if not soon remedied, may force us to reconsider the ultimate educational value of the JYA

France remains for us less accessible, more enigmatic than for you British. You tangle with the French in Brussels concerning *les montants compensatoires* and cooperate on the "Chunnel", although given the disagreements between France and the UK in the EEC, you may not be as close to continental Europe as we Americans think !

In conclusion, the cultural context of America as regards the teaching of French Civilisation is quite different from yours; our population is insular, provincial and dismally ignorant concerning European affairs. Most of our French departments do not (yet) accept the social and cultural dimensions of modern France as of prime importance in our pedagogical programme, and the inter-disciplinary approach is not as developed as it seems to be in British institutions, particularly the polytechnics and the "new" universities. In spite of all these factors, I have confidence that French Social and Cultural studies will increase in importance as our universities move away from structures inherited from the past and develop more inter-disciplinary programmes, where Social and Cultural studies *in the languages of the region concerned* will be the common model.

DISCUSSION OF HOMER SUTTON PAPER

Linda Hantrais asked to what extent American students actually chose the courses they took, as the evidence in Britain was certainly that students were making a choice, thinking about the courses available and opting for those which they saw as being relevant. She recognised that in the American context students were paying for their studies in a way that was visible to them. In the British context, fees were always paid by the local authority. Quite a high proportion of British students received a full grant, so they were not aware how much it cost, whereas in the American context they certainly were, which meant that the teachers had to be a lot more accountable.

Christopher Pinet replied that in small private colleges the accountability question was not as large as it was in public institutions. He thought that in these the accountability question was imposed by the State legislators, and they tended to look very strongly at what professors were doing. He also thought a major crisis of social class was very close in the US because of what it cost – to go to Yale cost $18,000. It cost almost more than what he would earn in a year to go to an Ivy League school, since he taught at a land grant State institution. The gap was widening like the gap between rich and poor: this had been fairly clearly documented. He thought that the question of accountability was important to the private schools and was becoming more so, but equally important were its consequences for what education consisted of; and referring to a remark by Brian Darling, added that we were seeing several cultures developing, which was to do with the incredibly increasing costs in schools.

As to choice, he thought that in the private situation students came in and were required to take a certain number of courses in different areas and did not really begin to specialise in their major specialisms until probably the beginning of their Junior Year. Therefore they had some choice within certain areas, but in a liberal arts college they were still required to take courses in certain areas.

Ed Knox went on on the same point to agree and said that it was perhaps not as clear as it might have been throughout the discussions that as regards American students reading French, basically the percentage of courses in French that they took in their four years at college would be a third, and certainly no more than a half. So the situation was rather different from the students being described by British colleagues. He then said he was getting a funny sense of the things that were pulling French Studies apart: the emergence of a high level of abstraction which would lead to a move away from national studies to either theoretical and abstract studies or inter-related international studies in a number of French Studies areas, and that some of the internal tensions the seminar had come together to talk about might be dwarfed by larger problems that had not been talked about.   In ten or twenty years' time, he thought we might not be studying French in similar numbers to now, and he doubted whether there was much that could be done to change this dramatically.

TEACHING FRENCH CIVILISATION IN SUNNY SOUTHERN CALIFORNIA

by Theda Shapiro, University of California, Riverside

What knowledge of France do American students bring to the college classroom ? Since Homer Sutton has ably described the current cultural context in the United States in relation to France, I would like to offer some personal observations about the cultural awareness of the current student population in America as I have seen it from the vantage point of the University of California at Riverside and while directing the University's study centre in Paris from 1982 to 1984.

Riverside is the smallest campus of the University of California, with currently about 4,500 undergraduates, including a sizeable population of Blacks, and of Hispanics and Asians from virtually every Pacific Rim country. The campus, located in an urban area of some 500,000 at the edge of the desert, some 60 miles east of Los Angeles, is now in a state of rapid growth after experiencing a difficult 15-year period of enrolment decline and stagnation. Our students are largely from the local area, which means that they are relatively poorer and less sophisticated than their peers in the larger cities near the Pacific coast. In Los Angeles, you can buy and eat all sorts of French products; in Riverside, anything French is usually mediocre or ersatz, and even French movies are almost never shown.

In 1972, when I joined the French programme at Riverside, enrolments were declining, and language enrolments were declining even faster due to a growing conviction on the part of American students and their parents that language studies were a waste of time and just not relevant to pursuing a successful career (inevitably defined, in America, by potential earning power). The number of French majors fell rapidly from a peak of about 50 to 20 or so. When asked by the programme chair, continuing students said they loved the French language and were very interested in France, but only mildly interested in literary studies. There was no easy solution, since the History Department did not - indeed, still does not - offer a survey of French history, preferring to deal more comparatively with the history of Western Europe. We proceeded to invent one of the first French civilisation majors in the country. Our "Civ track" includes a four-quarter survey course going all the way from Lascaux to to-day, a course on the history of Paris, and a senior seminar on a different topic each year, most of it taught by me.

An additional complication nowadays is that we still have few majors and we encourage those we have to spend a year at one of the seven University of California study centres in France, where they complete a considerable part of their course requirements. So we cannot rely on majors to fill the empty chairs; we must attract an additional public to these courses by giving them in English (advanced majors are expected to do their reading and papers in French). I am thus constantly contending with a new clientele, many of whom take one French civilisation course for enrichment and then move on. Typically, my students have been Caucasian and female; but now that the push is on to learn languages for international trade, they are becoming ethnically more diverse, though still in great majority female.

Now, what do these students know about France when they take their first course with me? The obvious, superficial answer is that they know almost nothing. Whether or not they plan to be majors, new Civilisation students typically cannot describe Charlemagne, St. Louis, Henri IV, absolutism, Versailles, the Bastille, Napoleon I or III, the Treaty of Versailles, Charles De Gaulle or François Mitterrand, and often do not even know these names.

At the same time, they bring many stereotypes about France. Americans tend to see France as a land of quaint peasants with moustaches, berets and *bleus*, glasses of *vin rouge* and crusty baguettes; as the country of gourmandise and glamour, art and aristocratic manners, elegance and romance; or as that vexatious ally who never does what the United States government wishes. These characteristics regularly appear in a survey-through-word-association I often conduct on the first day of a new class. Question: "What do you think of when you hear the word 'Paris'?" Answers: bread, croissants, cafés, red wine, Montmartre, paintings, *amour*, fashion, cuisine, the Arc de Triomphe, the Tour Eiffel. True, these stereotypes have served a useful purpose: the French language is still perceived as the language of the highly civilised, so enrolments in French classes have held up much better than those in German or Russian. But when it comes to cultural awareness, even those students - quite a few - who have already been to France, and those who firmly plan on a junior year abroad, have no substantial geographical or historical knowledge of France when taking their first Civilisation course. Indeed, as is finally being widely discussed in a national debate about the deficiencies of the American educational system, college freshmen in this country scarcely know *anything* about the history and geography of any country outside our borders, and know precious little about our own. Alarm bells are now continually ringing in reaction to the perceived ignorance of the young, their inability to express themselves orally or in writing, and the lack of shared cultural content in the education they receive from our locally-run, non-standardised school systems (1).

While it is clear that the decline in educational rigour and in parental co-operation in education has been drastic in this country during the last 20 years, Americans' deliberate insularity and ignorance about the world are of long standing. I am aware how little I knew as a high school student in a small Northeastern town in the late 1950s. Yet, in part because I and my friends were the offspring of European immigrants (Italian, Irish, Jewish, Polish), in part because we lived on ground where the French and Indian War and the American Revolutionary War were fought, in part also because plates of *knishes* and *conoli* were continually being carried from house to house, we did have a basic knowledge of European customs and an intuitive feel for (Caucasian) cultural diversity. In California in the 1980s, however, I am very conscious of being far from Europe (though not perceptibly nearer Asia for that). Paradoxically, I find myself in an environment of equal (perhaps greater) ethnic diversity to that of London, where students live in one culture (and often language) at home, another at school, and yet somehow the fact of cultural difference has not registered on them — they do not readily go from their daily reality to insights into yet another (French) culture. It is as if the famous American "melting pot" leaves various immigrant cultures intact on one level while removing consciousness of them on another.

Perhaps one cause is the "laid-back" California lifestyle, where acceptance and assimilation are easy, questioning difficult. Perhaps the contrasts among Black, Hispanic, Asian and Caucasian cultures are so extreme here as to be unbridgeable, and people therefore assimilate as they must, but do not actually communicate as we Europeans did 30 years ago. While directing the UC study centre in Paris for two years, and responsible for about 150 students from many American universities, I noted (unscientifically) that the students from California were the least adaptable to French standards of formality and *politesse*, the least willing to sacrifice their natural informality to the customs of the country and the demands for conformity by professors and landladies.

Judging by the recent literature denouncing our educational inadequacies, the situation I am observing in California may just be an extreme manifestation of a national phenomenon. Have we simply failed to teach our young the **facts** about France (or anywhere else)? Certainly, young people know less about the world than they used to, though more about technology and practical living.

Or, as I believe, are these recent inadequacies a magnification of long-standing, recurrent traditions in American culture which make for an anti-intellectual, utilitarian attitude to knowledge, at least outside the intellectual elite? *Habits of the Heart*, a recent, acclaimed sociological study of the current American ethos, relates long-term individualism and utilitarianism to the current ultra-individualism and the social fragmentation evident in work and community, as well as education (2). Alan Bloom's recent diatribe about the inadequacies of American education blames an extreme cultural relativism for youth's lack of interest in seeking out the True and the Beautiful through philosophical study and reflection (3). On a more trivial level, perhaps, a recent article in *The French Review*, comparing French and American guidebooks, contrasts the Frenchman's insistence on careful, detailed planning with the American's adventurous and unstructured approach to travel (4). These characteristics are not new, although they have been greatly exacerbated in the later 20th century with the arrival of so many diverse immigrant groups and the achievement of widespread prosperity. They have much to do with the social and economic, as well as the educational mess we are now in, but they have also contributed greatly to our particular brand of democracy, our extraordinary openness to diverse customs, ideas and initiatives.

In my view, therefore, the problem of young Americans' "ignorance" will not entirely go away, even with more rigorous educational discipline. But fortunately, I **do** have students who are genuinely interested in French civilisation. They need to be taught to see the parameters of cultural singularity before they will be able to integrate specific material about France into a meaningful structure. The insight that "the French perceive things differently than we do", or that "they **really** thought differently about child-raising in the 17th century", comes as a pure revelation. I can deal with my students' lack of factual information if I can just get them to read (not obvious in this time of audiovisual culture); I can also show them many things through slides, films, videos and tri-standard TV. But how do I conquer their resistance to seeing what culture is and how cultures differ? How, without requiring a couple of years of language study, do I instil that elementary fund of knowledge without which further understanding is impossible? Where do you start with the French, if your students haven't really noticed that they are different from us, or from the characters in a science-fiction movie?

FOOTNOTES

1. Since 1980 there has been a spate of task forces investigating the deficiencies in our educational system at all levels. Just two of the major recent reports are: *A Nation at Risk: The Imperative for Educational Reform*, Report by the National Commission on Excellence in Education (April 1983); BOYER, E.L., *College: The Undergraduate Experience in America*, report of a study by the Carnegie Foundation for Advancement of Teaching (New York, Harper and Row, 1987). During 1987, two books on the subject have become best-sellers: HIRSCH, E.D. Jr., *Cultural Literacy: What Every American Needs to Know* (Boston, Houghton Mifflin, 1987); and BLOOM, A., *The Closing of the American Mind: How Higher Education Has Failed Democracy and Impoverished the Soul of Today's Students* (New York, Simon and Schuster, 1987). Hot off the press as I write this is RAVITCH, D., and FINN, C.E. Jr., *What Do Our 17-Year-Olds Know? A Report on the First National Assessment of History and Literature* (New York, Harper and Row, 1987).

2. BELLAH, R.N. et al., *Habits of the Heart: Individualism and Commitment in American Life* (Berkeley and Los Angeles, University of California Press, 1985).

3. BLOOM, op. cit.

4. ROWLAND,M., 'Michelin's *Guide vert touristique*: A Guide to the French Inner Landscape', *The French Review*, 60:5 (April 1987), pp.653-664.

DISCUSSION OF THEDA SHAPIRO PAPER

Theda Shapiro remarked about the effects on one's research when one was surrounded by *littéraires*, which most of her colleagues were in the department. She felt that while one's colleagues were not necessarily unkind in making judgements that affected one's advancement, they were not knowledgeable either and one felt rather an orphan without intellectual soul-mates. Her own closest colleagues were not the near ones but various linguists, anthropologists, historians and art historians.

She also remarked, in response to the view that there was a wide age spread among the faculty in American departments, that on her campus many people were nearing retirement, so that on the one hand there was the idea that the campus after 15 years of hardship was actually going into a period of growth, that one could be optimistic since there would be a lot of renewal: on the other hand the renewal had not happened. She belonged to a younger group of professors in mid-career. She concluded that it did not seem universally true that there was a wide age spread. A lot of schools had a large faculty that had just stayed put.

Christopher Pinet, referring to the age-group of students, added that in many States, particularly in State universities, the age of students was rising. They were no longer 18 to 22: the average age of students at Montana State University was 23, and at the University of Montana, the local Arts School, it was 25. So he felt the American universities were beginning to deal with a wholly different demographic situation from what they had known before. He added that perhaps all the uneducated students **Theda Shapiro** complained about would eventually be educated because they would return to the University at the age of fifty, which might be one solution...

Alice Kaplan took exception to the use of the word "ignorant" and remarked that it was clear that American students did know a great deal, to which **Theda Shapiro** replied that she agreed, but they could not seem to verbalise what they knew, nor did they have a sufficient factual base of French lore to think clearly about what they learnt at first. Both agreed that E.D. Hirsch's trivia list, *What literate Americans know* (see footnote (1)) was pretty silly. On the other hand,**Theda Shapiro** maintained that the lack of factual knowledge in her students was appalling. **Christopher Pinet** thought this raised the problem of American students' general education; he thought that again went back to the 1960s. At that time, the traditional Western Civilisation course existed, so that Americans like him came out those courses as freshmen having read some of the basic texts in common. There was some commonality, people could discuss some things - maybe not all - but there were some points of contact between students. Since the 1960s, the situation had changed to a very considerable extent. There were

31

no real requirements today; at his university, there were no prerequisites for any of the History courses. People came in to the junior level History of French Civilisation course without having taken a History course of any kind. There were now universities where you could study very specialised topics at the higher level in History without having to have any form of historical training. So what had happened since the 1960s had been an abandonment of all requirements, including language requirements, and there was now an attempt in Harvard and other places to go back to the notion of core requirements and a core curriculum, where people might share some things. The debate on curriculum had re-opened because of all the vested interests, the vested interests of the old school who wanted to bring back things as theyt were in the old days. But there were also new lobbies like the formerly disenfranchised Feminist Studies in particular. As he noted the reactions of his female collleagues, he felt that if these new requirements came in, the commonality would be at the expense of some of the gains that had been made, so that it seemed to him that a real battle was going on in academia over some of these questions. The reason was the pendulum had swung back in the opposite direction.

Alice Kaplan recounted the story of one of her best students who, in presenting her dissertation on Le Pen in the course of her Final examination, had so far succeeded in internalising French culture that she had managed to produce a perfect mimic of the persona of a *polytechnicienne*. She argued that this was undesirable, and that the aim of teaching French should not be to make an American student adopt a completely different cultural identity. She also felt that teaching in French was often intellectually limiting: students tended to take courses like tourists preparing for trips, whereas they would look to History or English courses for serious intellectual work. **Christopher Pinet** wanted to say like Alice Kaplan that her brilliant student was simply playing a role, like so many Americans who went to Oxford and came back speaking an English that even people in Oxford could not understand. It seemed to him that that was a particular role that someone was playing. He would still maintain with Zeldin that there was no French "type" to be aimed at; the important thing was to have one's own personal identity. Having been a student of foreign culture who had lived in France for several years he was no longer the same individual. He did not see America the way he had done before. He could not therefore be an American "type" either. That was not to say that someone else who went to France and came back was not going to be different in another way, and was also not going to change. He simply did not think that you could apply a formula or an equation about how students should acquire French culture. He thought that being aware of one's own identity was terribly important, that you had to recognise that it was one thing to adopt the persona of a *polytechnicienne*, it was another to bring some French methods to bear on the problem of Le Pen. You were not going to get away from being an American.

Joe Coutts confirmed the problem of loss of identity and of a difficulty in integrating into the native country: the students he had surveyed had not only spent some time in France but had also been in the work situation, and this made it all the more difficult when they had to change countries and return to being students: the more successful the integration was in France, too, the more difficult it was for the student to return to his or her native land.

Nick Hewitt thought that the vocational nature of degrees being taught was crucial in the discussion, and that in order for a graduate to get a job where he or she was going to use their language, they would need as much language input and functionality as they could get. Of course, for those students who were never going to return to France, the issue was very different; for them what was needed was an intellectually coherent type of course of whatever type, literary or otherwise. If the aim was to make the course intellectually demanding, and if that was what students' employability was going to be based on, the ability to manipulate a certain amount of data, whether linguistic, literary, political or whatever, would take course-planning in a rather different direction. Laurence Wylie was thinking of the implications of this in terms of the American students who managed to study British politics, history and so on without a British accent. How far did the process of integration into French culture need to go ? Eric Cahm said he still felt unhappy about saying there was something wrong with the foreigner who was able to handle an academic subject like a Frenchman, as he supposed that was ultimately what one was trying to achieve; he would be inclined to cry "Hurrah" if the student came back and was able to write and speak like a Frenchman about Le Pen. What was actually wrong with the situation was not that it had happened, but that the change had not been adequately digested and the student's new identity had not been properly related to the whole of French culture and to her own basic national identity. The objective in itself did not seem undesirable and that sort of student was going to get an outstanding mark on the dissertation. One would not want to be too negative about the situation.

Peter Findlay noted the recent debate about dividing German Studies into two branches, the home-grown endo-Germanists and the xeno-Germanists, who were those who worked from outside Germany on German matters. He felt these two actually had fundamentally different premises. The xeno-Germanist, the extra-national, had to have comparison and translation at the centre of his work; quite simply moving between two cultures was not the same as living within the one. He thought that in many ways translation was the essential discipline of Area Studies and he wanted the answer to a few questions related to the whole issue. If the students ought to work in French the whole time, why were our major textbooks for them in English ? Many of them were in English. **Nicholas Wahl** interjected that the reasons were certainly commercial...

Jolyon Howorth felt there was a serious issue about the naturalness or foreignness of the whole enterprise of French Civilisation teaching. There was something of the freak in all those involved in it, an element of schizophrenia in the very nature of the work they were doing. There was a danger of that being written into the work that was being done with the students. He felt it was very important to remember that one was an American, precisely in order to do a better job on Le Pen. He felt that the objective should be to make students functional in the French setting, so that they could go over and know the works really. It was never going to be possible to make them into French people, of course, because the French would never allow this; but it would be possible to do the next best thing by making them functional. Students had to be given the barrage, the immersion, and they had got to cope with the foreign nature of French culture. He felt all those involved had to cope with that problem, and it was not necessarily the role of the teacher to take it on board. **Adrian Rifkin** added that, while he sympathised with making students functional, one also had to see that for a student to become French like Alice's student was for that student to adopt a particular position within French culture, which called for analysis. It also involved taking apart and understanding the kind of position the teacher had adopted within that culture, which was socially structured in terms of various forms of power and social relations. He thought that if one were simply thinking that becoming functional was useful in itself, then one was in a sense denying the inter-disciplinary nature of the whole enterprise of combining philosophy and culture and social analysis.

Laurence Bell felt that the question of whether or not to teach in French was closely linked to the question of inter-disciplinarity. When teaching a subject which was strongly empirically based, it was not necessarily a great problem to teach in French, since the language would not introduce a screen between the student and the material; if one were teaching a theoretically-based subject, the question would be whether to present **Marx, Weber**, Durkheim and their successors in French. Did you present something that was probably problematic and opaque to the students in French ? They had a difficulty in approaching such material, and he felt it was wrong to lecture in French on material that was quite difficult already. It distanced the students from that material purely in terms of understanding. This could quite easily be overcome, given enough time, but he also thought somehow they would perceive all theory as belonging to the French; they might think Weber was a Frenchman...

In relation to the language of instruction, **Peter Findlay** asked whether the ideology of the subject as it had grown up in the student's home country – what it meant to talk about French as a finishing school, German as a kind of world of philosophers and technocrats – should not be something the students studied; and if the lecturer were to ask about the meaning of the discipline within the home-grown culture, he wondered whether it were realistic to do that in the target language. Should this not be taught in English ? The kind of theoretical sophistication involved meant that the topic needed to be discussed in the student's native language: for example, the prejudices governing the image of France in Britain. He felt that to talk about preconceived notions of France in French was actually going to consolidate them rather than put them up for analysis.

Homer Sutton said that he thought that until French teachers came to a point when they realised that their real uniqueness was in being able to teach about French Cultural and Social studies in French, they were not going to earn their *lettres de noblesse*.

THE TEACHING OF FRENCH CIVILISATION IN THE UNITED STATES

by Jean Carduner, University of Michigan
and Claude Duverlie, University of Maryland

This paper attempts to describe a rather complex situation and it may be useful to start by insisting on its limited scope.

If one thinks in terms of "Area Studies" (or what is known in the US as such), teaching about France is divided along the disciplinary lines generally accepted in the Social Sciences. Most departments of History or Political Science have on their faculty scholars who specialise in "French Studies", and who write and teach on French History or French Politics. Most of the other Social Sciences (Sociology, Economics, Anthropology) ignore France. It may happen that France is sometimes included in European Studies, but one must say that Area Studies are usually the exclusive property of scholars interested in Asia (e.g. "Chinese Studies", "Japanese Studies") and in the Middle East. There are good reasons for this, but here is not the place to discuss them. What is more important is that a professor of French Language and Literature may often obtain help from a department of History or Political Science. But for most of the students who discover French culture through the learning of language, it may be difficult to take advantage of courses offered in English on France in the Social Sciences Departments because these courses do have pre-requisites. It is interesting to note a strong tendency in many Language departments to encourage students to have a double major in French *and* in one of the Social Sciences. But there are also a large number of students who hardly know any Social Science and need to discover French Civilisation.

What is most interesting today is that everyone involved in teaching French Language and Literature has become convinced that it is crucial to teach French Civilisation to the students who specialise in French. This is what this article is about. One can say that in the US we are discovering something that European teachers have known for a long time: that Civilisation is a legitimate subject matter which cannot be ignored when one wants to train language and literature specialists. If American students preparing a "teaching certificate" in French are not yet required to take Civilisation courses like the French students who want to become teachers of English, the general trend is in that direction and it will only be a matter of time before it becomes general practice.

To make generalisations when discussing pedagogical practices is always hazardous, especially so when it concerns the US. It is important to keep in mind the sheer size of the country, the complete decentralisation of the educational system, the lack of national standards in education and the peculiar (should I say marginal) status of foreign languages in academia. Any comparison with European countries is bound to be difficult if not downright impossible. What follows must be read for what it is: an attempt to describe the situation as it is perceived by colleagues involved in teaching French Civilisation. In the spring of 1981, Edward Knox and Jean Carduner published in the *AATF National Bulletin* (circulation 10,000) a rather simple questionnaire. The answers we received were synthesised by Knox in the *French Review* (issue 56, 1983). This article is a fairly comprehensive description of a situation which is not very different in 1987 as a follow-up questionnaire confirms. I quote its conclusion:

"When asked what their own concept of "civilisation" is, the vast majority of the responses break down into four more or less equal categories: the everyday-anthropological, the historical, a context for language, and whatever-leads-to-an-understanding-of-difference. The first and the second represent, of course, the rather strongly entrenched little "c"/big "C" (for culture) antithesis, but the third and fourth are integrated parts of the same effort, which becomes clear when the respondents are asked how they would justify the teaching of civilisation in a language programme. Seven point out that it gives students access to great humanistic achievements. 24 stress understanding and insight. 60 assert, many with indignant exclamation marks, that it is essential to the teaching of language. And finally when these teachers of language and civilisation are asked in an open question what place the teaching of civilisation should have in the training of language teachers, the answers tend overwhelmingly in the same direction: a larger, more important place (28); an "essential" place (nine); a required place (11); a status equal to that of literature (17)".

Another source of information is the excellent dissertation written by Marie-Christine Weidman-Koop on *L'enseignement de la culture française contemporaine dans les universités américaines* (Michigan State University, 1987). The author offers a quite exhaustive treatment of the problem, and her work is methodologically sound, having the great merit of never simplifying issues. It is required reading for anyone interested in the American way of dealing with the "teaching of French Civilisation" issue.

In a decentralised country, most changes in education are a response to a *need* manifested through a *demand* coming either from the public (students and/or parents) or from the teachers. Therefore I will now present the development of the demand for Civilisation courses, then one of its consequences: the Literature/Civilisation opposition. I will conclude by presenting the problem of resources and material available in the US.

The demand for Civilisation

It can be said that all the methods on the market today for teaching foreign languages, whatever their diversity, have a common feature: they focus on the learner. This hypothetical "learner" wants to learn a language in order to communicate with the native speakers of that language, and, in order to do so, he needs a functional knowledge of this culture. This is why there is such a strong demand for Civilisation courses. Such a demand is quite justified, but it is based, in part, on a misunderstanding. Somehow a "Civilisation Course" is perceived by many students as an easy "in" course more attractive than the other courses offered in a Language and Literature Department. The opposition Literature/Civilisation pervades implicitly the learning as well as the teaching of Civilisation. Students tend to understand "Civilisation" in television terms, and TV documents, whatever their strength as *"documents authentiques"* generate a passive, receptive attitude which seems opposed to the type of active, critical thinking associated with reading. As a result the "Civilisation courses" are considered "soft" by students who take them and by colleagues who do not teach them. This creates serious problems for those who teach them and may explain, in part, why the evaluation of those courses (assessment of knowledge) is still rather primitive. However, it is perfectly true that recent developments in Civilisation courses have been generated by a strong demand from the learner.

Put in a broader context, this demand is after all one of the manifestations of the new methodological dogma in foreign language teaching: the acquisition of functional competence in the second language. The foreign language is conceived (often narrowly) as a tool of communication, while in the past it was viewed in humanistic terms as a vital part of *"culture générale"* Consequently, learners and teachers alike are interested in contemporary life, political, social and cultural events; culture is the main source of language practice. The popularity of the teaching of Civilisation owes its strength to the desire of the learner to communicate rapidly and exclusively in the foreign language medium .

Another factor explaining the present demand for Civilisation courses is the development, under a variety of names, of programmes in "intercultural communication". The term "intercultural" covers a wide array of pedagogical practices which are rather similar to those involved in Civilisation studies. Is this simply a change in vocabulary or is it a deeper modification of the traditional concept of Civilisation ? Generally speaking, one can define the "cultural" as the result of "social practices" and of a series of "constructed discourses" on these practices. Very sketchily, one could say that the area of "intercultural" seeks to understand how social structures, social attitudes and language practices (verbal and non-verbal) determine the type of communication which can exist between individuals belonging to different cultures. The notion of "intercultural" integrates the perceptions that a community develops of another community. To work on the "intercultural" means to become conscious of the subjective, culture-determined point of view of any understanding of culture. All this is very well put by Jean-François Brière:

> "Starting in the late 1960s, the teaching of foreign cultures won its autonomy and, with the rapid expansion of the social sciences, sociolinguistics and semiotics, its perspective has been considerably broadened. The revolt against all forms of cultural imperialism has brought a relativisation of the concept of culture and has drawn attention to the immense problem of relations between cultures. Humanists as well as social scientists have become aware of the subjective and culturally-defined nature of any point of view and any discourse on culture - one's own or that of others. They have come to realise that in order to apprehend cultural realities, one could and ought to start thinking about the observer's status and his tools of analysis. Relativism and subjectivism have led to an emphasis on understanding rather than knowledge in the problematics of intercultural relations." (BRIERE, J.F., *The French Review*, vol.60, No.2 (December 1986), p.203).

The Literature/Civilisation opposition

It seems that the Literature/Civilisation opposition is central. It is not a conceptual opposition, but rather a typical power struggle which is going on in all departments of foreign languages. The power structure belongs to the literary scholars who try to block, or at least slow down, the development of civilisation courses. Higher education in the US is severely affected by financial restrictions, and no one is inclined to share stagnating resources: creating Civilisation courses does mean taking students away from existing literary courses. Therefore, the power structure is fighting to maintain the status quo. This is most visible if one looks at a) faculty recruiting, b) university library budgets and c) departmental resources available for subscriptions, books, lectures etc. Without winning the confrontation at this level, the Civilisation "lobby" (let us call it by its name) is unlikely to become very successful.

One important ally is the very large group of high school teachers. Schools are very sensitive to student demands and it is clear to them that present students want to get from their language studies a solid knowledge of the socio-cultural realities of modern France. School administrators complain that the universities do not properly train future language teachers (they are right), and universities often tend to answer that schools should teach more literature. This type of *"dialogue de sourds"* is, unfortunately, very familiar to all of us. We can hope that some day universities will wake up and take seriously their responsibilities in this area: after all without good high school students to recruit, what would they do ?

One could suggest that there is a dividing line between Literature programmes and Civilisation programmes which works approximately in this way: if one considers a long scale in which the most prestigious universities would be at the top, followed by various state and less distinguished private universities, technical schools and finally the community colleges, one would probably notice that the number of Civilisation courses offered in a language department increases as one goes down the scale. Like all generalisations, this one is at best only partially true even if it reflects the present situation rather well. Fortunately, there are a number of prestigious universities which have opted to create a highly visible "French Studies programme" and are in many ways considered as the leaders in Civilisation. I shall just mention, as examples, Brown, Middlebury and New York University, with its now well-established graduate programme. However, the development of civilisation programmes in those schools has not hurt (far from it) literary studies because financial resources were available to develop new areas without suppressing old ones.

The problems of resources and materials

Civilisation programmes have the reputation of being insatiable in their demands for new teaching resources. This all the more apparent since the nature of those resources is different from those needed by literature programmes which rely on books, that is on a traditional library system which fulfils its mission at the university level for the whole institution. Quite different are the needs of a Civilisation programme: by its very

40

nature it requires constantly new and authentic (sometimes ephemeral) material: newspapers, magazines *and* films, as well as video cassettes. Now if we must repeat that the very nature of the American system of education precludes a generalisation that is not based on very thorough research, we must still make three important observations:

1) the amount of resources available for the teaching of Civilisation depends on the financial health of a given college or department, on the status of foreign languages in that institution *and* on the status of civilisation in *that* department;

2) most departments have a chronic deficit of materials of any kind;

3) a major obstacle, even when resources are available, is the difficulty of obtaining access to the French sources. It is hard to imagine for anyone living in Britain how difficult it is to find French magazines, newspapers, video programmes and films outside of New York and the East Coast.

A Civilisation programme offers a number of courses on the history of France and those courses need a good, traditional library. But a larger number of courses is devoted to contemporary France, and these courses have different needs: a constant flow of current information is necessary to keep up with current trends and events. There are two ways of responding to that need: 1) to have visiting experts coming from France on a regular basis to teach courses and seminars, and 2) to purchase on a regular basis all the material available (printed and audio-visual). But only the most prestigious universities and the wealthiest can do this. Most of the others have to restrict the variety of courses they can offer because of the paucity of materials at their disposal. This is why there is usually, at most, *one* course on contemporary France, and why it is so difficult to develop quality programmes in Civilisation. However, the recent development of television (cable or beamed by satellite) offers tremendous possibilities for the very near future.

From "Bibliothèque" to "Médiathèque".

The impact of the new media is such that one can no longer consider them as a simple complement to the "noble" printed documents which have been the cornerstone of our teaching. The medias and telecommunications are creating a "window" which makes *direct* access to French life and society possible.

The video era

The rapid development of video has created a market and a distribution circuit in the US in the last four years which makes available, at low prices ($60.00 for a feature film) a wide variety of programmes:

1) Classic and more contemporary feature films in American TV standards. The number of French films available keeps growing but not as fast as one might hope.

2) Plays, documentary films on a wide variety of subjects, video clips etc.

3) Video courses on French language and culture coming from public TV (PBS) or from university TV stations (Nebraska, Oregon).

Pilot programmes

Many universities have launched ambitious efforts to organise *vidéothèques* of televised materials, coupled with distribution networks. One of the most vigorous is the Project of International Communication Studies (PICS) started in 1982 at the University of Iowa. It aims at encouraging the diffusion and the pedagogical exploitation of video documents coming from foreign TV networks. PICS purchases and stocks programmes coming from a variety of Western European sources. The French part of their catalogue proposes news programmes, a variety of documents on French society (youth, immigrants, trades, the Francophone world), and a number of programmes coming from Antenne 2. PICS is currently developing a pedagogical supplement to distribute along with the video.

TV by satellite

International TV beamed by satellite is a tremendous source of information and documentation. We have not yet quite realised all the implications of this new phenomenon nor its potential impact on the teaching of civilisation. But it is clear that the classroom teacher does not know how to use this wealth of authentic documents efficiently .

Many universities have equipped their language lab with a dish and they receive TV programmes from Canada and Quebec, and Quebec TV shows not only local productions but also a number of French productions (news, *Apostrophes*, etc.).

The legal problems concerning the copying and use of international TV programmes are rather complicated and often act as a deterrent. No doubt they will be solved some day and the general use of this type of material will soar.

France TV Magazine

France TV Magazine is a monthly programme originating from Antenne 2, which consists of 60 minutes of news and features on French life, selected by a team from the University of Maryland Baltimore County. The programme broadcast from UMBC campus in the States on January 8 this year consisted of about 11 minutes on the Gorbatchev-Reagan summit, 20 minutes about the release of two French hostages from Lebanon (Auque and Normandin), seven minutes of news (mine workers' festival celebrated by Polish immigrants, failing agriculture and a declining village in Aveyron, women oenologists), five minutes on the film industry (Chabrol, Beneix), five minutes on sports in elementary schools and three minutes on what children read between ages 8 and 13. UMBC produces a *"cahier pedagogique"* in order to facilitate the exploitation of the material by the classroom teacher. In the spring of 1987 about 300 schools, colleges and universities were receiving this programme. The programme seems to have a major impact on the development of civilisation teaching in the schools which receive it.

Such a packaging has a tremendous advantage: the programme is free from copyright and can be copied and stocked for one full year.

The training of teachers

Video programmes are going to become more and more important in the teaching of Language and Civilisation. But, unless the language teacher is properly trained to use these materials, nothing important is going to happen. We have to be careful that the mistakes which were committed when the language laboratory was massively introduced in the schools are not repeated. Not only do we have to invent a didactic approach to those materials, we have to upgrade the linguistic and cultural competence of the teachers. In order to react correctly to videotapes which show raw samples of contemporary society (without the help of any guide) one has to be extremely well-informed about contemporary France and to be completely fluent in the use and understanding of the language whatever the regional differences (the speakers from Bordeaux and Marseille for example, have heavy local accents). The teacher will also have to develop the kind of skill which permits the fabrication of a pedagogical approach geared to the linguistic level of the class. The pitfalls of video pedagogy are infinite, if only because television material is part of the normal life of students (far more so than the printed material), and we must warn everyone that the mere fact of using TV material will not be sufficient to generate the enthusiastic reaction of our students.

In the next few years, the profession will have to develop well-conceived multi-media packages including videotapes and pedagogical apparatus. It will also have to develop a variety of pedagogical techniques ("*une vraie 'didactique' au sens français du terme*", and retrain old teachers, while insisting that new teachers be trained appropriately in their university. In one sense the development of video materials will push to its logical conclusion the evolution which leads teachers to take into account the diversity of the needs of their students. It could lead to "*les lendemains qui chantent*"; it could also lead nowhere. As usual, it is up to us.

DISCUSSION OF JEAN CARDUNER AND CLAUDE DUVERLIE PAPER

To **Jolyon Howarth** the fundamental problem that came out of **Jean Carduner's** paper and a number of others was that of inter-disciplinarity. The reason why French Civilisation specialists had a difficulty in establishing themselves as a serious group of teachers was that they were not restricted to a particular discipline.

Nicholas Wahl agreed and added "from the other side" that inter-disciplinary programmes in the Social Sciences, the old Area Studies programmes, had had the same kind of problems. French Civilisation had the double problem of being inter-disciplinary both in the Humanities and in the Social Sciences.

His answer was a direct comment on something **Jean Carduner** had pointed to: the trend for some of the more successful undergraduate students of Civilisation to have a double major in French and Social Science. The most successful graduate students would come from undergraduate experience which was bi-disciplinary. Such students would get data and language from the French side and the concepts to deal with them from the Social Science side. Students on a bi-disciplinary programme could not get all the concepts of the Social Sciences but they could get those of Political Science and Economics which were the most solid. In a way, he felt this would offer a way into analysis on the French side too, because there both History and Language would be included.

Jean Carduner agreed that disciplinary range was a problem for students and felt the problem was equally real to the colleague who regarded himself as a teacher of Civilisation. He was thinking particularly of the outrageous amount of specialisation in the Social Sciences, as witness the number of journals of every kind published in a single discipline. It had been said that there were today 147 journals in Sociology alone, with five or six issues a year, each full of brilliant new articles. Publishable articles were becoming more and more narrow and esoteric and less and less interesting. The poor fellow teaching Civilisation was bound, on the other hand, to be a generalist, and his classroom work was at a quite different level. He was also quite despised, particularly since it was research and not teaching that was rewarded in the profession. This was a situation of which all those present were victims, unless an extraordinary review could be launched publishing generalist articles.

John Roach asked whether it was graduate programmes which were the prestige programmes in the United States since most of the papers seemed to refer to undergraduate teaching and Nicholas Vahl confirmed that all American papers but one were about undergraduate teaching. John Roach then asked whether Civilisation featured on graduate courses in the US, to which Nicholas Vahl replied that they were almost exclusively based on a single discipline, and in the case of French departments, this meant Literature, although there were some offerings of Civilisation, for example at Middlebury. A student interested in French Civilisation would not go into a French graduate programme but one in the Social Sciences. Those who did go into a Civilisation programme at that level were those eager to become secondary school teachers in French since Civilisation loomed large in secondary school teaching. They would take an MA which was all that was needed for that purpose. The MA of that kind at NYU was called "Language and Civilisation": it played down Literature in favour of Civilisation and included a good deal of grammar. It was not meant to take the student any further; those who wanted to go on to University teaching had to get in through Literature, except where there was a separate department dealing with Civilisation teaching.

In response to a question comparing student demand for Civilisation courses in Britain and the US Jean Carduner felt there was a real need in Britain for a university graduate to have the sort of competence which would allow him to work with the EEC because of its proximity. This gave a real objective, whereas in the US what could be done with a degree in French ? Many people combined it with a degree in Business Administration so as to find a use for it, but the immediate need for people trained in French culture to go into an administrative career was far less than in Britain.

UNIVERSITY OF CALIFORNIA, RIVERSIDE

The Major in French
The core of the major is the study of French culture, literature, or language. Students will work in consultation with their advisors, developing their interests in relation to French literature, civilisation, or language. Attention is drawn to Education Abroad Programmes in Bordeaux, Grenoble, Marseille, Montpellier, Pau-Paris, Poitiers, and a special programme in Paris.

French Civilisation
    Language Proficiency: All students concentrating in French Civilisation must complete 12 upper division units (or equivalent) of work in French.
    Civilisation: In addition to the language proficiency requirement, students must complete a minimum of 40 upper division units, as follows:
a) *European Culture 114A-114B-114C-114D (French Civilisation)*: b) 8 units of work in French literature: c) 4 units in European Culture 191: d) 4 units, either in French Literature or in upper division French Language (*French 100 or French 104*):   and e) 12 units of electives, either in French Civilisation and French Literature, or, with approval of the student's advisor, in courses outside the French programme relating to French Civilisation. Related History courses are strongly recommended. At the outset, *European Culture 25* is also strongly recommended.

The Minor in French
The Department offers a Disciplinary Minor in French with these requirements: 24 upper division units distributed thus:
         12 units of *French 101A-B-C* (Advanced Grammar and Stylistics)
          4 units of *French 100* (Advanced Conversation)
          8 units chosen from *French 109A-B-C* or
          8 units chosen from *European Culture 114A-B-C-D*:
    European Culture 114A.   French Civilisation in the Middle Ages
    European Culture 114B.   France Between Renaissance and Revolution
    European Culture 114C.   From the French Revolution to the Belle Epoque
    European Culture 114D.   The Twentieth Century
    European Culture 115F.   Paris.

The BA in French requires 8 semester-long courses above the language studies level and must include the 2-semester introduction to French Literature. All these courses are conducted in French. Between 12 and 15 courses a semester may be offered. The following is a list of undergraduate courses in the Duke French Department that involve cultural, rather than strictly literary studies:

French Civilisation: The department core course in civilisation. The institutions and culture of France from the Middle Ages to the present. The basic text: Jean Thoraval, *Les Grande étapes de la civilisation française*. Taught by Marcel Tétel.

Freshmen and Sophomore Seminar in Contemporary Ideas: Readings and discussion of French works which have provoked political or intellectual thought in recent years. (Taught most recently by Alice Kaplan, who taught half the semester on occupied France, half on the Algerian crisis, using radio tapes, documentary and narrative films, essays, newspapers, novellas.

Freshmen Seminar in French Theater and Theatricality: 3 plays studied in detail; includes intensive work in the production history of each. Taught by Alice Kaplan or David Bell.

Problems and controversies in today's France. Seminar in French for current affairs taught by staff.

An introduction to French commercial and legal practices and vocabulary: French for business and law. Taught by Anne-Marie Bryan.

French Women: Myths, Realities, and the Law: Influential women writers of the last forty years: Beauvoir, Duras, Yourcenar, Sullerot, Veil, Halimi, and others. Cross-listed: Women's Studies. Taught by Anne-Marie Bryan.

Topics in Renaissance Literature and Culture: Seminar. Topics may include: Women writers, love and self-knowledge, carnival and the grotesque, in search of Rome, text as political and religious pamphlet. Taught by Marcel Tétel.

French and Creole in Canada, New England, Louisiana, and the Caribbean: French in the New World: origins, history, linguistic characteristics, current political and social issues. Taught by Alex Hull.

Life in Eighteenth-Century France: a course based on period documents - books, memoirs, newspapers, scandal sheets - designed to give a picture of life in a large French city before the modern era. Taught by Philip Stewart.

Contemporary French Life and Thought: Major writers of the 20th century and their historical and cultural circumstances. Taught by Alice Kaplan.

The French film: taught by Staff.

History and Cultural Studies are also taught within the French Literature curriculum by David Bell, Fredric Jameson, Linda Orr, Helen Solterer and Jean-Jacques Thomas.

Faculty from other departments teach the following courses in French under the rubric "The French curriculum"; these courses have proved very successful with our students:

Art History: *Gothic cathedrals*. Caroline Bruzelius.

History: *Europe to the 18th century*. Ronald Witt.

Music: *The Humanities and Music*. Bartlet or Seebass.

Sociology: *Paris and Montreal in 1900 and 1968*. Tiryakian.
Many French Majors at Duke complete what is called a "double major" in conjunction with a programme called Comparative Area Studies, defined in the university bulletin as "the interdisciplinary study of societies and cultures of a particular region of the world". The French-Comparative Area Studies Major requires that the student take the Seminar in Contemporary Ideas, Contemporary French Life and Thought, French Civilisation, and Life in 18th-century France, as well as a selection of courses on France and Western Europe in the Departments of Anthropology, Political Science, Public Policy, History, Economics, Sociology, and Art History.
Students in the French Department are strongly urged to spend 1 or 2 semesters in France. During the academic year 1986-87, Duke students went to France on a variety of study-abroad programmes. Duke's own programme in France is centred at the University of Paris-VII, Jussieu. Students on the Duke programme are fully matriculated at Paris-VII. They take 4 courses a semester, 3 of them at either Paris-VII, Paris-IV (Art History), the Ecole du Louvre, or the Institut National des Sciences Politiques. The fourth course each semester is taught by a Duke faculty member; one of the traditional offerings is a course on Paris in French Literature.
Duke also offers summer programmes at Paris-VII, Paris, the University of Montreal and the University of Morocco, Marrakech.

MIDDLEBURY COLLEGE

Undergraduate
There are courses on French Politics and French History in other Departments, in English. In the French Department and in French, a freshman/sophomore introduction to contemporary France is offered on the same level as the introductions to French Literature (poetry, drama, prose). A second course offers thematic approaches to the contemporary French press. There is an advanced course, often offered as a senior seminar, on *French civilisation in the twentieth century*.
In Paris, students are enrolled at Nanterre and may also choose from a dozen courses at Sciences Po'. The "favourites" are French History, Art History and International Relations. These courses may count toward the French major, and our numerous students in Paris who are not French majors, may count courses taken there in French toward other majors.

Graduate
Our MA in French may be done through a series of summers on the Vermont campus or a summer there followed by the academic year in Paris. In both cases at least two of the twelve courses they take must be in civilisation. Here too the "favourites" would be History, Politics and Art History. In Paris, where we require a *mémoire*, many (a third?) choose to do them on topics in the area of Civilisation.
We feel good about including Civilisation specifically in the MA but a certain unease that there is no particular rationale or structure beyond that. For instance, should all MAs not be required to take an introduction to contemporary France ? Moreover, they are not historians, etc., and one can legitimately ponder what should go on in civilisation at the graduate level with students who are otherwise legitimately at that level.

Programmes of Study.
Qualified students may choose one of four programmes of study. They may concentrate in French Language and Literature, Language and Civilisation, Romance languages, or they may major in French and Linguistics.

Programme 1. Emphasis on French Language and Literature: nine courses. This plan of study normally consists of three courses in advanced language, four courses in literature, one course in civilisation, and the senior seminar.

Programme 2. Emphasis on French Language, Society and Culture: nine courses. This plan of study normally consists of three courses in advanced language, four courses in civilisation, one course in literature, and the senior seminar.

Programme 3. Romance Language Major.

Programme 4. Major in French and Linguistics: eight courses. This plan of study normally consists of the following courses: one course in spoken contemporary French, one course in advanced written French, and two courses in French literature to be determined in consultation with the director of undergraduate studies.

Civilisation Courses

French Society and Culture from the Middle Ages to the Present: French civilisation from early period to World War Two through the interrelation and interaction of the arts, philosophy, and history. Study of major trends, personalities, and events, search for a meaning and a definition of what constitutes the cultural heritage of France. To achieve a perception from within, this course avoids an anthological approach. Primary sources and documents, such as *chroniques, mémoires, journaux, revues,* and *correspondance.*

Contemporary France (formerly *Modern France*). The concept of "French Civilisation" in both its mythical and real aspects. Gives the student considerable knowledge about the economic and social features of contemporary France. The comparative approach between French and American Civilisation is used.

Versailles: Life as Art in the Age of Grandeur. Fabulous Versailles, the synthesis of Baroque and Classical aesthetics and the cult of kingship, introduces study of major aspects of 17th and 18th-century culture and French influence on European civilisation. The intellectual, artistic and social complexities of the period are viewed through the works of contemporary philosophers, dramatists, artists, memorialists and historians from Descartes to Voltaire. Films, field trips, multi-media presentations of music and art.

La Belle Epoque: Modes of Artistic Expression and Life. Focuses on the dazzling cultural life of the turn-of-the-century Paris. Explores the ascent of Symbolism, Post-Impressionism, Art Nouveau, Cubism, Futurism, and other creative concepts. The social, intellectual and artistic aspects of the period are viewed through the works of contemporary writers, dramatists and artists such as Zola, Huysmans, Maupassant, Proust, Colette, Apollinaire,

Toulouse-Lautrec, Cézanne, Picasso, Debussy, Diaghilev, Sarah Bernhardt and Gertrude Stein. Extensive use of audio and video material.

French Cinema - French Culture. A study of classic French films, their contribution to French culture, and their relationship to France's international role in the arts. Films are discussed and analysed in the context of socio-political events, and placed in cultural perspective.

Topics in French Civilisation. Courses on subjects of special interest by either a regular or visiting faculty member. Spring 1988: *Paris in History, Art and Literature.*

THE BRITISH EXPERIENCE

THE ORIGINS OF FRENCH CIVILISATION TEACHING IN BRITAIN: WITH SOME REMINISCENCES

by Eric Cahm, Université de Tours

From its earliest days at the beginning of the 20th century, the teaching of French in British higher education has been dominated by an almost exclusive concern with the literature of the past. French has been, and still is, largely taught in British universities through the medium of the master works of the literary canon into which even the writers of the most recent decades were only slowly admitted. It is not so long since French was taught almost entirely on the model of Classics, as if it were a dead language, in degree programmes to which oral proficiency and knowledge of the present state of France were thought only marginally relevant. Actual study in France, as opposed to vacation visits, was not an integral part of the study of French in Cambridge when I was an undergraduate there in the 1950s. I actually learnt to speak French properly only after graduating, by the lucky chance of spending a year at the rue d'Ulm as an *élève étranger*, which was an opportunity open to only one Cambridge graduate per year !

The teaching of French "Civilisation", still spontaneously put into quotation marks as an unfamiliar concept by British participants at the seminar, remains to this day strongly marked, in British universities, polytechnics and colleges, by the traditional approach to France based on literature. Civilisation teaching here - and I will now boldly drop the quotation marks - began as a mere instrumental adjunct to Literature teaching, and it developed initially by diversifying away from Literature. It has frequently been seen principally as an instrument of language teaching. It remains, more often than not, opposed to, or at least exclusive of, Literature - as witness the definitions offered by British participants at the seminar. But to vary Péguy's comment on atheism: *"Présence de la littérature, absence de la littérature, c'est toujours la littérature".* The very rejection of literature in the definitions offered here, and in most of the polytechnic French teaching programmes, still bears witness to its persistence and to the strong *réaction de rejet* it has engendered.

France outside the literary field was traditionally relegated in the university department of French to the status of "background", and this opprobrious term, which used to cause me paroxysms of rage, did duty for any analysis of French civilisation. France was simply a background to Literature, and if its Civilisation was taught at all, this could only be so that French Literature could be better understood and served. The noble studies of French History, of French Art and Architecture, and even of French thought were not recognised in their own right, and even the masters of French thought were seen through literary spectacles, so that the *Discours de la Méthode* and the *Lettres persanes* might appear in French syllabuses, but not the *Méditatations métaphysiques* or *De L'Esprit des lois*, which smacked too much of the technicalities of philosophy or social thought. The most that might be expected of the student of French, say in the late 1930s, was that he or she should complement his or her literary studies by reading R.L.Graeme Ritchie's classic *France: a Companion to French Studies* (1936), a survey of several centuries of French literature, history, art and philosophy, the conception of which was based on the traditional *cours de civilisation* as Laurence Wylie has described it in his paper. The title of Ritchie's book *en dit long sur* the position of civilisation in Britain at this time in relation to the study of literature. The gesture towards Civilisation, however, points to an early realisation of a need, and marks a sort of beginning. It is also worth noting that at Manchester, a major university of Victorian vintage, Eugène Vinaver had introduced history *à part entière* into the French degree syllabus before 1939, so inaugurating the approach that came to be labelled French Studies. Professor Vinaver, who first appointed me to a teaching post in French, continued to believe that all aspects of France could be legitimate subjects for academic study.

The first overall conception of French Civilisation to emerge in Britain, as exemplified by Ritchie's book, and derived from the old *cours de civilisation,* implied that the study of past literature could or should be complemented **but still wholly or mainly as background, outside the teaching syllabus** by a diversification into areas of French culture parallel to that of Literature, across the literary centuries. This conception of Civilisation as what to-day would be seen as a part of cultural history (*see* my conclusion at the end of this book), embracing at least Literature, History, and the History of philosophy and the arts, was from the 1960s actually to inform the French syllabuses of the so-called "new" British universities such as Sussex, Warwick and Lancaster, and, for example, to lead to the introduction by George Lehmann of both History and Philosophy strands into the French syllabus at Reading, (which also by now included a compulsory Contemporary Politics and Society course in the First Year). The Ritchie model is still reflected in the more recent editions of *France* (Methuen, 1972), edited by Donald Charlton of the University of Warwick, which also, however, include a chapter on Politics, Society and Institutions, which looks forward to the most recent trends.

Meanwhile, as far back as the late 1940s, the appointment by Eugène Vinaver of a French citizen to a joint post in History and French at Manchester to teach partly on the French Studies degree (a post later held with distinction by Norman Hampson), and the introduction into that degree of a Final Honours special subject on the French Revolution, also anticipated things to come in older universities.

Civilisation was beginning to move from background to foreground and to look towards the Social Sciences. However, the persistence of traditional attitudes related to the idea of background can be seen even in the 1980s in the fact that some lecturers in French Literature still regard the Civilisation area as a mass of unstructured fact, which does not lend itself to serious academic study.

More recent institutional developments from the 1960s: the founding of the technological universities with their modern and vocationally-oriented syllabuses; the march of the polytechnics from sub-degree technical training institutions to para-university status, with a predominance of degree work, in the Arts and Humanities as well as in the dominant areas of science and technology, but equally with a vocational flavour and a strong concern with efficient teaching; the transformation of many teacher-training colleges into institutions teaching at degree level mainly in the Humanities - all these developments have offered fertile ground for the emergence of radically new and generally non-literary, not to say anti-literary concepts of French Civilisation teaching, under the aegis, for the polytechnics and colleges, of the the Council for National Academic Awards (CNAA), a national degree-awarding body, which has had the task of

53

approving degree schemes for national recognition and has done much to facilitate the new approaches to French teaching at degree level.

By the early 1960s, I found myself teaching at the beginning of my career alongside Norman Hampson in the French Department at Manchester, where he taught a compulsory Second-Year course on Ancien Régime history and thought as well as the Final-Year option on the Revolution, while I was able to introduce a Final-Year option on political thinkers of the Third Republic.

The newest British conception of French Civilisation teaching has emerged, in the last two decades, in the strongly vocational atmosphere of technological institutions, and as an essentially non-literary approach, based on what is sometimes called in an ugly phrase "societal studies". Theoretical elaboration being always rather primitive in the context of British culture, the search for theoretical origins for the new approach must remain a vain one. The CNAA's national body for languages, the Languages Board, satisfied itself with insisting on a "theory and cerebration" element in degree syllabuses in French. Empirical enquiry shows however that the new concept remained and remains wedded, to an extent, to knowledge of France as instrumental to language-learning; and since for vocational purposes practical skills in the use of the contemporary language replace academic study of the History of the Language as a priority, the emphasis is shifted to France to-day, and *France Today*, ed. John Flower (Methuen, first edition, 1971) is the title of a very successful collection of essays, partly aimed at schools, which again does something to exemplify the newest approach, covering as it does politics, society, education, religion and the press.

The France of the past is not abandoned, but in view of the strong reaction against Literature, it is represented essentially by History. History is here seen in the context I have described essentially as a means to understanding present-day France. This implies that remote periods should be abandoned, more and more emphasis laid on the most recent past, and that history can now cover periods leading right up to the present, as is increasingly accepted to-day by the more adventurous historians of France in the country itself. My book, *Politics and Society in Contemporary France (1789-1971)* (Harrap, 1972) was a documentary history emphasising post-1958 France, and even reflecting events up to a few months prior to its publication. This approach inevitably provokes the question raised at the seminar as to where French history starts for our purposes and produces answers varying from about 1760 to 1981 !

As to the France of the present, this is seen essentially through the prism of the Social Sciences: Economics, given priority in the vocational climate I have mentioned, Politics, now strongly and almost universally represented, Sociology, and less often Geography.

French Civilisation teaching in the technological universities, polytechnics and colleges has thus come to be an **inter-disciplinary** activity, based on a collaboration between History and the Social Sciences, from which Literature has in many cases been eliminated: the typical Language degree syllabus outside the older universities spans two languages, of which French is one, and covers the History and Society of the two language areas, often in a European framework.   The disciplinary basis is frequently strongly language-oriented, with an admixture of Linguistics, and a continuing concern with Civilisation as an essential means to language learning (Polytechnic of Central London).   French may also be combined with one other principal discipline, such as Law or International relations (Surrey University), History (Cambridgeshire College of Arts and Technology), politics or another Social Science (Loughborough University, Sheffield or Kingston Polytechnics).

French Civilisation has thus now begun to emerge in Britain as an inter-disciplinary approach to the study of France.   It is not perhaps yet a fully autonomous discipline in its own right.   But it has come a long way from the traditional Literature-based model.   This can be illustrated by the French Studies degree at Portsmouth Polytechnic.   Portsmouth is one of the very few institutions in Britain where a single-subject degree in French Studies has been developed since the mid-1960s, based wholly on the notion of French Civilisation (the concept used is actually that of **Area Studies**).   Area Studies in Portsmouth, whether applied to France, the two Germanies, the USSR, Spain or Latin America, spans History and History of Ideas, Politics, Economics, Geography, and in some cases - though not in French - Sociology.   It should be noted, however, that the Portsmouth degree syllabuses also include Literature and Cinema, and have equally included History of Art or Music.   The Portsmouth experience, therefore, points to a more all-embracing concept of Civilisation teaching, covering History, the Social Sciences and Literature and the Arts.   This is perhaps already the beginning of the *menu gastronomique* for which Geoffrey Hare and John Roach call in their survey of French Civilisation teaching in the

British universities to-day. For if French Civilisation still remains, as they show, on the periphery in the older institutions, it has become mainstream in the newer ones. As Hare and Roach say, the direction of change is unequivocal, and the march forward continues, despite the financial constraints of Britain in the 1980s.

It will be sensed from the Hare and Roach survey that, despite traditionalism, few or no universities in Britain have remained unaffected by the wind of change that has, as a result of pressures from government and student demand, transformed the teaching of French in the newest institutions.

The founding in 1979 of the Association for the Study of Modern and Contemporary France, soon followed by that of its own inter-disciplinary review *Modern and Contemporary France*, is another sign of the growing numbers of British teachers in higher education concerned in an inter-disciplinary way with France, whether they work in Languages, History or Politics departments, in newer or older institutions. Its success bears witness to their self-awareness as a group with common interests, who both need and can support a forum for the exchange of ideas and information about France. It is no accident that the Association for the Study of Modern and Contemporary France has been centrally concerned with supporting and planning the Portsmouth seminar. However hard the times, there is indeed for all of us in Britain only one way forward, towards more degree programmes wholly based on an inter-disciplinary approach to French Civilisation and that implies more academic interchange of ideas and experience.

BRITISH CULTURAL CONTEXTS FOR FRENCH CIVILISATION TEACHING
by Michael Kelly, University of Southampton

Diversity of Cultures

There is no homogeneous culture in the British Isles which might provide a unified context for teaching French Civilisation. Diversity rather than unity is the hallmark of our culture. It is easy to identify the main axes along which the diversity may be traced; they include those of class, ethnic group, age, sex and region. Since our universities, polytechnics and colleges teach only a minority of the population, much of that cultural variety has only a marginal impact on our work in practice. We could be lulled into feeling that a degree of homogeneity exists, sufficient at least to be able to trace a general context. The white, Christian, middle-class cultural values may well be dominant, but they are far from exhausting the real richness of our cultural environment.

Class: It is true that our students are drawn from a narrow class band, predominantly from the middle strata of salaried, managerial and professional groups. In most institutions of higher education, the children of miners, dockers or cleaners are as rare as the children of industrial magnates or high financiers. But even within this narrow band, there is a degree of diversity, reflected in the differing educational backgrounds: from a private boarding school to an inner-city comprehensive can be a significant cultural distance.

Ethnic background: Our students are still mostly white, from Christian or post-Christian families. But the White Anglo-Saxon Protestant dominance was always moderated by Catholic and Jewish students, often from Irish or Eastern European backgrounds. To them are now added a small but growing number of students from the Asian and Caribbean communities, with different cultural and religious references again.

Age: The majority of our students are still aged from 18 to 22, with the cultural specificity of that transition from adolescence to young adulthood. Lecturers have always had to bridge a cultural gap between their own age-group and that of their students. But as the economic circumstances bite, the gap has widened. Staff are growing old together, with very few younger colleagues appointed who might have greater affinity with students. One third of university French lecturers are aged between 43 and 47, reflecting the expansion of the 1960s, but very few departments can claim a colleague under 30, and under-35s are thin on the ground, reflecting the contraction of the 1980s. There are signs that the number of mature students is slowly increasing, adding a further dimension to the age-profile of higher education.

Sex: Students of French are predominantly women. This fact, often remarked on in common-room banter, is rarely analysed for its cultural or academic implications. There is a tacit view that French must therefore be a "soft-focus" subject, fulfilling the functions of a "finishing school", a point which was alluded to earlier in this colloquium. What is often felt to be the guilty secret of Modern Language departments, an academic stigma almost, could be an occasion to address important issues of women's education. Paradoxically, the staff in departments are predominantly men, especially at senior levels, and the gender-based differentiation of culture is usually overlooked, when it is not actively denied and repressed.

Region: Taking the British Isles as a whole, it is evident that Scottish, Welsh and Irish students belong to quite distinct national cultures. Most important for Modern Language studies, they have a different relationship to language, since in many cases they speak French as a third language (after English and Welsh/Irish/Scots Gaelic), and their English differs significantly from the received standard southern English, not only in pronunciation. Moreover, their culture reflects quite different historical relations with France: in the case of Scotland and Ireland, France was historically very often an ally in the struggle against English domination. Within England, such regional particularites as do exist are largely neutralised by the "exogamous" character of higher education. That is, students normally leave home to follow degree courses at an institution other than their local ones.

Staff likewise rarely lecture in their home area, though they may develop local affinities over a period of time. The frequently cited town-and-gown tensions reflect the relative lack of local roots among the students and their lecturers. This extends to non-academic staff, in direct proportion to their status. The result is a greater degree of cultural homogeneity in higher education establishments than in English society as a whole. But the "national culture" which results is mainly an abstract and generalised extrapolation from the ethos of the South East, which exercises its domination in the cultural field as it does in the economic and political fields.

The cultural role of French

Bearing in mind these factors of cultural diversity, there are several identifiable factors which have a major influence on the teaching of French and French Civilisation. Chief among them is the role of French as a discipline in the British education system. But this role in turn springs from the wider relationship between Britain and France, in terms of their history, their economic and political ties and the cultural impact of France in everyday British life.

History: The long history of Franco-British relations is sufficiently familiar to us all not to need rehearsing. Whether we go back to the Roman Conquest, the Norman Invasion, the Napoleonic Wars or the two World Wars of the 20th century, these relations are an integral part of European history This century, the two countries have mainly been allies, but, as a stroll around the fortifications of Old Portsmouth graphically reminded us, for much of our history, France has been the main continental enemy of England, though not necessarily of Scotland or Ireland at the same time. History is not easily shrugged off, and accounts for much of the love-hate relationship between the two countries. Any colleague will confirm the curious mixture of Francophilia and Francophobia which makes up the typical French department (and the typical French lecturer) in England.

Economics and politics: The close trading links between Britain and France have been intensified since the mid-1970s by British accession to the EEC. The ineluctable advance of European integration has brought common agricultural and fisheries policies, a common passport (coloured "Burgundy"), a common driving licence, and the promise of a Tunnel. The Single European Act will in due course bring common laws (already partially achieved) and a common currency, among other things. The growing co-operation in defence, strategic research and foreign policy areas is also plainly visible. If the two countries are tied more closely together, it means that a great deal more contact takes place, though it does not necessarily follow that France and French things are any more popular in Britain. In some respects the economic and political integration has been offset by an ideological and cultural offensive aimed at protecting British national identity, and perhaps, through the American connexion, aimed at asserting British aspirations to regional pre-eminence.

Everyday life: Notwithstanding the mutual jostling by governments, there are ever-growing practical links with France in the areas which affect people in their daily lives. British tourism in France is expanding. Britanny, the Dordogne, the Loire valley, the Vendée, and the Côte d'Azur are flooded with GB plates every summer.   Winter sports attract growing numbers of British visitors with the requisite level of disposable income. And at the lower end of the market, "booze cruises" and shopping trippers cross the Channel in large numbers on day-return tickets.   Through the shops and supermarkets of Britain, the food and drink of France are rapidly becoming part of our staple diet.   Paris fashions have a long record of popularity, though far from unchallenged, and many French products are prominent in the field of consumer durables.

Secondary education: French has long been the main modern language taught in British schools.   In 1985, 152,000 pupils sat French "O" levels, 23,000 sat French "A" levels. This compares with German (43,000 and 8,000) and Spanish (12,000 and 2,500). The number of pupils studying Languages is declining both absolutely and relatively, but the pre-eminence of French is overwhelming, and likely to be exaggerated further by the government's new education legislation, under which all secondary pupils will study a Modern Language up to age 16. French has, to a large extent, succeeded Classics as the main non-national culture in the school curriculum. For many years, it retained the same syllabus structure, based on Language (mainly formal grammar and prose translation) and Literature (mainly set books, studied word by word)   -   though French Literature did draw to some extent on the methods of English Literature. The revolution of the last 10 years or so has been to replace the grammar and prose by an approach which emphasises communicative skills, especially oral ones, based on the use of authentic French materials. Concomitantly, literary texts have yielded place to the study of contemporary French society through particular topics of interest.

Higher education: In the universities, French is the major modern language, studied often on its own, but increasingly in combination with other disciplines. Over the past ten years, pressure from the University Grants Committee and elsewhere has led to many French departments joining other Language Departments in federal structures known as Schools. Traditionally, the syllabus was based on Literature, but this core has been pulled in two significant directions.   On the one hand, it has moved towards a broader cultural range, taking in the visual arts, especially Film, and the French intellectual tradition, especially Critical Theory:

this approach is particularly identified with the "new universities" of the 1960s. On the other hand, the literary core has been supplemented, and in some cases replaced, by the study of contemporary French social, political and economic topics likely to be of use in a commercial environment: this approach is particularly associated with the "technological universities" of the 1970s.

In the polytechnics and colleges, French is also the main language, but usually located in a Modern Languages Department, where students normally study French in combination with another Language or a Social Science. Courses concentrate on study of the Language and of Contemporary French Culture and Society, often integrating the two strands. The same kinds of pressures exist as for universities, though there have been (perhaps isolated) instances of literary courses being reinstated, implying possibly a measure of prestige assigned to such, less applied, courses.

Conclusions

The current climate in Britain is undeniably to accentuate the vocational nature of education, promoting business-related courses for undergraduates, and encouraging higher education establishments to offer customised language-based courses for industrial and commercial enterprises. The reduction of education to mere training is inevitably narrowing French sylllabuses. Whereas it may appear to be supporting the growth of French Civilisation teaching (as against literary teaching), it effectively limits the scope of Civilisation courses, cutting off the historical and the cultural dimensions without which the political and economic spheres appear rootless and disembodied.

It is clear that, outside Oxford and Cambridge Universities, the traditional literature-based syllabus is in decline, as it deserves to be. But there will be no cause for rejoicing if it is replaced by a narrowly commercial syllabus tailored to train bilingual secretaries and export managers. There is no inevitability that this will occur, though the pressures towards it are considerable. But if it is to be averted, it will be necessary for the French teaching profession at all levels to define the aims and objectives of teaching the French Language and Civilisation. The definition of purpose must include broad social and educational aims as a context within which vocational objectives can be included in proper perspective. Then we shall be in a stronger position to promote and defend our purposes through the various professional and academic associations which, for the most part, have not distinguished themselves in providing coherent leadership in the difficult circumstances of the past six or seven years. It may well be one of the merits of this colloquium that it has stimulated us to reflect collectively on the issues, as a necessary prelude to concerted action.

DISCUSSION ON MICHAEL KELLY PAPER

In response to a reference by **Neville Waites** to a diminishing pool of applicants going on to universities to read French, **Linda Hantrais** reported that her information was that from this diminishing pool the technological universities, which offered non-literary courses, were recruiting an increasing share, to the extent that five or six universities were now recruiting over 50% of applicants to higher education courses including French, specifically to courses of this type where the Civilisation or Area Studies element was dominant. One of the interesting features she had noted was that Aston offered Modern Languages courses combining two languages but also the same package with one language plus another subject. If one looked at the gender mix on these different combinations, on a course on modern languages only or languages in their social context, you would find 90% of the students were women. Whereas if you looked at Combined Honours with Languages and Business Studies, you were getting a 50-50 ratio; so this certainly demonstrated the points mentioned in discussion about the socialisation of women to read languages, but there were certainly balancing effects. Really the dominant male area was still Science, and that meant that the occasional male student who combined Science with Languages had exceptional job opportunities, because of being very rare and an excellent product. She also mentioned that certain universities recruited from all round the country, while in fact others did not accept students from their local areas, or did so only reluctantly.

Eric Cahm raised the class issue in English higher education which had already been discussed in the American context. He felt that it had to be recognised that there was an area of class distinction in French Studies in England, epitomised by the difference in status between universities and polytechnics. He reminded the seminar that polytechnics were set off on their path of offering vocational courses with a view to training rude mechanicals as opposed to the education of gentlemen. He was conscious that his formulation was a little provocative, but class distinction, though it had been declining for many years, remained real, and it would be interesting to survey the social background of students of French in different institutions in Britain. His impression was that there was a hierarchy between institutions, in which the ones which were more vocationally-oriented had the least middle-class students. As far as Portsmouth Polytechnic was concerned, the social background of the French Studies students was rather varied, the female students being generally drawn from a wider range than the male students who tended to come from lower social groups. This did not mean, however, that the women came to Portsmouth as a finishing school but simply that they might have missed university entrance because of their examination grades, or that they might have a particular interest in the course. He suspected that on balance there would be some social gap in Oxford between the university and the polytechnic. Referring to the origins of polytechnics, **Tony Harding** added that what still affected people's attitudes to them was that they had been created from existing institutions which quite clearly had lower status than the universities. He quoted his former college, Bristol Polytechnic, which, formed from Bristol College of Commerce, was still known locally as the College of Knowledge, since it was where you went for your evening classes. The polytechnics in some cases got off the ground with quite a different identity very quickly. He was not sure **Eric Cahm** was right about the social distinction between university and polytechnic students in Oxford; his hunch was that the pattern would be much more original. The social level of students at Oxford Polytechnic was probably a cut above what it might be at an unpopular university. He remembered, however, that once Oxford was the only Polytechnic that appeared in the Yuppies' satirical guide, the *Sloane Ranger's Handbook*. **Eric Cahm** remarked that he had "Oxford" in his title. In England that immediately gave prestige. **John Harris** added that the Cambridgeshire College of Arts and Technology had also appeared in the Handbook...

Alice Kaplan objected to the term "finishing school" used by several speakers and to hearing teachers say "You know, most of my students are girls. They're very nice and so on ...". She thought that some kind of perspective from feminist scholarship should be used to look at this population of women students, and there ought to be a more interesting way to talk about their majority position. It might be asked why women got socialised into studying or ghettoised into studying France, or in a more positive way, how French Studies were for women an instrument for class mobility or social change. **Siân Reynolds** added that the problem was compounded, since the crisis in British higher education meant that the teaching faculty were predominantly men and (like all those present!) middle-aged. So there was a certain disjunction between teachers and students which had the result of a) reinforcing parental/paternal authority (fathers and daughters) and b) causing anguish among teachers which surfaced in the "finishing school" image that French Civilisation was a "soft" subject. This anguish meant they were all too ready to **agree** with hostile critics who attacked it in these terms. The gender question was for her therefore fairly fundamental in the debates at the seminar on French Civilisation, in that it required analysis rather than lamentation.

Christopher Pinet said that he had been teaching at university for 16 years and his experience was that women were now doing different things. In his estimation, the women he taught, particularly the bright ones, were now not just doing French but combining it with Business Studies. Good students now wanted to go on, maybe to mixed institutes.

Adrian Rifkin, referring to the issues of class and gender, said that French Studies in polytechnics would have to look at the polytechnic situation in a slightly wider context in the light of the kind of people who had started the newer type of course in them, precisely that group of lecturers who were now in their early forties. They had become squeezed in at the top end of the scale and very few people had been recruited below them. They clearly came out of a completely different background from the kind of course they set out to create, that is from traditional university backgrounds, at a time when universities were sunk in the utmost conservatism. The polytechnics expanded and developed in a whole series of disciplines in a way that a variety of universities were largely incapable of doing, except in the case of isolated examples like Birmingham with its Cultural Studies. The field of Cultural Studies had actually been taken up by the polytechnics, not by the universities. The problem lay, for example, in respect of the inter-disciplinary studies which had been developed, for example in the impact of gender studies. What had happened in recent years with financial cuts had been that the people who were students on the new polytechnic courses had not gone on to teach within them and develop them further. He felt there was now a crisis among the original group affecting their ability to appreciate the consequences of the changes in which they had been involved, or to accept the consequences of those changes on themselves. He felt that there had in fact been a real failure to take on the consequences of some of the changes that had been brought about. This could be looked at in narrow terms as a return to the finishing-school type of education, but he thought the future of French Studies, like any other discipline, needed to be looked at in terms of the financial crisis in British education. Universities and polytechnics could not be collapsed together because the situation was not the same, and what worried him greatly was that the new notion of drives for excellence, pushing polytechnics back to the mythical purpose which they were supposed to have had, to be technically good at training, would be dangerous for the preservation of certain forms of culture.

Eric Cahm then remarked in this context that one of the strange features of the discussions so far had been that so little had been said about the current political situation in Britain, to which **Adrian Rifkin** was referring which, as he said, was having a disastrous effect on the possibility of cultural development, on teaching standards and on prospects for the future. Survival had become the main concern of many, and although it was necessary to look forward, the situation was very constrained, with funds and posts disappearing.

Geoffrey Hare thought that the series of questions raised by Adrian Rifkin were the most important ones; it had obviously been quite a dramatic period over the last few years and there had been clearly a very concerted and orchestrated attempt to restructure the entire education system. To his way of thinking, it was an attempt to roll back the gains of 1944, and possibly those of 1908 or even further back. He felt that as long as French Civilisation teachers did not develop a coherent and coordinated response, then they would continue to be victims, picked off one by one and driven into competition with each other. For **Linda Hantrais**, what most universities were now looking at was who was getting the most applicants: "Heavens! University A is getting more of the cake and ours is declining. What shall we do ?" was the cry. **Geoffrey Hare** agreed that this was the competitive strategy universities were being driven into, rather than a cooperative one. He felt there was a danger of being eaten alive if that route was accepted. There was a need for some kind of coordinated response which he felt would have to come from outside. The institutionalised bodies like the Society for French Studies, the Standing Conference of Heads of Modern Languages in Polytechnics and Colleges and the Association of University Professors of French had been in complete dereliction in the present situation. Not only had they not organised any response, but they had not even organised any comprehension of the problem. There had been very few gatherings like the present one, where there was an opportunity to say: "Look what's happening in our universities, in our country; look what's being done to them." More of this kind of meeting was needed and a more organised approach towards building up some kind of effective organisation.

From the American side, **Nicholas Wahl** said that although there was no comparison between the British situation and the so-called crisis in American higher education, there had been some tough times: student choice had been reoriented in America at the undergraduate level. Even before Reagan, there had been a cutting back of a number of Federal grants-in-aid to universities and to students, which meant that the very small amount of government aid that Americans had had in the past had increasingly been cut back; this had happened even more brutally under Reagan. It must also be said, he added, that in a long period of austerity, and with salaries moving ahead so slowly in higher education, a lot of good people had been turned away from the arts side of education and this had caused harm to the profession. In all the Social Sciences and the Humanities, the number of people applying was far lower, and a lot of the best students did not come. They went directly from undergraduate studies to Law School, to Business School, to Schools of Administration of various kinds, so that in that sense American colleagues had had problems too, leaving aside some of the more interesting problems raised by Alice Kaplan, for example, that

French Studies and Letters programmes generally had very few people from
graduate level of the male sex because they could go to professional
schools and he thought this was directly linked with the sharp decline in
Federal support for post-graduate education.
On the British political situation, **Tony Harding** thought that references to
bankcruptcy probably referred to the Committee of Directors of
Polytechnics, which had been very ineffective in planning the public sector,
just as the Committee of Vice-Chancellors had been ineffective on the other
side. The system as a whole had been unable to defend itself, irrespective
of subject. He thought that within the public sector people had accepted
that they were going to be cut, but that linguists in the polytechnics and
colleges, had grouped together to try to protect the interests of Languages
as an area through their own pressure group, which had been in existence
since 1972, via a variety of formal and informal initiatives, for example
attacking proposals known to be coming e.g. on raising the staff/student
ratio to 14.5:1 as the target for work in Languages. The group had tried to
work with the universities as well, through the National Council for Modern
Languages, a binary group which had gone dead in the 1970s and which the
group put some life back into at the beginning of the 1980s. It had been
the National Council for Modern Languages which had put in the application
for the Nuffield Survey. The idea of this survey had been that what was
needed more than anything else was a clear map of what was going on before
the cuts started raining in, so that there might be some chance of actually
introducing a degree of rationality. The body he was talking about was in
the public sector: it was called the Standing Conference of Heads of Modern
Languages in Polytechnics and Colleges and he himself was Chairman. On the
university side, there had always been a tremendous variety of
organisations, and that had been part of the problem. When the SCHML
joined the National Council for Modern Languages, they were surprised to
find that the Association of University Professors of French had not really
begun to think about what steps to take. It was therefore no surprise that
polytechnics and universities had been picked off separately. The
universities had gone through the small departments rationalisation
exercise without any real thought about what rationalisation in that
context meant, and without any real look across the binary divide to see
what was going on in the polytechnics. On the polytechnic side, it had
been, apart from one or two successful battles to protect the subject as a
whole, a matter of battles within institutions, and those with any sense
had made sure they were in the right place within the institution to stop
the cuts coming their way. It had been really that kind of damage-
limitation exercise in departments which had survived: they had done so
because they had known their way around their institutions at the top. It
had become as crude as that, and it was not going to become much better.
One speaker added that a vast collaborationist mentality had emerged, which
meant either keeping quiet and ducking or waiting for somebody else to take
a blow on the back of the head. **Eric Cahm** remarked that American
colleagues would have perceived in the preceding discussion some of the
differences between polytechnic and university discourse, and no doubt that
in itself was a weakness. **John Roach** thought that the problem was one of
people not geared to co-operating and working together and of a split
between polytechnics and the universities, of which there were 44 and which
were not a single entity.
Adrian Rifkin suggested that the split in the discussion had an impact on
some of the theoretical issues being discussed at the seminar. Speaking
for his own part, he said that in terms of the Cultural History he had been
working on, a great deal of his energy over 17 years had been devoted to
attacking the canon, and the whole notion that certain kinds of cultural
language study were a means of accession to social status. He had been

critical of that process, trying to develop new methods of study of cultural questions. In the current political situation, however, the terms of reference of the debate had changed, and if accession to the canon as a means to social status was being denied to students, in that context he would be inclined to defend the canon. He explained he would certainly no longer be prepared to be one-sidedly critical of a traditional method of organising knowledge, if accession to that form of knowledge had become the real area of social conflict. He thought that came right back to some of the points that had been made about access to knowledge. He thought the situation in Britain at the moment was that government policy actually seemed to be aiming to produce a very ignorant and uneducated population. In reply to a remark that the government was obsessed with technology, he replied that they were obsessed not with technology but a certain low-grade technological capability. The main obsession was to increase social differences through deprivation of any access to knowledge through traditional cultural values. **Linda Hantrais** pointed out to the seminar that it was the technological universities that had been cut most heavily in 1981: Aston's budget had been cut by one third, which meant reducing staff, students and books by one third. When looking at universities facing dire straits in a very competitive situation, it always had to be remembered that it was precisely the technological universities that had suffered most. There were cases in the public sector of some of the best degree courses in the country vanishing without reference to their quality, because in one particular institution at that particular time it had been politically possible to do so. Judgements had not been made, had never been made, in the series of cuts in the public sector, on the criterion of quality or even on the question of balance of provision.

Ed Knox intervened to say that all the American visitors had been impressed with both the quality and the quantity of the work they saw being done in French Studies in Great Britain. He said they would dream of a situation like the one British colleagues enjoyed in that respect, and he thought it was terribly ironical because they saw the downside of things. He thought all American colleagues would wish they were some day to be entrenched in anything like the same way that British colleagues were, with legitimate offerings. in Civilisation. They would not care whether it was in postgraduate work or undergraduate work; they simply wished for more. So British colleagues must be the judge of how bad their situation was. Much of it was a subject of envy from the American side. **Tony Harding** agreed, and said that if one looked back 20 years, there were virtually no Civilisation-based degree courses, whereas in 1987 the situation was that a very substantial proportion of the students doing Languages degrees in Britain, not only in French, were actually − particularly in the public sector − doing courses which came under the Civilisation umbrella. So yes, British colleagues were very depressed, but there were of course a lot of positive factors and growth areas. **Brian Jenkins** pointed to the approval at Portsmouth Polytechnic of a part-time MA in Contemporary French Studies. This point prompted **Tony Harding** to remind the seminar about the need not only to train people to come into higher education; he thought it was probably more significant in the long run to re-train those teaching in secondary education. **Geoffrey Hare** suggested scope for being very much less ambitious, in this area, by running conversion courses for teachers teaching the new A-level syllabuses, and wondered whether there were any similar moves in the United States to set up shorter blocks of MA-level training which could be very useful at a local level. **Ed Knox** answered that there was something of a movement in the US, but it was more for linguistic immersion than for French Studies. **Linda Hantrais** noted an interesting trend was that fewer of the graduates from the new degree courses were going into teaching, but she thought that the tendency among

Aston graduates was that they went in other directions immediately after graduation but ten years later decided that teaching might not be all that bad.

TEACHING FRENCH CIVILISATION IN BRITISH HIGHER EDUCATION:
THE POLYTECHNIC MODEL

By Stuart Williams, Wolverhampton Polytechnic.

"French Civilisation" as a teaching subject is a Gallicism or Americanism,
at least as far as British polytechnics are concerned. It has been defined
as "societal" study as opposed to literary or linguistic study. In this
paper, I shall refer to the Social Sciences, Business Studies, Language
study and Literature, as all contributing to the study of France in our
courses. However, if the debate in the USA has essentially been about "big
C or little c culture ?" (1), in our polytechnics it has largely been about
"which Social Science(s) shall we include?"

Why should there be a "Polytechnic Model" (like Cromwell's New Model Army)
? The idea goes back to the virtual en bloc creation of the polytechnics
in the late 1960s and early 1970s, to their academic tutelage by the
Council for National Academic Awards (CNAA), and their financial government
at local level by the Local Education Authorities (LEAs). The 1966 Crosland
White Paper intended them as "a distinctive sector of higher education
complementary to the universities" (2). I would interpret this as more
directed to teaching, less to research, more business and industry-oriented
than the universities.

The CNAA rigorously vetted all the polytechnics' degree and diploma courses,
which had to be submitted for its approval. In fact, the CNAA system
considerably determined how and what they would teach. The attachment of
each polytechnic to its LEA as purseholder - though most of the money came
from the national Advanced Further Education Pool - did not significantly
influence teaching, as far as I am aware. The annually updated SCHML (3)
Guide to Language Courses in Polytechnics and Similar Institutions lists, in
1986, 20 polytechnics and 15 other colleges doing similar work. Of course
the "binary line" dividing public sector higher education (polytechnics and
some colleges) from universities is not a Berlin Wall. Polytechnics are
both different from each other and sometimes quite similar to the so-called

technological universities, but there is enough coherence, determined by origin and governance, to make it possible to describe a model (4).

So the **typical** degree course in British public sector higher education, the locus of its French Civilisation or French Studies teaching, has been and is, some kind of European Studies degree with Languages. This means a package, for the student, with one or two European Languages and some of History, Economics, Politics, Sociology, Geography, or International Relations etc. These ingredients have been very carefully selected, dosed and structured; they had to be to pass the stringent requirements of a CNAA degree submission, with its attendant visit by a team of experts in the different fields selected. (I well remember being amazed at a conference in 1972 by a university teacher admitting that his European Studies degree had begun, but that its Final-Year courses were not yet determined. In the CNAA system this is strictly not possible (5). Literature, not Social Science, could have constituted the "theory and cerebration element" of these courses (to use an older CNAA concept). In fact however, Literature was marginalised, being represented on such degrees either minimally or not at all.

This is not to say that the combination of French and Literature is excluded from polytechnics altogether. Looking at the SCHML guide, I can see four strategies for retaining Literature. Firstly, "French" may be constructed of thin strands of Language, Literature, Politics and Society; the subject French may be the vector of nearly all the French Civilisation that the students receive, as at Oxford Poly. Secondly, students in their first year may have to study several different subjects, including Literature, which they may continue or drop in subsequent years; this is the case at Portsmouth Polytechnic. Thirdly, there is the BA Humanities style of degree, which offers all the Social Sciences already mentioned plus other subjects like Drama, History of Ideas, Philosophy, Psychology, Society and Culture; the students serve themselves, à la carte. Fourthly, the institution may offer an array of "named degrees" aimed at different clienteles. For example, Wolverhampton has a BA Humanities (as above (6)), a BA Languages for Business (Languages and Business Studies), a BA European Studies (one Language and a lot of Social Science), and a BA Modern Languages (two Languages and less social science). The last is the type that I am mainly describing in this paper.

I intend now to deal with two problems and two questions. The first problem is that of selecting and paring down the disciplines involved in

69

your degree. Of course, we all began having debates about "my subject versus your subject" many years ago. However, in preparation for this paper, and in order to show that the protectionist spirit is still alive, I circulated a simple questionnaire to my Social Science colleagues. They replied, quotably and only partly tongue-in-cheek: "Economics is the basis of Civilisation"; "power and decision-making seem to me to be second only to the economic system in their centrality to Civilisation"; "Sociology has been called the queen of the Social Sciences"; "History should be the core subject (but not as traditionally defined (7). Despite these pretentions, and because of our very thorough (and time-consuming) course planning, my colleagues all thought that the CNAA model tended to allow their subject its just deserts. They had some reservations e.g. (Politics) "Political Systems are covered very well but there is less scope in our courses for Political Theory etc.", (Economics) "any multidisciplinary course tends to dilute the disciplines offered".

My second problem concerns the integration of the diverse parts of our "Area Study". We strive for coherence, and our solution is to build many "bridges", links between the parts. Our degrees are structured over the four years (Year Three abroad) so that for example descriptive politics precede systems studies etc. All courses are Europe-focussed: Rueffian economics not Galbraithian, one might say. There are country-specific options, especially just before and after the period of residence abroad. Booklists contain foreign-language texts. Some lectures are given in the foreign languages. Numerous seminars are conducted in the foreign languages. Finally, the language instruction classes are often related to surrounding disciplines (more about this later). Any of these mechanisms may work imperfectly: the complaint about students being as silent as Trappists during seminars is frequently heard etc. However, I would say that several such mechanisms have to be operated if the parts of the degree are to "gel".

Of the several questions that such a system may raise, the first of my two concerns the congeniality of this context for the French Civilisation teacher, as opposed to the not entirely disgruntled Economist or Political Scientist referred to above. What is her/his role in this structure, apart from the teaching of French Language? Well, (s)he may of course be a product of just such a degree, in which case *"il/elle baigne dans l'huile"*. If however (s)he was trained for Literature then his/her most usual response in our system has been partially to convert to Social Science, by means of an MA in European Studies or Politics etc.. This "topping-up", as it is sometimes slightingly called, then enables the subject to share in the Social Science teaching. (It is incidentally rarer for a Social Scientist to feel the need to top up in Language). Those who wish to teach Literature do not, as I have said, find much scope for it in our model, although they have a place in our public sector system, in the BA Humanities type of course also referred to previously. Wolverhampton's BA Humanities has, quite typically, courses like: *Le Théâtre de l'Absurde, Le Nouveau Roman, Le Théâtre Politique de Sartre, Quelques Romancières Françaises, La Littérature de la Résistance et de la Collaboration.* And courses in French Cinema, *"le septième art".*

I leave the question of whether it is right that Literature should have been marginalised in polytechnicss, since it is not part of my brief, and pass to my second question concerning the role of Language. If the economist is broadly happy that our students leave us Economics-literate, how do we ensure that they are French-literate?

It may be said that Language teachers in this system set themselves three goals. Firstly, to teach all-round language competence, these days with a renewed emphasis on "communicative competence" and "communicative capacity" (8). The second aim is that of inter-disciplinarity between Language and Social Science, already referred to as bridge-building. The third aim might be called *"culture générale";* it may be logical in the system I am describing to relate all language work to the other (social science) subjects of the course, it is however both *"agréable et utile"* to deal with several more subjects than are covered (or even dreamt of ?) by the Social Sciences. In this way we may produce, in one person, a competent linguist, an economist/political scientist and someone who has rubbed shoulders with Frenchness.

Much more could be said. Some might say that I claim too much for the system I am representing. It is certainly true that change is constant; CNAA is on the wane, notions of free student choice or ease of transfer may militate against structured integration etc. Since I support the model I have described I can only say, like Napoleon's mother *"pourvu que ça dure"* .

1. Edward Knox (Middlebury), during the seminar.

2. I am quoting a 1979 pamphlet, *The Polytechnics: Vision into Reality* issued by the Committee of Directors of Polytechnics. See also ROBINSON, E., *The New Polytechnics* (Penguin, 1968).

3. Standing Conference of Heads of Modern Languages in Polytechnics and other Colleges.

4. Polytechnics: Birmingham, Brighton, through to Teesside, Wolverhampton. Other Colleges: Cambridgeshire College of Arts and Technology, Colchester Institute, Ealing College etc. Technological universities: Aston, Bath, Loughborough, Salford, Surrey.

5. There is an amusing parody of the CNAA visit in the novel *Wilt* by Tom Sharpe. *Wilt* is loosely based on CCAT above.

6. The BA Humanities type occurs frequently in the SCHML institutions; there are 12 such in the Guide. Their products are necessarily heterogeneous.

7. My historian colleague does not much like the usual formula of Political History plus History of Ideas but prefers "History from below, Social History, T.S. Eliot's boiled beef and carrots."

8. See for example WIDDOWSON,H.G., *Teaching Language as Communication* (OUP,1978).

THE TEACHING OF FRENCH "CIVILISATION" IN BRITISH UNIVERSITIES

by Geoffrey Hare, University of Newcastle-upon-Tyne
and John Roach, University of Aberdeen

The survey

Our paper is based on a survey carried out during the academic year 1986-87, covering 31 university departments where courses on some aspect of French "Civilisation" are offered in the context of a degree course involving French language study. All university departments in the British Isles were circulated and 36 of them responded, approximately three quarters of the whole. We circulated the polytechnic sector too, but our brief for the present paper was limited to the university sector.

In a covering note which accompanied our questionnaire, we explained the purpose of the survey as being to provide us with information on "Civilisation" courses on France offered in higher education in the British Isles, in the hope of creating a data bank available to all those interested in this area of French Studies, and providing the material for an analysis of the range and nature of the courses available with a view to publication. One of the stimuli towards our interest in gathering information in this area was the imbalance we perceived in a questionnaire circulated, in the context of the Nuffield Enquiry into Modern Languages, between the sophistication of the questions on the teaching of literary periods, authors and genres, and the relative lack of detail being requested on societal or Area Studies courses within Language degrees.

Within the context of the questionnaire, we defined "Civilisation" as societal, i.e. non-literary and non-linguistic, studies, of France or French-speaking areas. The distinction was not totally unproblematic however. For instance, we had respondents who felt that a course on the sociolinguistics of French could well have been included. We were also somewhat tentative about including as course content topics French Philosophy or "The Intellectual Life of France", since these have been more commonly included in traditional literature and philology-based courses. In

order to iron out in advance some of these difficulties, we conducted a
pilot survey in order to test the questionnaire. From the pilot reponses,
it emerged that there was a great diversity of courses and approaches
(content, duration, level etc.). We did not therefore try to cover
explicitly every possible variation in the final version of the
questionnaire, but, following comments from respondents, we added an
Appendix sheet with general headings relating to sections of the
questionnaire, which could be used to amplify information on any aspect of
courses. We asked for course description handouts as an alternative. We
should like to record here our grateful thanks to those colleagues who were
generous with their time in responding so fully.

Results

31 of our 36 university departments offer "Civilisation" courses wthin
Language degrees involving French, four of these at MA level. We identified
87 different course units at these 31 institutions, some being compulsory,
some optional, some lasting one term, some throughout the whole course. It
is clear therefore that few university French degrees now have no
"Civilisation" aspects at all in the course.

3412 students follow such courses out of a possible total of 5452. These
figures are somewhat inflated by the phenomenon of double counting, i.e. the
same student being counted twice where he or she is following two such
course units in the same year. Nonetheless, there are obviously many
students involved in such courses, mainly of the French Studies or Modern
Languages (Double Honours/Joint Honours) type, with a small number on
European Studies or (International) Business Studies with French courses.
The success of the Association for the Study of Modern and Contemporary
France and the number of publications in this area in the last five or ten
years had indicated a growing market, and one suspects that in view of the
numbers involved, publishers will continue to see French "Civilisation" as a
growing market at the undergraduate level.

What was already well known was that there are a few technological
universities, where the study of "Civilisation" may be regarded as central
to the degree course, for example Aston and Bradford. What is less obvious
is the type of "Civilisation" course available in other university degree
courses. It appears that in addition to those courses on degrees where all
content study is of the "Civilisation" type, there are two main types of
course unit: on the one hand, the survey course or introduction to (usually

many offer a broad range
** *others offer few*
only a

74

+ *v. few univ. Fr. degrees now have*
no CF aspects at all in the course.

imposs.

contemporary or modern) France, and on the other the special option, a narrowly focused study of a particular aspect of French "Civilisation".

Within all the types of course mentioned above, the topics or disciplines covered are as follows, the figure in parenthesis referring to the number of times the topic was cited as being included in the course unit concerned (out of 87 course units, remember):

    Government, Politics, Institutions, Administration (68)
    Society, social institutions and   structures (e.g. family, education)
    (52)
    History (37)
    The Economy, Economic Geography (e.g. industry, regional planning)   (36)
    Current Affairs   (13)
    Demography (13)
    Media Studies (11)
    Commerce, French Business Practice, Commercial Law   (10)
    Geography (9)
    Film Studies (8)
    International Relations   (7)
    Intellectual Life (6)
    France within European Community Studies   (6)
    French Law and Legal System   (5)
    Other types of study which got a mention were for instance *Bande
    Dessinee* and *Chanson*, which might find their way into
    non-traditional literary courses.

It is clear that the fields of Politics and Society, either contemporary or historical, are well ahead of the field, with the French Economy making a respectable showing, and the discipline of History far from being swamped by the newer disciplines of Political Science or Social Studies.

As regards the periods covered in these courses, we find the almost universal coverage of contemporary France or France post-1945 in some kind of course in those universities which offer one or more "Civilisation" courses.   Four-fifths of the courses claimed to cover periods ending with the contemporary situation, their starting points being many and varied, but the most popular being post-Second World War:

    1789 (7), 1848 (2), 1870/1871 (2), 1900/1914/1918 (18), 1945 (25),

    1957/1958 (12), 1967/1968 (3), 1981 or later (4).

A small number of course units covered the 19th century only, e.g. *Politics and Society in 19th-century France* at Newcastle University and *Aux origines de la France contemporaine* - Lancaster, or perhaps 1789 to 1945 (*Histoire sociale et politique* - Bath), but in all cases they were complemented by other course units covering the modern period.

Some courses are very narrowly focused in terms of time span: *Paris and its Culture in the 1920s* (Swansea), or *Occupation, Collaboration,*

Resistance - 1930-1947 (Hull). Other courses covered very wide time-spans: *Art and Society from the Middle Ages to 1870* (Hull), *History of French Civilisation, 1500 to the present* (Trinity College, Dublin), and one beginning in 120 BC on *Occitania Past and Present* (Southampton).

It could be argued that the term "background" course marginalises the study of French "Civilisation", and the term does not appear in the overwhelming number of course descriptions. Seven-eighths of courses are described as stand-alone or independent courses, with one eighth as "background" courses, i.e. background to literary studies, several of these being in Ireland, but also in London, with varied starting dates again. One is explicitly labelled in this way as *20th-Century France and Modern French Literature* (Edinburgh).

This should not lead us to believe that the marginalisation phenomenon has ceased to exist, since the number of teachers on the courses labelled as independent suggests that the opposite may often still be true. There are a high number of one-teacher courses (48), and 20 (survey) courses where four or more teachers are involved. Our tentative conclusion is that where the course is an independent course, either it has only been recently introduced - we should have included in our questionnaire a question such as : "When did "Civilisation" begin ?" - or that "Civilisation" courses are treated as discrete parts of the degree course (*see* below the frequency of options) rather than an integral part of course planning. In consequence, "Civilisation" becomes colleague X's equivalent of the "period" or "author", their own patch of academic territory, from which others will happily exclude themselves. Where several colleagues share the teaching on a course, it is often (but not always) likely that their contribution is a non-specialist one, or at least is not based on any research interest and is an introductory survey course, the non-specialist aspect again leading to a marginalisation of the subject area.

Nonetheless, it is clear that over one hundred different teachers are involved in the teaching of one aspect or another of French "Civilisation" on language degree courses in British universities. Many more of course teach aspects of French History or Politics from within History or Government and Politics departments.

The relationship of the "Civilisation" teaching to the language teaching was another aspect explored, insufficiently no doubt. In response to the question: "Is teaching of content study *integrated* with teaching of language skills ?", 33 course units were described as being *integrated* and

76

54 as *not integrated*. A large proportion of these positive replies can be accounted for in the technological universities like Bath and Aston (18 out of their 20 course units described). These results beg several questions about how the integration is conceived and effected, especially in other universities, and this is a promising area for further research. It is understandable that very few colleagues were able to find the time to add explanatory detail about this in their submissions. However it is of interest to see how many of these courses are taught through the medium of the French language (*see* below).

Looking at how the course units are organised within the structure of the degree course as a whole, it emerges that students are twice as likely to embark on "Civilisation" courses in their first year as they are in their final year – this more a function of supply than demand – but it is in the Second Year that the courses last for the longest amount of time:

> Year One: 1720 students on 34 course units for total of 98 terms
> Year Two: 1610 students on 32 course units for total of 152 terms
> Final Year: 825 students on 33 course units for total of 120 terms

It comes as no surprise that it is in the First Year that we usually find the large compulsory survey courses, with the narrowing down to more specialised optional courses in the Final Year. Of the 325 obligatory courses (followed by some 2100 students), 25 are obligatory in the first year of study, and 13 are obligatory for Finalists. The duration of these courses varies from one term (e.g. for some first-year survey courses, but equally for some final-year options) to three, six or nine terms. Most typically a course unit lasts for one academic year, which is often described as two terms in the Final Year.

Pursuing further the mode of teaching and examining, every year some 1300 lectures are given in British universities on "Civilisation" topics – scope for some rationalisation perhaps, or for the marketing of video lectures on popular topics ? A further 1000 or so tutorials are attended by students on these courses. Insofar as such tutorials are probably repeated two or three times by tutors for different small groups, then we can say that there exists a great deal of small group teaching on "Civilisation". Picking up the point about integration of content and language teaching, it is encouraging to see that 55% of lectures given are given in French, and (perhaps surprisingly) 60% of tutorials in French. 60% of all students receive their "Civilisation" teaching mainly through the medium of French. Basing our idea on no more evidence than a hunch or hearsay, we feel it is likely that these percentages for the use of French language in the context of "Civilisation" classes are much higher than those for the use of French in the context of literary studies. It would be interesting to explore further this supposition that the "Civilisation" teacher is closer to France and to the French language than his or her literary colleagues. It may be true if it is linked, as looks to be the case, with innovation in general, innovation in syllabus design (extending coverage to include "Civilisation"), perhaps going hand in hand with innovation in teaching methods (a move in the direction of teaching through the medium of the French language). This is merely speculation. It is clear from the survey, however, that those course units which have teaching mainly or exclusively in French tend to involve higher teaching loads and longer courses (in terms of the "Civilisation" components) than those courses where teaching is done in English. This suggests that where "Civilisation" is done most seriously or where it accounts for a major part of the course, as opposed to being marginalised, is in those courses where it is taught through the medium of French. The link between the teaching of "Civilisation" and the teaching of the language is probably not coincidental, but part of a coherent philosophy of language teaching. A lot more could be said about the necessary link between Language and "Civilisation", but similar results are found as regards students' written work, slightly more students being required to write in French than in English. As to the number of essays or written assignments per year per course unit, the most common was two:

No essays: 11;   1 essay: 18;   2 essays: 35;   3 essays: 17;   4 or more essays: 6.

Seven courses involved dissertations, but three were to be in English.

The pattern of assessment reinforces in a small number of cases the marginalising effect of some survey and background course: 18 are assessed by course work only, six of these being first-year survey courses, three of which were described as Background Studies. On the other hand, 37 course units are examined by a written paper in Finals, only 12 of them in French. This means there is a fall-off between the number of courses where Final Year teaching is done in French and those where the examining is done in French. The same phenomenon is seen in other aspects of examining. Whether First Year or Final Year, there are a number of courses where teaching occurs in French, and examining is done in English. It is an old argument about the use of the foreign language in teaching, and in many places working practices have been established. However it seems to have been harder to break down the barriers of the examination system, where, especially in the case of a department running a system of options, it is more difficult to be the odd one out, and where the notion of "fairness" as between students following different options has meant that uniformity of examining mode (in English) has won the day. One interesting and unique return, from Manchester, was where a "Civilisation" course was examined in the Finals oral.

Bilan et perspectives

The statistics brought out by our survey show a very positive and healthy growth in the number of "Civilisation" courses taught in institutions of higher education. However, the figures also reveal a more negative element, namely, the ad hoc nature of university courses, with some obvious exceptions in certain institutions. The reasons for this will vary from one university to another, but for the most part the fact is that "Civilisation" courses have been grafted on to existing, long-established university undergraduate degree courses so that they find their place on such degree courses either as bolt-on components or, frequently, as optional extras. The presence of "Civilisation" on a degree course may have been brought about through various factors, such as a response to student demand, and the need to keep up with other institutions and thus meet the challenge of rival and, increasingly, competing institutions. Sometimes a "Civilisation" course has been introduced in order to accommodate the interests of a member of staff, or as a result of a desire to widen the curriculum and to be perceived as "relevant", whatever that vague catch-all term may mean.

The fact which emerges from our survey is that within the presently constituted degree courses, that is, within a traditional or conventional or even partially revised Language and Literature degree, "Civilisation" is not a fully integrated component of that degree. Even when "Civilisation" is a compulsory part of the degree course, examined in Finals, it remains a discrete element. This has major consequences, not only for what is taught under the label "Civilisation", but also for how it is taught.

Given that the majority of university "Civilisation" courses are taught over one or two terms, or, at best, a full academic year (very rarely two, and not across the full degree course), we consider it to be impossible to construct a cumulative curriculum for such courses. Consequently, those who teach "Civilisation" courses (and such courses are very demanding in preparation and teaching time) are frequently forced to offer only a segment of the subject they are concerned with. They have to concentrate on a narrow, highly selective coverage of a historical period, of politics, economics or sociology. Hence the popularity of "Contemporary France" courses, that is France since 1958. These seem to have the advantage of being "relevant" and self-contained, but, even leaving aside the fact that there was a France before 1958, as the years go by and 1958 recedes, such courses can no longer offer even the superficial attraction of being self-contained. Thus the lecturer is faced with the problem of deciding what is manageable within the time allocated, what to include and, increasingly what to leave out, as the period extends and the issues widen and the complexities deepen.

Pedagogically, faced with the time restrictions imposed, the "Civilisation" lecturer has to perform the almost impossible task of initiating students to subject areas with which they are, at best, unfamiliar if not wholly ignorant. At the same time as informing students, the lecturer has to engage them in analysis of the material so as to stimulate intellectual debate and thus encourage original work. Further constraints arise from the fact that most "Civilisation" courses do not have set books, or at least not a set book. They demand a wide range of reading on the part of students if they are to acquire the necessary information and confront the variety of intepretations which will enable them to conduct intelligent discussion of the subject (2). But since a "Civilisation" course is only a part and usually a minor, subsidiary part of a student's degree, the lecturer, to be fair as well as pragmatic, has to create a course which has to meet almost impossible demands. The material has to be intellectually and even factually accessible, and yet the lecturer has to promote an understanding of the complexities of the issues which arise from the material. The lecturer has to produce a course which can be readily assimilated without being pre-packed and therefore undemanding of the student.

The present restrictions on time which circumscribe "Civilisation" courses mean that it is extremely difficult, if not impossible, to plan a course which will allow for a process of building and consolidation. Within the prevailing conditions, students cannot be prepared properly so as to enable them to benefit fully from the potential richness of the material with which they are dealing. Too much is expected of them in too little time. Nevertheless, given the inherent difficulties which arise from the conditions in which "Civilisation" courses operate, it is a measure of the interest of students and of the commitment of lecturers that the courses should continue to enrol such large numbers of students. But the popularity of "Civilisation" courses should not mask the fact that such courses have to fulfil too many objectives in too short a time, they have to inform, to promote knowledge and stimulate understanding, to engage the student in debate, to draw out connections with other parts of the degree course, to extend linguistic awareness and competence etc. The restriction on the time allocated to "Civilisation" means that it is extremely difficult to achieve any, let alone all, of these desirable goals. One consequence, and a very damaging one, which in the present circumstances has become almost a self-fulfilling prophecy, is that "Civilisation" courses run the risk of being perceived by students and more particularly by colleagues in the department as interesting but "soft", that is, as intellectually undemanding and thus unworthy of further development.

"Civilisation" courses will be open to such charges for as long as they remain peripheral rather than core within a university French degree. For "Civilisation" to move from periphery to core there has to be a structural change in the degree course. Merely adding "civilisation" courses to an existing degree will not change the situation, indeed it will only make it worse by creating further confusion in the guise of diversity, and by compounding the problem of a lack of coherent development through increasing the sense of bittiness, so that in the end "Civilisation" courses would be even more marginal. Weight of members is not the answer. As long as "Civilisation" continues to be merely a component of a degree course rather than the conceptual starting point for a degree course, determining not only content but development and pedagogy, then "Civilisation" will continue to be relegated to its present peripheral role. From our survey we feel that university degree courses are in a period of transition and rethinking, most particularly with regard to the place and teaching of "Civilisation". But if "Civilisation" is to be more than a token presence on a degree course then departments must stop thinking of "Civilisation" as "a course" and start considering it to be the core of the degree. It will not be easy.

A degree which takes the teaching of "Civilisation" as its starting point has to be a fully integrated course, language-civilisation-literature, in which each component interconnects rather than existing, as at present, as one of a series of discrete elements. There has to be a move from the present illusory "à la carte" degree menu which has only the vaguest rationale for its eclecticism, to a carefully conceived and structured *"menu gastronomique"*, rich and varied, but which above all is coherent and explicit about its objectives. The present structure, for the most part, pretends to offer choice and diversity, while in fact being designed to protect the multiple *"propriétés privées"* which have long been established and which have come to be accepted, without proof or challenge, as constituting what is essential to a "proper" French degree. As many of those who teach "Civilisation" know, these *"propriétés"* are zealously guarded by energetic *"chiens méchants"* - *"défense d'entrer"* ...

This should be a time for innovation, but, given the present conditions in higher education (in Britain at least), we are not hopeful that the restructuring which needs to be done can in fact be accomplished. Our survey brings out the fact that "Civilisation" courses are increasingly perceived to be desirable because of demand factors or even per se. Yet the contraction in higher education and in Humanities in particular, the dearth of resources in personnel and materials, and the climate of hesitancy not to say fear, prevent rather than stimulate the kind of structural changes which are required. Under present conditions, conservatism will prevail and the danger is that though the goods displayed in university departments' shop windows will be attractively rearranged and relabelled, in reality, University French Departments will continue to be essentially concerned with reproducing themselves rather than with restructuring themselves. Departments will seek to answer the question: "What is it that we have to offer in order that we may continue to be what we have always been ?" rather than start from the fundamental question: "What is it that we have to do in order to make our degree meet the needs of to-day ?" Without such a fundamental shift, it may well be that whatever the calendar entries show, once again it will be a case of *"plus ça change..."*. And yet as the survey on "Civilisation" demonstrates, we have seen the future and it belongs to us.

FOOTNOTES

1. For some thoughts on the issue see HARE, G.E., 'L'apprentissage des langues et l'étude de la civilisation, tandem inséparable' in BATES, M. and HARE,G.E., *Communicative Approaches in French in Higher Education, AFLS Occasional Papers*, No.1 (AFLS, 1986).

2.　"Civilisation" courses are dependent on access to a wide range of publications. Given the cut-backs inflicted on library resources throughout higher education in Britain, it is essential that departments (e.g. Languages and Social Sciences) should collaborate in order to achieve maximum efficiency in ordering so as to provide as wide a coverage as possible.

DISCUSSION OF GEOFFREY HARE AND JOHN ROACH PAPER

In reply to a remark by Siân Reynolds about the freeze on posts in British universities, Nicholas Hewitt pointed out that even if a lot of posts were coming up it was not at all evident where the qualified candidates would come from. What came out of the survey as very significant from his position, was that there were 29 out of 34 universities doing undergraduate courses in French civilisation, but only four doing graduate, MA courses, and he suspected that the overwhelming majority of PhD candidates in French were working in literary or intellectual or critical areas. Very few were actually coming on-line with actual PhD specialisms in "Civilisation", which meant that they would have problems at a job interview. If they got the job they would have to recycle themselves and their Civilisation courses might begin by covering the French Economy; the following year it would become Writers on the French Economy, and in the third year, Writers...

On the difficulty of developing postgraduate courses in French Civilisation in Britain, John Roach wondered if it might be possible to overcome some of the difficulties in staffing them by a system of buying in staff from other institutions, so as to lead to a genuinely collaborative postgraduate system. Tony Harding remarked that there had of course been quite a considerable growth of postgraduate courses based on Civilisation, such as the Reading MA, courses at LSE and so on, but the financial arrangements in British higher education were going to make it difficult for students to obtain the support needed to take these courses. John Roach added that in any case such courses had to offer a fairly convincing menu of Politics and Economics, which meant that they were open to a very small number of students in any one institution. Nicholas Wahl remarked that there had been traditions of that kind of collaborative thinking - the best-known had been in Germany, where before the war you could go at doctoral level from one university to another, picking out the specialisms of each. The city of New York had a doctoral consortium so that the PhD candidate could pick up language in one institution, and Civilisation elsewhere. For **Linda Hantrais**, this was difficult to achieve in the British system, because in order to obtain credit, the student had to follow a complete course in one institution: otherwise he or she would not get the postgraduate qualification. In answer to a question about recruitment to civilisation-based postgraduate courses, she said that, for example, the MA course in French Area Studies at one polytechnic where she had been external examining had had enormous problems in recruiting because of the financial burden throughout the educational system. They found it impossible to get secondary-school teachers released at all, even on a part-time basis. The Association of University Professors of French had done a survey about four years ago on French Departments, which showed that any department which had a postgraduate population of more than about four was really doing extremely well. **Tony Harding** pointed out that until about two years ago, teachers in higher education who chose to enter the type of postgraduate programme they were talking about had up to 75% of their salary refunded through what was called the "pool" system. But that no longer existed and the number of students who could be recruited in that way would be significantly reduced. Until two years ago, staff release of this kind had been the most popular method of staff development, and of encouraging lecturers to acquire another discipline to add to their original training. One speaker added that you needed a very strong lobby within a French Department for Civilisation in order to obtain a reasonable level of support for postgraduate work. The possibility of postgraduate students coming in on a part-time basis was mentioned as a solution. **Laurence Bell** reported finally that Surrey had launched an MA two years ago, hoping that it would attract overseas and American students, but this year it seemed to be attracting a lot more British students: one of the features was that the course was conducted in English. But he found approaching French politics and society difficult without the benefit of using texts in the language.

THE TEACHING OF FRENCH "CIVILISATION" AT THE UNIVERSITY OF EDINBURGH
by Vaughan Rogers, University of Edinburgh

The programmes concerned are: 1) MA in French with Business Studies

2) MA in French with Contemporary European Institutions

3) BCom in Business Studies with French.

Introductory remarks concerning the concept of a Combined Honours Model and its applicability.

The concept seems to imply the existence of an integrated programme of courses, drawn up and administered jointly by the departments concerned, with the specific educational needs of the students following such a programme in mind. Although this may well be the case in institutions where combined programmes are a well-established phenomenon, in institutions such as Edinburgh, where the establishment of Joint Degrees is a relatively recent initiative, efforts to set them up have had to contend with long-standing departmental structures and loyalties which have militated against the emergence of properly integrated courses. As a result, the Joint Degrees under discussion are made up of parts of courses already on offer to other students in the departments concerned. The French Department, therefore, requires students following these programmes to complete the same "main course" in Language and Literature as students intending to specialise in French alone, but in Year Two a special element is provided which seeks to correspond more closely to their studies outside the French Department. Any search for overall programme coherence, in line with the implications of a "Combined Honours Model" would, therefore, be fruitless.

In Scotland, students are admitted to "Honours" only after two years of study, the decision as to whether they will proceed to the Honours stream or the shorter and less prestigious "General" programme being taken on the basis of their performance, not so much in the special component provided for them, which they have only to pass, but in the end-of-year examination concerning the "Main" literature and language course, in which they must

85

normally obtain over 60% to qualify for Honours. (Continuous assessment is in the process of being introduced.) This 60% target causes students to concentrate their efforts where they will best be rewarded, with damaging consequences for the status of the special component.

The special component on Politics and Institutions of Contemporary France: aims and objectives.

This component, offered by the French department, is the only part of the programme concerned which has been devised specifically to meet the requirements of students embarking on them. (Since this report was originally presented, a major review of the MA in French with Contemporary European Institutions has been undertaken by the Departments of French and Politics and the Centre of European Governmental Studies in order to provide an integrated course.) In two hours per week (one lecture and one tutorial) it seeks to introduce some of the main issues relating to the political and social systems of contemporary France, looking in Part I at the organisation and functioning of government, both central and local, and the role of political parties, before moving on in Part II, in week four of Term Two, to the operation of social institutions and the position of specific social groups in the context of economic and social change. The course begins with an examination of the questions of legitimacy and authority in connection with the Vichy régime and the Fourth Republic, before concentrating on the Fifth Republic, divided up into topics. Each week, after the introductory lecture, the corresponding small group tutorial discussion addresses itself to a specific question, in an effort to make tutorial discussion a problem-solving exercise.

The very literary training which students receive elsewhere in the French Department at Edinburgh tends to encourage the perpetuation of the myth that social and political enquiry is about "facts". Students are therefore cautious about expressing opinions in this area, convinced that one cannot argue about "facts". The problem-solving approach helps to weaken the hold of this myth. Students are asked to prepare short introductory papers, identifying the issues which arise from each "problem" and, frequently, a discussant is called upon to comment on the introductory paper and encouraged to disagree with it. This device is intended to avoid the painful silence which can follow the presentation of a paper and appeals for a response from the other students.

Language

All of the above activities take place in French, although the examination, in line with departmental policy to examine language and content separately, is normally written in English. The argument is frequently advanced that manipulating complex ideas and technical concepts is rendered almost impossible if French is employed. In my experience, tutorial discussions in French are somewhat stilted, not because of the technical or complex nature of the material, but because students' basic French is halting and inaccurate. Constant practice is the only solution to this problem.

Content and student response

The fact that this course, taught by two people, has to cater for the needs and interests of students pursuing different curricula has necessitated the search for a compromise over content. Although there are excellent academic reasons for the inclusion of all the topics studied, by and large Part I corresponds to the interests of students of Contemporary European Institutions and Part II to those of Business and Commerce students. By far the least popular of the elements, as far as all students are concerned, is that concerned with social welfare and the limits of "social capitalism". Any assumption that students of Business will be better trained in or more enthusiastic about the use of quantitative methods in analysing contributions to social welfare or benefits paid by it is quickly revealed to be a mistake.

La civilisation dans un ghetto ?

Although the special component is perceived by students as "useful", the status of "Civilisation" remains relatively low, given the small number of staff engaged in teaching on the Contemporary France element. However, a considerable improvement in the position of this area of study is slowly being achieved by integrating it into the Year One course taken by all students of French. A large part of this course is concerned with France in the 1930s and 1940s, studied through Politics/History, Literature and Film. Although one lecturer presents the Politics lecture, tutorials are taken by the majority of the staff in the department, despite their main interest in literary matters. This has been achieved by putting together a dossier of political texts (speeches by Pétain, De Gaulle, articles by Brasillach) which can be exploited by using semi-literary techniques to gain insights into political issues. In response to criticisms such as those advanced by Nicholas Wahl at the seminar, to the effect that

"Brasillach is not in the history books", it must be stressed that the writings of Brasillach employed in this context are part of his very considerable output as a political journalist on the collaborationist newspaper *Je suis partout*, rather than literary texts. Furthermore, Brasillach is very much in the history books, having, for example, been the subject of an important political biography *The Fascist Ego* by Robert Tucker and figured prominently in *Je Suis Partout: les Maurrassiens devant la tentation fasciste*, by Pierre-Marie Dioudonnat.

These texts are studied in conjunction with the memoirs of Raymond Aron, *Le spectateur engagé*, facilitating a concentration on problems of interpretation and point of view according to the ideological, social, political and ethnic position of the commentator. Study of *Le Spectateur engagé* is reinforced by use of a video in which two members of the Department subject Dominique Wolton, one of Aron's interrogators in the televised *entretiens* which led to the *Spectateur engagé*, to the same kind of treatment, pointing out inconsistencies in the line of questioning adopted, and highlighting the ideological underpinnings of the encounters betwen Aron and Wolton and Missika. Film, as a point of convergence between the study of socio-political and aesthetic questions, has an important place in this course, and Malle's *Lacombe Lucien* and Resnais' *Stavisky* are studied first and foremost as films, but also serve as a basis for consideration of the historical significance of the Stavisky Affair and February 6th, as well as the collaboration, using historical studies and the texts alluded to previously. In this way, those unfamiliar with material of this kind have become willing to teach it, with a corresponding reduction in student and staff impermeability to the introduction of "Civilisation" into the Department of French.

Building on this increased familiarity with social questions, the Department has introduced a Final-Year option, taught to a small group by one person, concentrating on the Extreme-Right Tradition in France. A further option concerned with relations between central government and local society, especially the regions, is in the process of being introduced. Both of these options rely almost totally upon the use of historical and political studies of a conventional kind. In the first two years of students' courses, however, where the aim is to introduce students to as wide a range as possible of manifestations, of French culture (literary, artistic, cinematic and social), the way lies foreward not in the creation of discrete units concentrating on "Civilisation", but in the development of interdisciplinary programmes, where the interaction between the diverse forms of French culture can be explored.

SYLLABUS EXTRACTS FROM BRITAIN

ABERDEEN UNIVERSITY

Year 1

Background course on the development of France 1789 to the present day. Lectures (one hour per week) throughout the year. The lectures are given by various members of the Department and occasionally by specialists from other departments, e.g. History of Art. The course covers the major changes in French political, social and cultural life. The lectures are mostly in English.

Year 2

Work on Civilisation is concentrated on live contemporary issues, using French radio news (France Inter) supported by videos of *Télé-Journal* and periodicals, *L'Express*, and *Le Nouvel Observateur*. Students have access to recordings daily and have a class (fortnightly, alternating with the *lecteur*) in the language laboratory where the news of the day is discussed. The objectives are: to familiarise students with France today, people, events and issues; to develop listening comprehension skills; to extend sociolinguistic, accent and register awareness. The discussions are conducted in French. The material is examined in the end-of-year oral.

Year 3

French 3 is a course for students not doing Honours but who wish to extend their French studies to Third Year level. The *Modern France* course lasts the whole year and is in two parts, Geography (taught by a member of the Geography Department) and Institutions (taught by the French Department). Broadly, Geography consists of demographic and economic changes in post-war France, and Institutions examines the constitutional and political framework of the Fifth Republic. The class is taught by lecture/seminar. It is examined by end-of-year examination.

Honours

All Honours courses (other than Language) are options or special subjects, the choice of which rests with the student. There is an option on *Contemporary France*, which is generally a popular choice. The structure and content of the course varies. In 1987, the course (taught over two terms, two hours per week) was in two parts: 1) Institutional Framework of the Fifth Republic; Administrative structure; Education (Lectures and Seminars in French for 10 weeks); 2) options within the Option: Immigration, Elites, Feminism, French Foreign Policy (Tutorials, 1 hour per week for 10 weeks). Some of these sub-options may be taught by members of other departments (e.g. International Relations for French Foreign Policy). Students have to do three essays plus tutorial papers. The essays may be in French or English. The course is examined by a three-hour paper in Finals. (There are proposals to introduce a special subject on specific aspects of Civilisation e.g. by expanding one of the "sub-options" and this would be examined by dissertation of around 10,000 words).

Students in the Department of Modern Languages reading French prepare for a BSc Honours Degree in a) **Modern Languages** b) **Combined Honours** or c) **International Business and Modern Languages** (IBML), where French is normally one of two subjects. A small number of students take Single Honours in French, but this affects only Final-Year courses. Whatever the subject combination, the content of the French course is roughly speaking the same.

In the **First Year** of the four-year course, all students of French follow a core course on French History from the Revolution of 1789 to the 1950s. The course is based on a weekly lecture in French over two terms, with fortnightly small-group supporting seminars in term two. Two weekly language skills classes are loosely related to the content of the core course.

In their First Year, Modern Languages students follow a course in Language and Communication in French, which examines the communication system, and contexts of communication and verbal interaction. The course is based on a series of ten weekly lectures in the second term.

In the **Second Year**, the core course focusses on Social, Economic and Political Institutions in Contemporary France. Students attend a weekly lecture in French over two terms, followed by a weekly seminar in a small group with a native French speaker. Supporting materials are used for individual study in the language laboratory, and written language exercises are based on situations and communicative tasks and strategies which relate to the themes of the course.

The **Third Year** of the course is spent abroad in a university or business school or in a work placement, either as a language assistant or in a firm. During the year abroad, students are expected to write a dissertation in French under supervision from the Department on some aspect of contemporary French society, or, in the case of a work-placement, on the work context.

In the **Final Year**, students follow the core course in Contemporary Affairs, which involves a 10-week series of open lectures in term one on aspects of contemporary social, economic, political and cultural events in France, with supporting small-group seminars by French native speakers. In the second term students work on projects under supervision on selected and approved topics, relating to contemporary events in France.

In the **Second and Final Years** of the course, students must choose from a range of options in French on different aspects of French studies. Options currently offered include: *French Political Discourse, The Extreme Right in France, Trade Unions in France, The French Economy 1981-86* and *International Marketing* (taught mainly in English but with projects relating to France). Options are generally taught over one term with three hours per week.

IBML students additionally follow a course on the International Business Environment in France in Years One and Two, and on the French Legal System in Year Two. In Year Two these courses serve as substitutes for the option. In the Final Year, the International Marketing course is a compulsory component for these students and replaces the option. Each course is taught over one term in French through a lecture and supporting seminar.

Approximately 90% of all French teaching is concerned with French Civilisation, although the exact amount is difficult to estimate, since Language and content are closely integrated. Only Modern Languages students follow compulsory courses in Literature and Linguistics in the first year of their studies.

UNIVERSITY OF BATH

"Civilisation" courses form an important and integral aspect of the main degree programme in the School of Modern Languages at Bath: **BA in European Studies**. Two languages and societies are studied to Honours level, from French, German, Italian, Russian and Spanish. Approximately 80% of all students in the School take French.

The mainstream "Civilisation" courses (code-named, at Bath, "Institutions") are as follows:

Year One: *L'Histoire sociale et politique de la France 1789-1945.* Compulsory for all students. Lectures and seminars (40 hours per year) in French.

Year Two: 1) *Les Structures économiques, sociales et politiques de la France contemporaine.* Compulsory for all students. Lectures and seminars (15 hours for one term) in French.
2) Options on *L'enseignement en France; Le Régionalisme en France sous les Quatrième et Cinquième Républiques; Les Partis politiques en France depuis 1958; L'Exercice du pouvoir sous la Cinquième République.* All students opt for one course taught in French by seminar for 10 hours over one term.

Year Three: Spent in France. Students prepare a 15,000-word research dissertation on an aspect of Contemporary French Politics or Society (in French).

Year Four: Options on *La défense de la France et la sécurité en Europe; Décentralisation et politique régionale en France; La Politique de la gauche depuis 1968.* All students select one option taught for 20 hours over one term.

In addition to these specifically French-oriented courses, all students follow, in Years One and Two, a compulsory lecture course (in English) on European Politics, Economics and Institutions (*Europe Today*) in which a great deal of attention is paid to France. In the Final Year, a "vocational" option on European Industrial Studies is available.
From 1988, a major new course on International Management and French is being offered, with exclusively "Civilisation" courses on the French side.

CAMBRIDGESHIRE COLLEGE OF ARTS AND TECHNOLOGY (CCAT)

The courses listed are all offered to students on the BA (Honours) Modern Languages (CNAA)and BA (Honours) Humanities/Social Studies degrees.
Language degree students take two Languages, the other being German, Italian or Spanish. Humanities degree students can combine French with a range of other subjects.

The courses below are taken by all the French students. Aspects of French Civilisation are studied in all French language classes (4 hours per week throughout). Topics covered include:

Year One
Les classes sociales
Les syndicats, le monde du travail
L'enseignement
Introduction à la vie politique

Year Two term 1 (followed by one year's study abroad)
La presse
La CEE
Les élections

Year Three term 3 (after year abroad)
Problèmes sociaux
L'urbanisme

Year Four
L'industrie française
Les partis politiques
La Résistance et l'Occupation

In addition the major core content of the course is a specialist course in French History, taught by staff of the School of History, with some input from suitably qualified linguists:

Year One term 1 *History Foundation Course*
terms 2 and 3 *Outline of French History 1770-1871*
Year Two term 1 *Stability and change in French Society*
1871-1916
terms 2 & 3 (Humanities students only)
France and the EEC
Year Three term 3 *France in the inter-war years*
Fascism and the Right in France
between the Wars
Year Four *Post-War France*
The Left in France

NEWCASTLE-UPON-TYNE POLYTECHNIC

BA (Hons) in Modern Languages and Political Studies
All students take courses in two Languages (from French, German, Russian and Spanish) and Politics.

First Year	*French Society through Literature*#	1 hour	7%
Second Year	*French History since the Revolution*#	1 hour	7%
	Political themes from French History	1 hour	7%
Third Year	Placement in French university#		
Fourth Year	*Contemporary French Politics*	2 hours	15%

BA (Hons) in Modern Languages and Economic Studies
All students take courses in two Languages (from French, German, Russian and Spanish) and Economics

First Year	*French Society through Literature**	1 hour	7%
Second Year	*French History since the Revolution**	1 hour	7%
	French Economic History	1 hour	7%
Third Year	Placement in French university*		
Fourth Year	*Aspects of the French Economy*	2 hours	15%
	* = courses common to both degrees		

BA in Secretarial Studies
All students take courses in Secretarial Studies, Business Organisation, Business Information and a Language (French, German or Spanish) or International Business.

Second Year	*Economic Background of France*	1 hour	6%
Third Year	*Business in France*	1 hour	6%

MA in French Area Studies
All students take the following courses -

Year A	*Socialism in France*	4 hours	100%
	Feminism in France	4 hours	100%
	France and Europe	4 hours	100%
Year B	*The Citizen and the State*	4 hours	100%
	Religion and Society	4 hours	100%
	Industrialisation in France	4 hours	100%
Year C	Dissertation		

UNIVERSITY OF NEWCASTLE-UPON-TYNE

All the courses below come under the degree BA (Honours) in French Studies, or French as Joint Honours, or **Major or Minor** subject in BA (Honours) in **Modern Languages**.
One Politics/Society course is offered per year of study, alongside Literature and Linguistics courses. In addition to language skills work, first-year students of Single Honours take the course in *French Contemporary Society* compulsorily as one course of four in total; in Year Two they may optionally take a course in *Politics and Society in 19th Century France* as one of two courses (choice of five); in the Final Year they may optionally take a course in *Politics and Society in 20th-Century France* as one of four courses from choice of six (plus courses not taken in Year Two). For students taking all these courses, civilisation = 33% of content studies, excluding language work; some Joint Honours students can avoid it completely.

First Year: *Société Française Contemporaine*
One hour lecture in French per week; five seminars in English during year in small groups. Taught by G.E. Hare and P. Powrie.
Lecture titles:
Introduction au cours et aux méthodes de travail, et introduction à l'étude de la population.
Tendances démographiques, évolution de la population au 20e siècle, taux de fécondité, taux de mortalité.
Evolution de la population active, sa répartition géographique, les migrations internes, exode rural, urbanisation.

L'immigration en France.
Structures sociales: la stratification sociale, les categories socio-professionnelles et leur évolution.
Les inégalités sociales.
Mobilité sociale ou reproduction sociale ?
Structures politiques: les institutions démographiques et gouvernementales.
Les partis politiques et les élections.
Féminisme et droits de la femme, la femme et la vie publique.
La femme dans la famille et au travail.
Le système d'éducation.
Les enjeux de l'éducation: l'égalité des chances, l'école laïque et l'école libre.
Le travail: le syndicalisme.
Travail et temps libre: l'industrialisation créatrice du loisir.
L'utilisation du temps libre, les fonctions du loisir dans la société.
L'information: la presse écrite.
L'information: l'audiovisuel.

Second Year: *Politics and Society in 19th-century France*
Outline Syllabus:
The legacy of the Revolution/French society in the early 19th century.
The Napoleonic era/The Restoration and the July Revolution.
The July Monarchy and the 1848 Revolution/The Second Republic.
The Second Empire/The Commune.
The Third Republic (up to 1914):
French Society : Changing class structures; Education and society.
Politics and government: The founding and consolidation of the Republican régime and Republicanism/The Radical Republic and Radicalism/The growth of the working class-movement and Socialism.

Final Year: *Politics and Society in 20th-century France*
   Term One: *Panorama of French history up to 5th Republican Gaullism:*
Pre-1914: la Belle Epoque/First World War and aftermath/The Twenties and Thirties/The Popular Front/War, Occupation, Resistance, Liberation/The Fourth Republic/De Gaulle and establishment of 5th Republic.
Le gaullisme ou les gaullismes ?/Gaullism and the Right after De Gaulle.
The events of May-June 1968: prelude and causes, interpretation and effects.
The Right in France after Gaullism ?
   Term Two: *Society and politics in France today:*
Demographic and Socio-economic change in France since 1945.
Social Structures and Inequalities in France.
How does government work ?: the Institutions of State and the Constitution of the Fifth Republic.
The interlinked roles of Government, Parliament and Civil Service.
The Party System and Bipolarisation, with particular reference to the parties of the Right and Centre Right.
Mitterrand and the making of the new Parti Socialiste.
L'Union de la Gauche: what was it for, and is it irrevocably over ?
Elections in France: what kinds are there, how do they work and what are they for ?/Voting behaviour: how far can the electoral sociologist explain why people vote as they do ?
Media and Politics: History of TV-State relations.
Socio-economic and Socio-political Bases of the Media in France to-day.
Women's rights in France/Economic analysis of the Position of Women in France.

Introduction

French Civilisation is taught at Oxford Polytechnic mainly within the Modular Course, one of the largest unit-credit schemes of undergraduate education in the United Kingdom, with students studying towards diplomas and degrees in over 30 subject areas. The Modular Course is offered on an undifferentiated full-time, part-time or mixed-mode basis. Students on the course are registered for study in one or two Fields, a single Field representing approximately half of a full degree course. The Field on which French Civilisation is taught is entitled *French Language and Contemporary Studies*.

French Language and Contemporary Studies

NB: All Modules have a maximum of 4 hours class-contact per week and are taught for one term of 11 weeks unless otherwise stated.

This single Field is designed to enable the student to understand the social and political developments of France since 1870 with a view to defining the tensions inherent in contemporary French life and the degree to which they have been attenuated or exacerbated during the period since World War Two.

All students must spend one academic year resident in France, following courses at one of the universities with which the Polytechnic has links, or working as English assistants. Stage Two modules are almost invariably taught in French.

Stage 1:

The compulsory modules are:

2100 *French Core Language I* (three-term double module)

2105 *Introduction to Contemporary France* (three-term double module)

The following modules are recommended, preferably in Stage I:

2400 *History and Historical Change 1750-1850*

7603 *Politics and Government of France*

Stage II:

The acceptable modules are:

2110 *French Core Language II* (three-term single module)

2116 *French Core Language IIB* (three-term single module)

2154 *Education and Society in France since 1882*

2157 *Mass Media and the State in France*

2159 *The Events of May 1968* (Synoptic module)

2163 *The Right in France since 1945*

2164 *The Trade Union Movement and the Left in France*

2166 *Post-War French Politics and Society*

2175 *World War II: the French Experience* (Synoptic double module)

2188 Independent Study (FS)

2190 Interdisciplinary Dissertation

2197 Dissertation (double module)

2434 *Republican Democracy and its Challengers in France 1871-1945* (two-term double module).

All students must take Modules 2434 and 2166, and must pass 2110, 2116 and 2159. Students are required to pass a minimum of seven modules (maximum 12) in each single Field to qualify for an Honours Degree.

PORTSMOUTH POLYTECHNIC

Single Honours (BA French Studies)

This is a four-year CNAA degree programme, of which Year Three is spent in France or a French-speaking country, either attending university courses or as a language assistant.The degree as a whole is largely (c.80%) devoted to French Civilisation. However, some of the courses listed below for Year One have a minor European or comparative dimension. Those in History and the Social Sciences are strongly discipline-based and may be taught partly in English. Year Two options relate wholly to France, but Final-Year options diversify into e.g. Belgian or EEC studies. Year Two courses are taught mainly in French, as are Year Four courses with the exception of e.g. the lectures on Marketing, Geography, Organisational Behaviour and EEC.

		% devoted to Fr. civilisation
Year One	*Language* (four hours per week)	(37%)
	Linguistics (two hours per week)	(50%)
	History (two hours per week)	(80%)
	Politics (two hours per week)	(60%)
	Economics (two hours per week)	(20%)
	Literature (two hours per week)	(100%)
	Thought (two hours per week)	(80%)
	Geography (two hours per week)	(100%)
	Tutorial (one hour per week)	
Year Two	*Language* (four hours per week)	(50%)
	Linguistics (two hours per week)	(70%)
	History, followed by *France contemporaine*	
	(term 3 only) (three hours per week)	(90%)
	TWO OF THE FOLLOWING:	
	Politics (two hours per week)	(100%)
	Economics (two hours per week)	(100%)
	Literature (two hours per week)	(100%)
	Thought (two hours per week)	(100%)
	Geography (two hours per week)	(100%)

Year Three

Spent abroad in France or a French-speaking country. Students are required to write while abroad a dissertation in French of 10,000 words on a French Civilisation topic.

Year Four

Language (four hours per week)	
France contemporaine (two hours per week)	
(current issues)	(100%)
THREE OF THE FOLLOWING:	
Belgian Studies (two hours per week)	
Cinema (two hours per week)	(100%)
EEC (two hours per week)	(20%)
German (two hours per week)	
Literature and Society (two hours per week)	(50%)
Marketing (two hours per week)	(30%)

>   *Organisational Behaviour* (two hours   (20%
>   per week)
>   *Spanish* (two hours)
>   *Theory and Practice of Translation*   (60%)
>   (two hours)

Combined Honours (German and French Studies/Russian and French Studies/Hispanic [i.e. Spanish and Latin American] and French Studies)

In these four-year CNAA degree programmes, the French Studies component represents exactly half the programme. It is made up virtually entirely of a narrower range of the same courses as are offered to Single Honours French Studies students, the groups being taught simultaneously for lectures and parting company only for seminars. This means that for each Combined Honours student the language element is doubled (two Languages), but the civilisation element correspondingly reduced : French Civilisation represents only 60% of the French component. Year Two or Year Three is spent abroad, attending university courses. Half the year is spent in each of two appropriate countries.

French component for all Combined Honours degrees

Year One   *Language* (four hours per week)
                            Linguistics (two hours per week)
                            History (two hours per week)
                            ONE OF THE FOLLOWING:
                            Politics (two hours per week)
                            Economics (two hours per week)
                            Literature (two hours per week)
                            Thought (two hours per week)

Year Two or Three   Spent abroad - half the year in France or a French-speaking country.

Year Three or Two   *Language* (four hours per week)
                            Linguistics (two hours per week)
                            History, followed by *France contemporaine*
                               (term Three only) (three hours per week)
                            ONE OPTION AS IN YEAR ONE

Students are required to write a dissertation in English (7,000-10,000 words) on a French Civilisation topic, to be completed by Year Four.

Year Four   *Language* (four hours per week)
                            France contemporaine (two hours per week)
                            ONE OPTION AS IN FRENCH STUDIES YEAR FOUR ABOVE.

Single Honours French
Year One, Terms 1 and 2
        Three courses, one on *Contemporary France.*
Year One, Term 3, and Year Two
        French History from 16th to 20th century (option)
Year Four
                FOUR COURSES FROM:
                Medieval Literature and/or History
                Renaissance Literature and/or History
                17th-century Literature and/or History
                18th-century Literature and/or History
                19th-century Literature and/or History
                20th-century Literature and/or History
                OPTION:
                Specialised literary or historical topic.

Combined Subject Courses (BA Honours) French and X, or X and French
The subject combinations include:
                French and Economics
                French and International Relations
                French and Management Studies
                French and Politics
                French and Sociology
                English Literature and French
                German and French
                Italian and French
                History and French
                Latin and French
                Music and French
                Philosophy and French.

Graduate courses
The following courses in French at MA level are also offered in the
Graduate School for European and International Studies:
                French Foreign and Defence Policies
                Left-Wing Political Novels
                Socialism and Social Democracy in Europe.

French Civilisation is largely taught in the French department, though there are also programmes in other departments touching on the area, notably in the History Department, and Education Faculty.

BA degree in French

First Year: *Culture and Society in Modern France* (two hours). Based on literary and non-literary material in five modules: *19th-century Paris; the Popular Front; the Resistance; Theatre of the Absurd; Women's Writing since 1960.*

Second Year: *Social and Political Structures in the Fifth Republic* (2 hours).

Fourth (Final) Year: 1981 (two hours).
A special subject based on weekly seminars, examining both historical and cultural developments during that year.

> *Le génie d'Oc* (two hours for 1 semester).
> *Mitterrand's Presidency* (two hours for 1 semester).
> *Intellectuals in Contemporary France* (two hours for 1 semester)

N.B. The above courses are also available to students in the Arts Faculty who are not studying French to degree level.

MA degree in Culture and Society in Contemporary Europe

The one-year postgraduate instructional course is taught in collaboration by the Departments of French, German and Spanish/Portuguese/Latin American Studies.

Core course: *Issues in Contemporary European Culture and Society* (three hours). Includes French material in several modules: *Geography, European Integration, Foreign Relations, Euro-communism, Culture and the State, Postmodernism.*

One from:
> *Contemporary European Cinema* (two hours)
> *Contemporary French Thought* (2 hours)
> *Language and Politics in Contemporary Europe* (two hours)

BA degree in History

Second and Third (Final) Year:
> *France 1871-1958* (2½ hours)

This course is also available to students in the Arts Faculty who are not studying History to degree level.

MA in Education

This is a two-year instructional course, taught in cooperation between Education and French.

Option:
> *Contemporary France: teaching and learning approaches* (three hours for 1 term).

French Civilisation at the University of Surrey is taught at undergraduate level within a form of Combined Degree lasting four years (BSc in Linguistic and International Studies). Students majoring in French also study a Subsidiary Language and either International Relations, Law or Economics. The latter are studied in the first two years on a purely disciplinary basis, but are integrated in the Third and Fourth years with Main Language studies so that students study either French Foreign Policy, French Law or French Economy.

From the Second year onwards, some of the courses listed below are taught either partly or wholly in French.

French Civilisation elements within the BSc in Linguistics and International Studies

Year One

French Main	*French History* (a survey course from the end of the Ancien Régime to Modern Times) (one hour) *Literature and Society* (a selection of literary and philosophical texts chosen for their socio-historical value (one hour)
French Subsidiary	*French History* (as above) (one hour)

Year Two

French Main	*Politics and Government in Contemporary France* (two hours) *French Social Theory : the Positivist Tradition* (one hour)
French Subsidiary	*Politics and government in Contemporary France* (one hour)

Year Three

French Main	*French Society and Institutions* (two hours) *The French Intellectual Tradition: Existentialism* (two hours) *French Foreign Policy* (one hour) *French Law* (three hours) *French Economy and the Economy of the EEC* (three hours)
French Subsidiary	*French Society and Institutions* (one hour)

Year Four

French Main	Options: *Césarisme in France from Bonapartism to Gaullism* (two hours) *The Left in Post-War France* (two hours) *Ideological Fiction* (Committed Literature) (two hours) *French Foreign Policy* (three hours) *French Law* (three hours) *French Economy* (three hours)

Surrey also offers a taught MA in European Area Studies which includes a French Area Studies option. The latter covers the Contemporary French Economy, Politics and Society in Contemporary France, French Foreign Policy and French Intellectual Life.

Introduction

At Sussex, each student follows a double track: one set of courses in the major subject - let us say French - and one set of contextual courses, that is courses shared by a whole School of Studies. The majority of students **majoring in French** are in the School of European studies. Thus half their time is devoted to courses on European Civilisation in a broad sense (History, Politics, Literature, Society) as their contextual programme. (A few students choose to major in the School of African and Asian studies, with appropriate contextuals).

Although "French Civilisation" obviously comes into courses on Europe, in the interests of simplicity only courses devoted entirely to France are listed here. These are mainly courses within the French major degree **(French Single Honours, French and Italian, French and German)**. The French major courses are divided between "Literature" and "Civilisation" - all students do a combination of both. Only the "Civilisation" courses are listed here (a). Also listed are a course done by scientists (b), as well as the French options in the History and Politics majors (c) and (d).

Teaching Scheme Outline

BA degree in French (French/Italian, French/German)

Year One, Term 1 or 2:
> *Introduction to Modern France 1870-1945*
>> (two hours, lecture plus tutorial)
>> (NB: to be modified from 1987-8, probably being more restricted and concentrated, provisional title, *France in the 30s and 40s*)

Year Two, Term 3:
> *French Politics and Society since 1945*
>> (two to three hours, lecture plus tutorials)

Year Three: Spent in France; may do courses at French universities on what could be described as French Civilisation. All write a 10,000 word dissertation, supervised from Sussex: a high proportion choose a topic in this area rather than a literary one.

Year Four, Term 1: Options Group I
> One course out of about seven options, five in the Civilisation area:
> *Language and Society in French-speaking countries*
> *The Making of French Public Opinion, 1789 to present*
> *Paris and the Parisians 1815-71*
> *Rural France*
> *Intellectual Situation of Post-War France*
>> (1 hour, sometimes more, a week)

Year Four, Term 2: Options Group: one course out of several Special
> Authors or Topics, two in Civilisation area:
> *Vichy France, 1940-44*
> *Women and French History, 1870 to present*
> Total: Two out of five survey courses in Year One-Two.

BSc Euro degree: (Science plus a Language)

Year Two, Term 3:
> *French Society* (two hours, lecture plus seminar).

BA degree in History
Year Two, Terms 2 and 3. Special Subject Option:
> *The Fall of France, Collaboration and Resistance*
> (one to two hours, tutorials)
> *The French Revolution, 1783-1793* (ditto)

BA degree in Politics
Year Three, Term 2. Option:
> *Politics of the Nation State: France*
> (one to two hours, tutorials)
Year Four, Term 1: Special Topic Option:
> *Presidential Politics in the Fifth Republic*

UNIVERSITY OF WARWICK

Teaching provision for French Civilisation at Warwick falls into two distinct parts: its place within the course content of the various French Studies and allied degrees within the Faculty of Arts, and the teaching offered by the Department of French Studies for a range of degrees of BSc in the Faculty of Social Studies.

French degrees at Warwick are modular to the extent that students follow throughout their three years of study a core of French Language and Literature courses, taught within the Department. In addition, normally one third of their study takes place in the form of courses offered outside the Department by the Departments of, for example, History, Politics, Law, Philosophy, Fine Art etc. Since the options in French History, Foreign Law, French Politics and Institutions etc. are extremely popular, students in French at Warwick have considerable exposure to aspects of French Civilisation, taught by specialists in the relevant subject areas. This is particularly true in the case of the degree in **French and History** and in the new degree, **French with International Studies**. Apart from students reading for the degrees in **French with Theatre Studies, French and European Literature** and the **Cultural Studies** variant of the French Studies degree, therefore, most students would have exposure to at least one course dealing with one specialist area of French Civilisation.

Recently, however, the Department has realised that we provide no overall framework in which to set these specialist subject-areas, and we have now introduced a survey course. Until this year, it took the form of a series of lectures on key areas of Modern French Politics and Social Institutions, but has now been formalised into a First-Year option, which it is expected most students will take. This option, *Modern and Contemporary France: Culture and Society*, taught by Nicholas Hewitt and Brian Rigby, will concentrate, as before, on major aspects of French Society since 1945, but will also explore cultural responses to those aspects, particularly in the form of mass or popular culture.

In addition, within the Department itself, aspects of French Civilisation reappear in the form of options or special subjects available exclusively to our own students. Examples of this are the special subject Brian Rigby offered until very recently, on *1848*, and Nicholas Hewitt's special subject on *Literature, Thought and Film in the Fourth Republic*. Considerable attention is also paid to intellectual and cultural history within the same time, for the last ten years, the Department has offered an , *Contemporary France: Language and Society*, taught by Nicholas Hewitt Irs. Claudie Cox, to Departments in the Social Studies Faculty. The course consists of a series of 20 lectures, ranging from the establishment of the Fourth Republic to the Contemporary Political Context, and dealing with a number of institutional areas, from Post-War Economic Expansion to Cultural Policy. In addition to these lectures, there is a parallel Language course, designed to foster skills in translation from French to English and in the comprehension of Oral French. It is a feature of the course that it is deliberately designed to complement the specialisms of the candidates, and we hope that they will use that specialism in the writing of the assessed essay project for the course: e.g. Economics students writing on the French banking system etc.. This option has now been extended to create a French variant of the Management Sciences and Economics.

WOLVERHAMPTON POLYTECHNIC

BA Modern Languages (BAML) (Four years)
Language Teaching Units (all years, 75% of students study French as one of their two languages).
Political Development of Europe (Year One, 25% France)
Economic Geography (Year One, 25% France)
Growth and Development in Europe (Year Two, 25% France)
Politics in France (Year Two, all students of French)
Year Abroad (half in each of two countries)
France, the Economics of Intervention (Year Four, 30% of all students in the year)
France in World Politics (Year Four, 20% of students)
Right and Left in Contemporary France (Year Four, 20% of students)

BA European Studies (4 years, each student studies one language, 40% study French)
Language Teaching Units (all years, teaching in common with BAML above)
Introduction to International Relations (Year One, 25% France)
Introduction to Sociology (Year One, 25% France)
European Thought (Year One, 25% France)
Introduction to European Politics (Year One, 25% France)
The Making of Modern Europe 1780-1890 (Year One, France)
European Economic Systems (Year Two, 25% France)
The Foreign Policies of the Powers (Year Two, 25% France)
Sociology II or European Thought II (Year Two, 25% France)
Europe since 1890 (Year Two, 25% France)
European Political Sytstems (Year Two, 25% France)
Year Abroad (40% of the students do French and go to France)
European Labour Market (Year Four: students choose three out of these five and three others, 25% France in these).
Security in Europe
Social Revolution in Europe
West European Political Parties
Comparative Communist Politics
Class and Social conflict in Europe (Year Four students choose one of these three, 25% France)
Women in Europe

Dip HE/BA in Languages For Business (Three years, each student does two languages)
Language Teaching Units (all years, 75% of students study French)
Introduction to Foreign Language Shorthand (Year One)
The Business Environment (Year One, 25% France)
Placement in French firm for the 50% of students who choose French as
   their main language in term 3 and vacation of Year One. 3-6 months.
Business in Europe (Year Two, 25% France)
International Marketing (Year Three, one of these three, 25% France)
European Business Law
European Economic Organisations

BA Humanities (Four years for students who take a language, a "modular" degree with French, German, Spanish, History, Geography, English)
Language Teaching Units (all years, 25% of students study French)
Zola and Naturalism (Semesters 3 or 5)
The Theatre of the Absurd (Semesters 3 or 5)
The Nouveau Roman (Semesters 4 or 6)
Year Three abroad, usually only one language studied, so in one country
French Women Novelists (Semester 5)
The Political Theatre of J.- P. Sartre (Semester 6)
Resistance and Collaboration in French Literature (Semester 6)
French Surrealism 1924-1930 (Semester 6)
Introduction to French Cinema (Semester 4)
French Cinema: The New Wave (Semester 5)

TEACHING FRENCH CIVILISATION WITH AN AUSTRALIAN ACCENT
by Karis Muller, Australian National University

In Australia, formal courses in French Language and Literature were
established before 1945 in the Universities of Sydney, Melbourne, Adelaide
and Western Australia. Beginning in the 1960s, courses in French
"Civilisation" or Society began to be introduced by some of these
universities and by the newer universities which had been established up to
a decade earlier. By the 1980s, these courses had become widespread. The
results from the survey described in this paper do not support any simple
generalisations on the contents of "Civilisation" courses offered by the
older and the newer universities, apart from a tendency of the latter to
adopt a broader approach to the subject a little earlier in the overall
course of studies (1). In 1987, a traditional literary programme has been
retained as the main emphasis of French courses in two universities,
founded in 1913 and 1970.

Since most Australian universities are based on the British model, with
separate departments and faculties, the trend towards an inter-disciplinary
approach has in recent years given rise to the creation of "centres", whose
function it is to facilitate inter-disciplinary and comparative teaching and
research.

Of Australia's 19 universities, 16 offer French at both beginners' and
post-high school level, as well as postgraduate and research facilities.
French is the most common foreign language offered and is followed in
order by Italian (taught in 14), German (12), Japanese (10) and Chinese (9).
The popularity of French over other foreign languages reflects Australia's
close historical links with Britain, where French is also the most commonly
taught second language. Since the Second World War, however, Australia has
become both culturally and linguistically diverse, with over 30 non-

aboriginal languages spoken. Because there has been no large-scale migration from France to Australia, French is not a "community language". Out of a population of some 16 million, only 15,000 were born in France (2) and even a generous estimate of 100,000 for the number of migrants from Francophone countries speaking French at home (3) would not account for its popularity. The importance of French, as opposed to its popularity, is commonly ascribed to Australia's relative proximity to Vietnam, Laos and Cambodia in the north, Réunion and other islands in the west, and New Caledonia to the east, with Wallis and Futuna, French Polynesia and Vanuatu beyond it. Tourism combined with trade and politics creates pressure for the emphasis on the direct and practical application of French Language teaching. How far university courses should respond to this pressure is naturally subject to debate.

In Australia at tertiary level, only 70% of students pursue a foreign language option. Some 85% of secondary schools teach a Foreign Language compared to 60% in the USA. A declining national competence in foreign languages in Australia is, however, evident from the low figure of 12% in 1986 for the proportion of school-leavers studying a second language in their last two years; in 1967 the corresponding figure was 40% (4). These figures are viewed with some alarm by the Australian government. In 1987, the Commonwealth Department of Education published a National Policy on Languages which analysed the languages situation in Australia and recommended strategies to effect improvements. The author, J. Lo Bianco, considered that "the tertiary sector greatly over-emphasises literature as distinct from practical communication skills" (5). This view was expressed earlier, in 1984, by Dr D. Hawley of Wollongong University, in his *Foreign language study in Australian tertiary institutions 1974-1982*. He concluded that university Language departments emphasised reading, written skills and literature at the expense of oral fluency and competence in skills useful in business and international relations. The survey described in this article has shown that there has been some progress in this area since these criticisms.

The purpose of my survey was to examine how French "Civilisation", be it Society, Culture or Business, is interpreted in universities on the other side of the world from metropolitan France. Although French Philosophy and History may be offered by their respective departments, the survey confined itself to French departments, from which it was anticipated that responses would be most likely. Two particular aspects of concern were:

    (1) content and method of "Civilisation" courses;
    (2) perceptions of France thus revealed.

Content and methods

As indicated earlier, two French departments prefer to offer Language and
Literature alone.   Of the remaining 14, 13 integrate "Civilisation" with
Language, seven with Literature and one with Social Sciences.   The figures
overlap because in many cases "Civilisation" has a broad catchment area.
In nine institutions, "Civilisation" is compulsory as it is integrated with
either Language, Literature or both.   Ten departments interpret
"Civilisation" as high culture or ideas, while four regard it partly or
entirely as myth.   In their teaching, five respondents concentrate on the
period after 1870.   Where departments offer specific modern themes, these
are predominantly Cinema, Women, Press/Media/Advertising, or Francophone
literature.   Finally, in three universities, students of French may undertake
the Theory or Methodology of Culture, History or the Social Sciences.
Universities follow a diverse policy regarding the language of instruction.
Two departments teach only in French (Adelaide, Australian National
University (ANU).   The ANU also insists that all postgraduate work be in
French.   The others surveyed teach mainly in French, and none uses English
for more than half the contact hours.   Policy in this respect appears to
be left largely to individual lecturers (except at Adelaide and ANU).   Five
universities have French "Civilisation" courses conducted in English at
first-year level, which are open to outside students.   This relative
prevalence of English is due to the fact that perhaps half of Australian
students arrive as beginners in the language, so that courses in English
may seem the best way to expose them to a foreign culture, in the First
Year at least.
Methods of instruction vary also. All universities but one use audio-visual
methods.   Three do not give lectures.   One (Flinders) examines the
"Civilisation" competence of its students by frequent interrogations in
French. The others all demand written work. Half the departments do not
use prescribed books, preferring to collate their own material in the form
of handouts or booklets. Of those that do set books for students, Ardagh
was the most popular (six departments).
In the past few years, certain new trends have emerged: courses in cinema
or the media, an interest in Francophone literature, offerings on France and
the Antipodes.   Four universities have, since the early 1980s, started

practical language courses in scientific, business, legal or political French. In sum, there exists in Australian universities a great variety of models of French "Civilisation" teaching.

Perhaps of more concern is the fact that no Australian French Departmewnt builds a year abroad into its degree structure. This has been discussed but never realised, owing to the costs involved and the high number of students studying part-time or in paid employment. Only two universities give students the option to spend short periods in France (Monash to Nice, Flinders to Sèvres).

Because of distance, general up-to-date information is not always easily obtained, although the Alliances Françaises, the Embassy and Consulates provide films, books and sometimes speakers. Radio-France Internationale broadcasts at inconvenient times and is not clear enough to record.

Perceptions of France

Cultural perceptions of France resemble those found elsewhere. Courses such as *The Middle Ages in France* (Wollongong), *L'Utopie et l'autre monde aux XVIIe et XVIIIe siècles* (Sydney) and *The Revolutionary Tradition in French Culture* (Queensland) do not reflect an Australian view. Students have a high opinion of French culture, whether artistic or scientific. However, they also have a negative attitude towards France as a world power. Class-based opinion polls and discussions indicate that they share their government's antipathy towards French policies in New Caledonia and Polynesia. They also complain of what they perceive as Gallic agricultural protectionism within the EEC. Culturally sophisticated yet deficient in moral principles: this is a common view of France, both in the press and among students. Admiration for the people, their history and their language is tempered by accusations of colonialism, and militarism.

Given this cultural context, it seemed of interest to investigate how far there might be a specifically Australian orientation to course choice, corresponding to public attitudes. In particular, I wished to test the hypothesis that the perception of France as a European power might be relatively neglected, in favour of her Pacific presence. Choice of tertiary courses would reflect different priorities, France's key role in the South Pacific featuring more prominently than her EEC membership, even though both greatly concern Australia.

Survey results showed that Queensland and New South Wales offer courses on Franco-Australian relations. The latter runs an undergraduate course in

English and an MA in French, both under the aegis of the French-Australian Connections Research Centre, which in turn contributes to that university's Centre for South Pacific Studies. The ANU has a large Research School of Pacific Studies, which encompasses French possessions in its fields of interest, while at undergraduate level the Pacific Studies Field Program is to prepare a course on France in the South Pacific. The French government supports a study centre in Nouméa for students of French from Australia and other Pacific countries. Nouméa is less than three hours' flight away from Sydney, and only two from Brisbane. There are five Australian French departments offering courses on New Caledonia; at least one more teaches a part-course on the subject. Four departments, all on or near the East coast, offer students the opportunity to spend a few weeks in Nouméa. Not many go. Furthermore, these courses, begun in the early 1980s, have all been unable to send their students to Nouméa since the 1985 troubles. On the other hand, postgraduate exchanges seem likely with the forthcoming establishment of the Université Française du Pacifique Sud, based at Nouméa and Papeete. French-Australian relations will be much in the news here in 1988, since the Association pour le Bicentenaire d'Australie (President, the French Defence Minister) is funding a variety of cultural events in honour of the historical links between the two countries.

Until the 1980s, the absence of France in the Pacific from French department teaching was matched by a lack of courses on France within the Common Market. While comparative European history and literature are common, and politics or law may also be added, the study of Europe and of the EEC as an area was not taught, and there was no integration of language programmes with any of these. In 1982 Wollongong initiated a Graduate Diploma in European Studies, for which students may choose Italian and/or French and a variety of courses taught in English, but excluding Politics. The University of Sydney's Centre for European Studies, founded in 1983, functions as a *"centre d'animation culturelle"*, holding colloquia and public lectures. At present, no tertiary institution in Australia has a cross-disciplinary European Studies degree incorporating Languages. It is this perceived disadvantage that Monash University intends to eradicate from 1989, with a new undergraduate programme consisting of short, intensive language courses (West European or Slavonic) plus culture and literature taught in English. The same university plans to launch an MA in European Studies, to include politics, EC law and institutions.

The government view now seems to be that in the 1970s the obvious strategic importance of Asia and the Pacific region was allowed to overshadow the equal importance of the EC in Australia. The EC is our largest trading partner after Japan. While it may not be advisable for universities to adhere too closely to governmental viewpoints, there seems to be no harm in recognising that the study of French has political and economic as well as cultural advantages. The relative slowness of Australian language departments to place their countries (where relevant) in their EC context may perhaps be attributed to the fact that European Australians detect a certain estrangement between Australia, the land of their birth or adoption, and the country of their cultural origins, a Common Market member.

Whether as a European or a South Pacific power, France arouses considerable interest in Australia, albeit also some hostility. The two countries share military intelligence over activities in their common "backyard". They have twinned, or soon will twin, several towns, and they collaborate on a wide range of scientific, commercial and cultural endeavours. Within universities, despite the decline in student numbers in languages, as outlined by the recent government report, promised support for foreign language study is a cause for optimism.

American and British experiences of French "Civilisation" teaching will also be on the agenda when, in late 1987, lecturers from the ANU and six universities in New South Wales are to meet to discuss, for the first time, the definition, strategies and objectives of our discipline. This becomes the more necessary and challenging in the Australian context since even to-day distance may inevitably hamper understanding (6).

FOOTNOTES

1. K. Muller, survey sent to French departments in Australian universities, May 1987.

2. The unofficial figure from the 1986 National Census is 15,074.

3. Figure from the French Embassy, Canberra.

4. Australian figures from *A National Policy on Languages*, p.26.

5. Ibid., p.190.

6. X. Pons of Toulouse and D. Camroux of Paris-VIII are among those teaching and writing in France on Franco-Australian and Franco-Pacific relations.

SYLLABUS EXTRACT FROM
THE AUSTRALIAN NATIONAL UNIVERSITY

I. **Third-Year "post-beginners"/First Year** (one year)
This course integrates Language, Literature and Society. One of the six weekly hours is devoted to a lecture on Society. A second hour is an oral class based on material related to the lecture (slides, video, graphs, articles); a third hour is a textual analysis also related to the lecture topic. Several colleagues collaborate in this course; the overall scheme is drawn up by the course leader. Obviously the content varies depending on staff availability; in 1986-87 the syllabus was:

A) 1. *Comment voyez-vous la France ?*
2. *Comment les Français se voient*
3. *Profil démographique de la France*
4. *Nuptialité/divortialité*
5. *Natalité et natalisme*
6. *Les exclus*

B) 7. *La France dans le Pacifique*
8. *Problèmes de la Calédonie*
9. *Problèmes de la Polynesie*

C) 10. *On est en République, non?*
11. *La Cinquième: d'Alger à Mitterrand*
12. *La gauche au pouvoir 1981-6: libertés et contraintes*
13. *La droite revient!*

D) 14., 15., 16. *La chanson*

E) 17., 18., 19. *Comment vivent les Français ?*

F) 20.-26. *Questions sociales et culturelles (les femmes, les immigrés, l'éducation)*

II. **Second and Third-Year Courses** (all year-long)
1) *The French Language Today* (two hours a week): taught by a Linguistics specialist. It covers topics such as:
   a) *le franglais*, language and gender, regional and social variation, position of non-French languages, different registers
   b) major variants of French in Europe and elsewhere
2) *Contemporary France* (two hours a week): alternates with (3) below. Usually taught by one person. Typical syllabus:
   1. *Les institutions de la Ve République*
   2-5. *Partis politiques, syndicats etc...*
   6. *Economie*
   7-8. *Démographie*
   9. *Les jeunes*
   10. *Les femmes*
   11. *Les DOM-TOM*
   12. *La France militaire/vente des armements*
   13. *La francophonie*
   14. *Nouvelle-Calédonie*
   15. *Polynésie française*
   16. *Algérie française*
   17. *Les immigrés*
   18. *La presse*
   19. *TV et radio*
   20. *Nouvelles technologies*
   21. *Crime/délinquance*
   22. *Terrorisme*

23. *L'Eglise catholique: dissidences catholiques*
24. *Juifs, Protestants et sectes*
25. *L'Islam*
26. *Bilan: l'image de la France en Australie et vice-versa.*

3) *Ideological Issues in Modern France* (two hours a week): alternates with 2) above. At present the syllabus is:
1. *Culture/idéologies*
2. *L'Intellectuel*
3. *Critique de l'intelligentsia*
4. *La mort des maîtres à penser ?*
5. *Cultures populaires*
6. *Prestige de la modernité*
7-10. *Gauchisme/mai 68*
11. *Ecologie et pacifisme*
12. *Tiers-mondisme/anti-tiers-mondisme*
13. *Féminisme*
14. *Mouvements autonomistes*
15. *L'individualisme des années 80*
16-17. *Novembre/décembre 1986: mai 68 à l'envers?*
18-19. *Gaullisme: du Général et depuis*
20. *L'Etat-spectacle*
21. *Nouveaux philosophes, phénomène médiatique*
22. *Nouvelle Droite et racisme*
23. *La fin de la gauche ?*
24-25. *La bio-éthique*
26. *Où va la France?*

DISCIPLINES AND INTER-DISCIPLINARITY

THE ROLE OF HIGH CULTURE IN THE TEACHING OF FRENCH CIVILISATION:
TEACHING THE MASTERPIECES
by Alice Kaplan, Duke University

I am responding to a complaint that is fundamental to many of us attending
this conference. Laurence Wylie put it with great wit this morning: it is
the feeling that "the literature people won't let us in" or that "my
university won't let me teach 'Civilisation'; I'm only allowed to teach
Literature."

For a way out of this dilemma, I'd like to shift our working definition of
literary or artistic high culture from a definition based on content
(certain works deemed eternally, unimpeachably great) to a definition based
on value.

To study the role of high culture in our courses means therefore to study
canon formation, the process by which certain works of art are deemed
"great". I have taken two of the textbooks on French literature we currently
use in the United States to introduce our students to the masterpieces of
French literature as my measure of canon formation in French Studies, and I
will only sketch here the results of a much longer paper about these texts.

The first anthology in question is Morris Bishop's *Survey of French
Literature* which was published by Harcourt Brace in 1955 and still sells
3000 copies annually. Bishop taught at Cornell, he published literary
biographies, light verse, and even a mystery novel over the course of his
career. It is clear from the editorial comments in his survey that he was
reacting against Gustave Lanson and against literary history: he believes
instead in "literary enthusiasm" and promises to select passages for their
vitality rather than their significance. He nonetheless organises the whole
of his text by centuries, and provides charts comparing events in French
literature, with events in history, and with other literatures.

Bishop's notion of what is vital in French letters is quite obvious in his
introductory remarks to each author treated. He writes in English

(remember, it is pre-sputnik America and still standard practice to read the masterpieces in the target language but lecture on them in English). Let me read you a phrase of Bishop on Rousseau:

> "When the undergraduate walks out at the end of the day to gaze at a sunset and feel the exaltation of beauty, or when he regards a mountain peak with emotional awe, he is imitating Jean-Jacques Rousseau, for Rousseau invented (as far as we are concerned) the beauty of sunsets and mountains."

A creationist notion of literary paternity indeed! Notice specifically Bishop's gesture towards his students' own personal experience and enthusiasm, his attempt to convince them that life really does imitate art. Bishop is a populariser and cultural enthusiast; he believes that great literature must communicate and it must stir.

Now let us turn to Schofer, Rice and Berg's *Poèmes Pièces Prose* published by Oxford Press. The year is 1973, and the authors, who have written the book in a collective, teach at the University of Wisconsin, a large public university and a centre of anti-war protest in the early 1970s. Their text is in French, it is organised by genres, not centuries, and the bulk of the editorial commentary comes in the form of questions the students are supposed to answer after reading each text. The tone of PPP is critically engaged and anti-authoritarian; an introduction begins "we do not want students to approach literature as a body of knowledge to be memorised." Robbe-Grillet, Valéry and Barthes are quoted in the preface: the banner being flown is clearly that of the new novel and structuralism. The message to students is this: reading is a **critical act**. The students are given only what critical vocabulary they will need to deal with each genre, "narrator" to read prose, "alexandrine" to read theatre and so on. Bishop's passion - the author as a personality or a mentor - is out the window, as is the lecture hall-itself. PPP cannot be taught as a big lecture, since what matters is student participation and response. The course using PPP has to be a seminar.

The irony is that this volume which claims no particular value system with regards to greatness, is in some ways more exclusionary than Bishop's. There are no women writers, no non-metropolitan writers and no medieval selections in PPP, because none of them would work as textbook examples of mainstream post-classical genres.

So while Bishop is dated, because we no longer perceive that clean superstructural universe of great men gathered in the literary salon, so is

Schofer, Rice and Berg: we are no longer comfortable either with the radical relativism implied in the idea that the creative work of literature is all ours, all the reader's, to shape and enjoy.

But we should not despair. The good news behind the kind of "textbook bashing" I am doing is the proof it offers that both these manuals are profoundly imbued with values about French and American culture - PPP with structural enthusiasm, Bishop with new critical idealism. Were we to take up Nicholas Wahl's suggestion and go back to teaching with Gustave Lanson's literary history, there would be plenty of cultural analysis to be done in the classroom in order to connect Lanson to the cultural values of his world. In other words - and here I am speaking to those of us who are institutionally discouraged from teaching courses called "French Civilisation", who teach instead the "masterpieces" of literature or of any other "high art"), allow me to suggest that the masterpieces course can itself be a wonderful entry into what we are calling "Civilisation" pedagogy. Teaching the masterpieces means teaching the way certain texts and authors have been organised, transmitted, and received in specific historical situations, with different works, authors, and forms playing distinct roles in a cultural patrimony.

Jean Carduner wonders why we still need to deal with anthologies; Edward Knox suggests, quite sensibly, that we abandon the notion of survey altogether. Michael Kelly adds that "coverage" is often a code word in French Departments for resistance to any substantial curricular change.

I ended my paper by announcing what I think is proof of a significant change under way in the French literature curriculum in the United States. Harvard Press, under the direction of Denis Hollier, is in the process of putting together a multi-volume *Encyclopedia of French Literature* organised not by genre, not by century, but by individual year or even date. My own assignment, for example, was February 6 1945: the date of Robert Brasillach's execution. Such dates, according to Hollier, are used as "safety pins" to connect books to institutional reality. The single year has also become the basis for Civilisation track courses at the University of Pennsylvania and Berkeley. It is a way of mapping culture which allows you to pay attention to history, society, and politics, to mix so-called "high" and "low" forms that often get separately tracked just as they did in this session, where Christopher Pinet was to speak on "popular" and I on "high" culture.

But at the introductory level, where we want to establish some kind of general cultural sensitivity to France, it is not clear that we would want to zero in on anything as specific as a single year - though the mixture of cultural registers and media is something we probably do want to hang on to. Nor is it the case - and here I am on much more controversial ground - that we should abandon even as dangerous a notion as that of coverage, given the sense we want to offer students of the vital importance in French culture of an official literary patrimony. It is terribly difficult to historicise an entire nation's relationship to its literature, though perhaps easier in the case of post-1870 France where education has been so highly centralised. Could we, for example, teach the Alexandrine verse in such a way that students might perceive it as a character, an historical agent, its glory day in Racinian tragedy, its distortion at the hands of Victor Hugo? Could we teach the history of the literary prizes, the *parti pris* of the manuals, could we teach something about the history of book publishing and copywright laws in France? Laurence Wylie suggests we read Lavisse for myths about history: can we use the literary anthologies and the survey course itself to teach myths about literature ? Then, when an author or a work is excluded - and exclusion is the rule, not the exception in masterpieces courses - at least we will have taught our students what is at stake in rejection or acceptance.

Adrian Rifkin posed what was perhaps the final challenge to a discussion of the masterpieces: do those of us on the Left want to abandon the canon at the very moment when universities and polytechnics in Britain and the United States are pushing disadvantaged students in strictly vocational directions and reserving literary studies for a few ?

(For the discussion on Alice Kaplan's and Christopher Pinet's papers, see below, p.123.)

THE TEACHING OF FRENCH POPULAR CULTURE
by Christopher Pinet, Montana State University

Popular culture has been defined in many ways. I take the term to mean primarily written texts which have been sold in the millions such as *Astérix*, *Le Petit Nicolas*, the songs of Georges Brassens, or more recently Renaud (1). I would also include movies seen by large numbers of people, for example, *Trois Hommes et un couffin*, the most "seen" film of the last 30 years in France or the recent *Le Grand Chemin*. I might add one more group of "texts" and that is television commercials.

I do not and would not claim that French popoular culture as I have defined it is either all of the story or even the most important part of it. I do claim however that it is essential to include "popular culture" in courses on contemporary France (especially those taught in French) if we are to give our students a sense of France *au jour le jour*. It is very much the point of contemporariness (though this does not prejudice continuity) that I want to underline here. Students must, of course, know about the past in order to have any chance of understanding the present, and what is to come. The past continues to preoccupy the French, as the Barbie trial so clearly demonstrates (this year also sees the 25th anniversary of Algerian independence). And yet students always want to know about what is going on in France now, what is *dans le vent*, what their peers are seeing, reading, listening to, saying, etc. It seems to me that popular culture is one of our best ways into France, and the "shock of the new" that intrigues our students, even if that "new" is not always so "new" as they or we would like to think. Personally, I shall always prefer Brassens to Renaud, but then Brassens was the discovery of my undergraduate year in France and in some ways Renaud is his direct descendant.

It seems to me that French teachers have an obligation to "keep up" and to devise ways to help students find the pulse of French life. One good way to do so is by integrating popular culture into our courses.

It is far easier for me to find a rationale for the inclusion of popular culture in a course on contemporary France than to tell how to do it. What

I will do is describe some of the things I have tried and how they have worked.

First, however, it is important, I believe, to make a distinction between courses taught in English and courses taught in French. (In the US I tend to do one or the other, as opposed to readings in French and discussions in English).

For the course taught in French, one can use a variety of texts depending on the level of proficiency of the students. Perhaps my most successful experience has been that of teaching *Le Petit Nicolas* at the intermediate level (2). I have concentrated on two stories from the first volume: *Le Bouillon* and *On a eu l'inspecteur*. The attraction of the stories is immediate, and students often recognise and identify with the characters such as Eudes, Alceste and Agnan who remind them of their own schoolmates of the grade school years. They react emotionally when describing the *chouchous* or bullies of their classes. (According to my students it is at least as difficult to be the *chouchou* as to be *le dernier de la classe*.

Along the way, I point out that a great number of changes have occurred in French education and socialisation during the past 25 years and that in many ways the series *Le Petit Nicolas* (1960-1964) is as much a book for adults, built on their stereotypical (at once exaggerated and condensed) memories, as for children. Thus I cannot claim that *Le Petit Nicolas* provides an accurate or even contemporary account of French school life. But I can say that many French people from diverse age groups continue to buy the books and read them avidly.

Though ranking in grade schools has been done away with, the French school system remains very competitive. There is no longer a system of "*bons*" and "*mauvais points*" nor "*leçons de morale*", but it is important to know that many French people experienced such a system. The "*surveillant*" still exists in schools and I have been told that though now often a college student, the monitor still symbolises negative aspects of authority. Organised disruption, the *chahut*, is also alive and well. The point I want to make here is that popular culture itself is very much part of a continuum, it is not cut off from the past, on the contrary, it may provide important links to the past and may function as a point of reference for changes that do occur in a particular institutional setting. I should add that I sometimes use *Le Petit Nicolas* in tandem with Zola's *Le Grand Michu* to provide a more literary perspective on French school life. Remember that the course I am describing is both a grammar review with compositions every ten days and an introduction to literature and culture. The idiomatic French of *Le Petit Nicolas* is a useful bridge to that of the 19th-century French of Zola. It also lends itself to pastiches. At a more advanced level I have used *Asterix chez les Bretons* also by Goscinny (3). I do so in order to discuss how the French stereotype the English (and vice-versa) as well as themselves (4). Although *Astérix* works reasonably well one should be prepared to present this comic book in more of an *explication de texte* fashion as students need to be initiated into the many double entendres and other word games which make the series so captivating. After the students have caught on, they enjoy the book.

In the same class, I used several strips by Claire Bretécher to good effect, especially *Clair Foyer*, about the dilemmas of modern motherhood. Although I don't really consider Claire Bretécher to meet fully my definition of popular culture, I include her because of her unique perspective on Parisian life and the way she skewers those who use jargon.

In other courses, especially language courses, I have used songs by Georges Brassens and Renaud (5). Once again, it is necessary to explain a great deal to students as well as to annotate the songs, but songs like *Le Gorille* and *HLM* never fail to intrigue students. The notions introduced in the songs always astonish my students for they are literally "foreign" to Americans.

Although I have used Roland Barthes' *Mythologies*, especially the essay on wine and milk in order, once again, to deal with stereotypes, a more accessible introduction for beginning language students is television commercials (6). For better or for worse, my students have been raised on television and pick up quickly on cultural differences or see them (nudity, for example) right away! Commercials also allow one to discuss the sources of French stereotypes of America and Americans, such as every American a cowboy or Californian or New Yorker or gangster. Students remember the commercials, and I sometimes have language students prepare skits based on them. A most successful one, ironically enough, involved a commercial for reading glasses and there were no words at all, simply a man and a woman lifting up their glasses to get a better look at one another and to flirt. At the end of the commercial the man has gone off on a train trip and is sitting across from another man who lifts his glasses in a similarly suggestive way. Our hero begins to respond in kind before realising the implications of his gesture. At an end of term party my students performed their version of this commercial in a local pub and brought the house down.

Television commercials, though sometimes useful, are too limited, especially as they become more American in conception and content. French movies, on the other hand, are rich in cultural content and work at all levels. Even when they are not "popular" as I have defined the term, they are extremely helpful in raising a multitude of issues. Among others I have used to introduce the French are Truffaut's *Les Quatre cent coups* and *Argent de Poche*, which treat school life and adolescent problems. This Fall I shall use the prize-winning *Le Thé Au Harem d'Archi-Ahmed* by Mehdi Charef in order to talk about the problems of second-generation French adolescents of Algerian descent (7). *A Bout de Souffle*, the great Godard classic is as good an introduction as I can think of to French stereotypes of Americans and vice-versa. *Cousin-Cousine* was useful in discussing the family in France and last spring I tried *French Postcards* (1979), which deals with Americans on a junior year abroad programme in Paris. Though not popular culture by any means, I have also had students view *Le Chagrin et La Pitié*, *La Bataille d'Alger*, *Ma Nuit chez Maud*, *Farrebique* and *Biquefarre* to deal with historical problems in French life. This Fall I shall show *Trois Hommes et un Couffin* and when it gets to the States *Le Grand Chemin*. An obvious advantage of films is that they are subtitled and can be used in courses taught in English.

I should like to close with a brief discussion of courses taught in English. Obviously, I do not believe that it is possible outside of movies and possibly television commercials to deal adequately with popular culture in these courses. What one can do, on the other hand, is to introduce popular social history in the form of books like *The Return of Martin Guerre* which can be used in conjunction with the movie version. In this way one can deal with popular customs and traditions of the 16th century like Charivari as well as questions of Protestantism, family life, literacy, the legal system, etc. I use this book in the course the History of French Civilisation.

In the course on contemporary France taught in English, I use Hélias' *The Horse of Pride*, which, like *The Return of Martin Guerre* was a best-seller in France. Both of these books exemplify the continuing preoccupation of the French with their own history. I continue to use Wylie's *Village in the Vaucluse* as well, along with a recent film made of the author on a return visit to Roussillon. Though these works are in many ways classics of their kind they do not deal with contemporary popular culture and frankly, chapters in Zeldin's recent title *The French* on contemporary cartoonists are not satisfactory in giving the flavour of the strips. John Ardagh's book does not really address the question either; so for me any serious treatment of popular culture has to take place in courses taught in French. Though I have no real conclusion to offer, I would make several suggestions: first, whatever difficulties one may have in expanding one's syllabus to include popular culture, the effort is well worth while because of the positive reaction of students and what they stand to learn. Second, though I have not yet done so in my own limited context, I favour a course on popular culture as a special subject or seminar on an occasional basis. Such a course would allow one to use a variety of materials including those outlined above, and others to present an overview of French popular culture since World War Two.

FOOTNOTES

1. *See* STARKEY,H., 'Bande Dessinée: the state of the ninth art in 1986' in HOWORTH, J. and ROSS, G., eds., *Contemporary France: A Review of Interdisciplinary Studies* (Frances Pinter, 1987) for an overview of the current state of the BD. The best analysis of a BD is Jean-Marie Apostolidès' brilliant *Les Métamorphoses de Tintin* (Seghers, 1984). One has only to read this book to be convinced of the potential of BD for learning about recent French history. *See* also my article, 'The ABC's of Popular Culture' in BERTRAND, M., ed.,*Popular Traditions and Learned Culture in France*, (Stanford, Anma Libri, 1985), pp.275-287, (Stanford French and Italian Studies 35).

2. *See* PINET, C., 'Teaching Civilisation with *Le Petit Nicolas*', *The French Review*, 56, No.4, (1983), pp.599-607 for a fuller discussion of the series.

3. *See* PINET, C., 'Myths and Stereotypes in *Astérix le Gaulois*', *Contemporary French Civilisation*, Vol. I, No.3 (Spring 1977), pp.317-336. Rpt. *Canadian Modern Language Review*, 34, No.2 (1978), pp.149-162.

4. An American studying the French must necessarily learn about the British, most noticeably in the *Major Thompson* series by Daninos.

5. *See* PINET, C., 'The Image of the French in the Songs of Georges Brassens', *Contemporary French Civilization*, Vol.VI, No.3 (Spring 1982), pp.271-294.

6.   *See* Katherine Lawrence's 'The French TV Commerical as a Pedagogical Tool in the Classroom', *The French Review*, Vol. 60, No.6 (May 1987), pp.835-844.

7.   *See* PINET, C., 'Le Thé au Harem d'Archi-Ahmed' in the forthcoming issue of *Contemporary French Civilization.*

DISCUSSION ON ALICE KAPLAN AND CHRISTOPHER PINET PAPERS

Micheline Herz referred to the question of teaching literature through anthologies, which had been raised by Alice Kaplan, and **Alice Kaplan** pointed out in response that there was a material problem, especially in big State universities where students could not afford to spend the $100 it now cost to buy six literary texts. She thought that anthologies were preferred for economic reasons, but obviously it would be better to be able to do without them. She also thought that anthologies were a fascinating way to look at the state of the discipline.   **Christopher Pinet** agreed, but was rather surprised Alice Kaplan had not called into question the whole notion of a survey, because it was survey courses that led to having recourse to anthologies.   **Alice Kaplan** replied that one had to decide where to fight one's battles; she had decided with co-operation from the Women's Studies Department to fight to put mainstream, non-metropolitan women authors into the survey course.   She felt that the survey course was so deeply entrenched in her university that it would be the last thing to go.   **Michael Kelly** remarked that survey courses had been inherited from the literary tradition and he thought they were something that would have to be refused in a radical way, in order to introduce the kind of courses that had been talked about on "Civilisation".   Survey courses were dominated by the idea of coverage, and he felt sadly from his own experience that the difficulties faced in introducing popular culture or ideas courses went back to this. Opponents would say: "Does that mean then that we are not going to be able to cover Renaissance literature ?   Or will we sacrifice the 17th century ?" Coverage tended to become a massive argument implying that there was some kind of eternal structure which the lecturer had to plough through, and it was only afterwards that peripheral things like popular culture and society could come in.   He thought it would be a disaster if that sort of approach were imported into Civilisation courses, since it could become a highly conservative force and was very well adapted to the most authoritarian forms of pedagogy. A survey course was brilliantly adapted for a magisterial lecture in which you simply, as it were, passed on a body of knowledge, but it was very badly adapted to stimulating critical reflection among students, getting them to solve problems and getting them to try and synthesise ideas. Survey courses did not allow enough time for such things.

Nicholas Wahl asked what had happened to the use in America and perhaps in Britain of some of the old French literary histories, which included a considerable amount of historical and History of Ideas material, along with the discussion of literature. He was thinking of Thibaudet's *Histoire de la littérature française*, based on the idea of generations, in which the author talked about the ideas of the generations as well as their literary works. Even Lanson did that, and Castex. Had they been completely thrown out, because it seemed they might now become useful again to connect the History of Ideas with literary figures ? **Micheline Herz** certainly thought they were going to come back because at the moment if you were to ask any student when Montaigne was writing he might answer: in the 19th century ... She thought it would be essential to bring such works back. **Laurence Wylie** remarked that the older ones at the seminar would have Lanson on their minds for a long time.

Peter Findlay thought the interesting feature of both **Christopher Pinet's** and **Alice Kaplan's** papers was the way they indicated that what could start to happen was a dismantling of the authority of literature as a discipline. He said he was very convinced that literature as a subject had to be a part of the work of language specialists, but he thought that in order to do that work properly, it was neecessary to start taking literature to pieces as a discipline, because of its authority. In order to do that, the literature specialist had to join hands with the sociologists among others, and that meant acquiring a new cultural breadth, arriving at a concept of culture which was much broader than that traditionally adopted and defended by literature specialists. The idea of the literary moment and its extension into a historical totality - Christopher Pinet's idea of hanging cultural study onto a date - seemed to him to be a fascinating development. Such an approach would of course then necessarily include the kind of aspects of popular culture he had been talking about. They would have to be included as part of the same texture of a particular moment. That seemed to him very much the way teaching ought to be moving. He himself also used songs, popular music and popular cultural texts quite a lot; he found them very important from the point of view of getting responses from the students, because these were cultural elements they were very much at home in. They were not frightened of them. It was also true in France, as in Germany, that an enormous number of political and social ideas were reflected in them, which could immediately be recognised.

Adrian Rifkin thought that the two papers, and Peter Findlay's intervention in particular, had raised the question of what in England, since the mid-1970s and the development of the Birmingham Cultural Studies Centre, had become a dominant academic issue, i.e. the whole question of the methodology of Cultural Studies and its problematic, about how within any given discipline a variety of methods could be applied, without themselves being undone by the particularity of that discipline. He felt both papers raised the question of how you unpicked the nature of the discipline as a kind of study and related that to other kinds of social phenomena, methods of analysis and so on. This was not a particular problem for French, but a general one about the academic division of labour; for example, one could ask why one discipline went in and out of fashion. He felt that if a meeting to discuss French Studies became too French-centred, this might undermine the possibility of inter-disciplinary approaches actually restructuring French syllabuses. He felt that it was more important, for example, to concern oneself about the more general culture of Western societies rather than about a particular canon like the French canon.

Jolyon Howorth, referring to the tremendous value of *Charlie Hebdo* as a teaching tool, said that his problem was that it was an impossible task to explain this to a class of British students unless they had had a year abroad, and, even in the Final Year, its use was very problematic. **Christopher Pinet** replied that he had tried to indicate in his paper that it was possible to use the songs of Renaud even at beginners' level; there was an explanation for them, but the more need for explanation, the less useful the text would be. This meant that some of the more interesting texts, such as Cabu for example, posed difficulties.

Nicholas Wahl then asked whether popular culture was maintaining its national identity, or whether television was not changing it so much that it would cease to have any value for learning about a particular national culture; he felt that video and press popular culture was getting to be the same in all countries. *Le Petit Nicolas* might not be possible in future; **Christopher Pinet** agreed that was certainly true of TV commercials, which had changed so much in the last five years that there was almost no difference between one in France and one in the States. **Nicholas Vahl** interjected that French TV commercials were better. **Christopher Pinet** felt that the problem was less acute where a text had

become institutionalised, like *Astérix*. As far as he knew, *Le Petit Nicolas* was still popular among children and adults as well; he felt that one had to be aware of the problem of homogenisation, but that there were features that were particular to popular culture, particularly written popular culture, that were not being homogenised down.

THE ROLE OF LITERATURE IN THE TEACHING OF FRENCH CIVILISATION
AT PORTSMOUTH POLYTECHNIC
by Tony Callen, Portsmouth Polytechnic

In their First Year on the French Studies degree, students normally have no options, so they have to study Literature, as well as six other subjects. The "Civilisation" (Area Studies) subjects attempt to keep in step chronologically, and *History* is the core course. Literary Studies therefore start in the same period (the 17th century) and stay parallel as far as possible through to the end of the 19th century.

At two hours per week, aims and content must be modest. We try to show how literary language manifests changes akin to those occurring in other areas of life, be they political, economic or philosophical. To take a quick example, Hugo's eclectic imagery is one feature that distinguishes his language from that of Racine, who has a more restricted repertoire. It illustrates his claim that *"Le Romantisme n'est que le libéralisme en littérature"*. At the same time, we try to tell the traditional literary history with all the usual -isms, introducing students to a selection of highpoint texts. This is clearly a compromise, and to effect it we make continual use of extracts to fill the gaps in that story.

Reproduced on the page following this is the first page of a booklet issued to students at the start of the course, showing the set texts for the year and setting out the autumn term programme. They illustrate the way the extracts are woven in (the early modern extracts are both an appetiser and the launching of a study of comedy - for we also try to cover the genres approach too!).

FRENCH STUDIES

YEAR ONE

French Literature Set Texts 1986-87

Molière	*Le Malade imaginaire*
Racine	*Phèdre*
Balzac	*Le Colonel Chabert*
Baudelaire	*Les Fleurs du mal*
Zola	*Thérèse Raquin*
Jarry	*Ubu Roi* (in *Tout Ubu* (Livre de poche)
Gide	*L'Immoraliste*

Programme - Autumn

Week 1	Monday	Lecture
	Friday	Prévert, Ionesco extracts
2	M	Lecture
	F	Queneau, Voltaire extracts
3	M	Lecture
	F	La Rochefoucauld, La Bruyère etc. and Boileau extracts
4	M	Molière
	F	*Le Malade imaginaire* Act 1 sc.5
5	M	*Le Malade imaginaire*
	F	*Le Malade imaginaire*
6	M	*Phèdre*
	F	*Phèdre* Act 1 sc.3
7	M	*Phèdre*
	F	*Phèdre*
8	M	de Lafayette, Marivaux extracts
	F	Rousseau extract
9	M	Romantic drama
	F	Boileau, Hugo, Beaumarchais extracts
10	M	Assessment (in class)
	F	Return of assessment

The Second-Year course is for students who *opt* to study literature. One consequence is that they have fewer courses in common. So although retaining links with the History course, and continuing with the -isms and highpoints approach, the Literature course can now pursue other aims. The programme can now find time to study aspects of popular culture, for instance: songs, comics and love stories:-

Autumn:

Apollinaire *Calligrammes*

Saint-Exupéry *Vol de nuit*

"Occupation Poets"

Sartre *Les Mains sales*

Spring:

Robbe-Grillet *La Jalousie*

Ionesco *La Cantatrice chauve*

"Les BD"

Sagan *Bonjour Tristesse*

Tournier *Le Coq de bruyère*

"Les Chansonniers"

Summer:

"Workshop"

Little in the way of methodology is offered for approaching these "non-literary" areas. There is no Sociology on French Studies, for instance, and the course still has only two hours per week in which to complete students' introduction to Modern Literature. Hopefully, though, they are, by the end of the year, in a position to make knowing choices about dissertations and Final Year options. Time was found last year to introduce what the students dubbed a "creative writing block". It is called "workshop" on the programme. Although having no obvious links with French "Civilisation" as such, it did involve language learning, group work, critical judgement and presentation skills (reading aloud, *mise en page*, etc.).

Literary Studies can offer great flexibility to students. Cross-disciplinarity is one opportunity certainly, but there are many others. The first year Literature course, for instance, formally assumes a responsibility for examining and practising certain study skills. The creative writing block emphasised many of the aspects of learning that all

129

too often only remain implicit in our courses. And it did not, of course, preclude learning about France: one of the pieces involved research on the Mont St.-Michel, for instance.

In Year Four, we offer a course that is overtly multidisciplinary: an option called *Littérature et société*. There are also a Drama and a Cinema option too).

Texts are chosen entirely from the post-war period and focus on major social issues such as immigration (Etcherelli's *Elise ou la vraie vie*, terrorism (Manchette's *Nada*), the events of May 1968 (Merle's *Derrière la vitre*) and so on. In this way direct links are forged with the core course: *France Contemporaine*, and this aspect is stressed by having one of the three course teachers concentrate on the contemporary history in the texts. Another team member stresses the ideological content and a third the literary qualities.

As throughout the literature teaching on this degree, up-to-date critical approaches make way for the other aims of the course, which is very much a jack-of-all-trades as a result.

The technique is largely pragmatic and exploratory, examining as they occur questions about the relationship between fiction and reality ("Civilisation"?). French Studies produces generalists. It has to admit this openly and be proud of it.

Here, then, to conclude, is a summary of the points I have been trying to make about the role of literature in the teaching of French "civilisation":

THE STUDY OF LITERATURE OFFERS:-

1) A great capacity for **integrating** with other subjects

2) An opportunity for **enriching** political histories of "Civilisation"

3) Ways of **accommodating** popular culture in the overall programme

4) The flexibility needed for **training** in study and personal transferable skills.

5) A powerful way of **learning** about all aspects of "Civilisation".

THE ROLE OF HISTORY IN THE TEACHING OF FRENCH CIVILISATION
by Jolyon Howorth, University of Bath

The following comments aim to address a number of basic questions raised
by the prospect of integrating a French History course into the
undergraduate curriculum in degree programmes such as those in Languages
and Area Studies.

Why History?

The arguments in favour of History are compelling. Of all the Human and
Social Sciences, History is the discipline which is the most
quintessentially French. The *Annales* school of historiography has been a
model to which historians the world over have aspired for much of this
century. Stanley Hoffmann recently observed that, of all the great Human
and Social Sciences, History alone still thrives in France (1). Moreover,
there appears to be an insatiable public thirst for historical knowledge.
To some extent, this is the case for all régimes with revolutionary origins:
the Revolution and its consequences become beacons of legitimation for the
present. In France, for almost two centuries after 1789, the key to the
meaning of life was to be sought in the ideological universals spawned by
the Revolution. History, it was believed, had a meaning and a directiomn
and must needs be studied, lest civil society stray from the revolutionary
straight and narrow.

History in France has always been an arena in which political forces have
locked horns over the "true" heritage of the past. The victorious Socialist
Party swept to power in 1981 amid a welter of historical hoop-la.
Ressusciter la mémoire et redonner un sens à l'histoire de France
proclaimed a chapter in the party's official project (2). As against the
efforts of Giscard and his education minister René Haby to exorcise what
they regarded as the "demons of the past" by downgrading History in the
school curriculum, the socialists, spearheaded by François Mitterrand,
proclaimed *"la mémoire est révolutionnaire"* (3). This tendency of
politicians to do battle over the meaning of the past, is mirrored by the

historians themselves, ever ready to engage in the cut and thrust of political polemic. In recent years, furious battles have been publicly fought over history books offering reinterpretations of the Revolution of 1789, the origins of French fascism and, of course, World War Two (4).

Those great systemic structures much loved by both politicians and historians have, of course, taken a beating in the last ten years, and few now look to history for an explanation of the present, still less the future. Yet history, paradoxically enough, remains as popular with the public as ever. Since the early 1970s, consumption of history books has increased by 10% per annum and serious glossy history magazines are scooped up with relish by an avid reading public, for whom the past, far from offering an explanation of the universe, now tends to be seen as a form of tourism (5). In short, for the French, an understanding of the national heritage (*"civilisation"* ?) without a solid grounding in history is, whichever way one looks at it, inconceivable. The next question is: at what stage should history be integrated into an Area Studies programme?

When?

There is a good case for offering History in the **Final Year** of an undergraduate Area Studies course. Since History (as understood in France) requires prior understanding of concepts and methods from a broad range of the Social Sciences, and since History aspires to an explanation of the **total** human experience, it could be argued that any attempt to tackle it before the Final Year is doomed to failure. In fact, the difficulties of teaching the other (contemporary) elements of an Area Studies course if the students have no historical background are even greater, and most courses elect, if only for reasons of chronological neatness, to begin with History *in the First Year*. In this way, the History course is perceived by students and staff alike as a necessary foundation for the remainder of the degree programme.

The constraints involved in this method are obvious. First, the students entering Languages and Area Studies courses reveal a considerable diversity of historical competence and/or interest. Many dropped history early on in their schooling, and only chose an Area Studies course because of a dislike of literature. Others have taken it at "A" level and are keenly and positively interested in the Social Science side of the course. The History course cannot be taught in the same way as it might to first-year undergraduates in a History department. To begin with, there are problems of methodological transition. Moreover, although there must of necessity be limitations on the content of the course, and although it cannnot be geared primarily to the training of future Braudels, the Area Studies History component should not be seen as an elementary service course - students from such courses have gone on to do history doctorates and become recognised historians in their own right. But given that the First Year is identified as the most appropriate point at which to integrate a History component, the course itself must be carefully geared to meeting certain specific targets.

The aims of a First-Year History course
The first aim, clearly, should be to offer the students the basic information: facts and dates. Much of this can be gleaned by them from background reading of basic texts. Such reading is all the more essential given the limited number of contact hours. Optimum results can only be expected if considerable structured guidance to the readings is given in the form of handouts offering chronological signposts, explanatory references and cultural topography. The main problem derives from the relative inappropriateness of almost all existing historical writing. Textbooks in French (especially such masterly overviews as the 16-volume series *Nouvelle Histoire de la France contemporaine* (5) are packed with allusions and cultural references which are way beyond the ken of the average British student. The standard British works are either too old-fashioned (Cobban, Brogan, Wright) or, as in the case of the most recent and by far the best (Magraw), somewhat too specialised for Area Studies students. The best texts are the Longmans "Seminar Studies in History" or a recent work like McMillan, which is more geared to first-year undergraduates. Other textbooks badly need to be written. Whichever material is chosen, however, the students will be expected to discover the basic facts for themselves.

Over and above this factual discovery, there are four fundamental aims in such a course. The first is to introduce the students to notions of historical casuality, to help them understand that, even if history is no longer believed to contain a universal blueprint for Nirvana, it does demonstrate how and why things happen. Without unduly complicating the explanatory framework, it is possible to take this opportunity of integrating the second aim of such a course: the introduction of concepts, approaches and methods from a range of the Social Sciences. Thus, when studying, for example, the Paris Commune of 1871, students can be brought to think about questions of social class (distinctions between artisans, proletarians and bourgeoisie), economic liberalism (the battle over the free or the controlled economy), geographical diversity (Paris and the main cities versus rural France), political philosophy (anarchism/libertarianism versus Jacobin or Marxist centralism), collective culture or psychology (the power of nationalism under conditions of extreme cold and hunger), and even diplomacy and military strategy. It is precisely the "totality" of history which makes it such an ideal vehicle for introducing notions from the other disciplines of the Human and Social Sciences.

The third main aim of a first-year Area Studies History course should be to encourage students to engage in independent analysis of essentially inter-disciplinary problems through their own participation in the controversial dimensions of the topics studied. British students, in particular, tend to be seeking the "correct" interpretation of events. For the most part, they are unpolitical if not apolitical in their approach (which means that they have never really learned to think in political terms). For students of France, this is a severe handicap. The history course is an ideal opportunity to help them to work out their own political views and opinions. They should be encouraged to take an active part in the great ideological clashes between, say, Robespierre and Danton, between Guizot and the Utopian socialists, between Marx and Proudhon, between Jaurès and Clemenceau. Contact with French history carries with it both responsibilities and rewards: it is an inevitably maturing experience.

The final objective of such a course must be to introduce students to the vocabulary and registers of contemporary French history and society. It is impossible to overstress the need for British students to begin to think about France and French society in the appropriate register. Concepts such as *le syndicalisme* simply cannot be conveyed by the use of English - indeed, for students to believe that what they are thinking about is actually **trade-unionism** makes understanding of the reality virtually impossible. One could suggest thousands of examples of this type of problem. We will examine the question of the use of language in the History course in more detail under below.

Course Content

Periodisation depends on programmatic emphasis. Unless the degree programme requires concentration on social, economic or industrial history (as in the case of French and Management degrees), in which case the start date might be as late as 1871 or even 1900, there is a solid case for following French historiographical convention and dating the dawn of *contemporary France* in 1789. Two problems arise here. First, is it possible to understand the Revolution, without first having understood the Ancien Régime ? The answer has to be pragmatic. If the course is pushed back well into the 18th century, the difficulties of coverage become well-nigh insuperable. One has to start somewhere and to begin with the Ancien Régime is to pose also the question of feudalism and to push the origins even further back into the mists of time. A flavour of the Ancien Régime can be given in an introductory session on the "pre-Revolution" and references back to the *philosophes* and feudal structures can be incorporated into the sessions on the Revolution itself. But therein lies the second major problem. The revolutionary period 1789-1815 is arguably the most complicated - and certainly the most exhaustively chronicled - in European or even world history. A narrow course needs to be steered between oversimplification and the overwhelming mass of detail. This is, in fact, extremely difficult, and the course requires intensive and sensitive preparation. But the other side of the coin is that the sheer complexity deters students from any temptation to believe that there is a single underlying truth behind historical phenomena. This in itself is an important lesson, which can help them concentrate, instead, on grasping the main lines and the main interpretative frameworks. The case for studying, in some depth, the period 1789-1815 does not need making.

Thereafter, 1815-1870 can be covered relatively rapidly, the successive régimes being seen at one level as slow-motion action replays of the various stages of the Revolution itself: Absolutism in danger, Constitutional Monarchy, Republican democracy, bourgeois "Directorship", pre-imperial Autocracy and finally Empire. The significant innovatory features of this period (beginnings of industrialisation, social class mutations, advent of mass literacy) can be highlighted in the relevant political framework. The period 1870-1900 offers immense scope for examining the emergence and evolution of 20th-century structures and problems, the period 1900-1945 (taken as a bloc) can be presented as the crystallisation and consolidation of those problems (the stalemate society) and their non-resolution. In this way, the post-war world, which will normally appear as a "contemporary" course in the second year, can be understood as the area of new issues and new approaches in which a "new"

France, profoundly influenced and shaped by her historical roots, is seen striving to break free of a number of the more constraining shackles of the past.

Content can best be dealt with thematically and allied to various disciplinary concepts and approaches. A fourfold framework facilitates the task of clearly identifying the wood, while never losing sight of the main groups of trees:
- sources of wealth and social actors (Economics and Sociology)
- politics and ideology (Political Science and Philosophy)
- foreign and defence policy (diplomacy and geo-strategy)
- culture and communication (Language, Education, Media).

Such a thematic structure constitutes a solid grounding for the move, in subsequent years, towards more concentrated work in the different Social Science disciplines.

Teaching Methods

Given the constraints and limitations mentioned above, the problem of teaching methods is crucial. **Lectures** should not be seen as the means through which to convey "facts" and basic information, but as an opportunity to stimulate, enthuse, fire and inspire through provocative comment on mainstream events which the students will necessarily have to have "read up on " in advance. The lectures can help crystallise and make sense of these selected background readings by drawing attention to major themes and by underscoring their historical casuality, continuity and evolution. There is no reason for not lecturing in French. Although students are slightly "destabilised" at the outset (and certainly need guidance on note-taking), experience shows that, by the middle of the first term, they can cope just as easily with a lecture in French as with one in English. It is also advisable to break them in early to the links between culture and language.

Seminars are another matter. They are of crucial importance in identifying problems and misunderstandings as well as in helping students to participate in the events they are studying. Since student participation is of the essence, there should be no hard and fast rules about the use of language. It is more important for the students to say what is on his or her mind than to say it in French (although experience shows that, if they are interested enough in a topic they will have no difficulty in saying it in the relevant register). Isolated mini-exposes, followed by group discussion, are a recipe for disaster. Far better is to identify a burning or controversial issue (say: *"L'Affaire Dreyfus: la France éternelle et la vérité républicaine"*) and devise two sets of readings. The first, covering a range of sources, should be prepared by all students in the group. the second should offer hard-hitting partisan interpretations from both sides of the ideological divide and should be used by two students to draw up their own speeches "for and against". The remainder of the group can then enter the controversy as they see fit. In this way, spontaneity and a lively interest are ensured.

Audio-visual back-up is indispensable. Excellent films (*Danton, La Grande Illusion, La Marseillaise*) not only bring the subject to life, but also consolidate student interest. Slide shows offering visual support (Daumier's cartoons for the mid-century, the events of the Paris Commune etc.) and tapes of, for instance, cabaret songs of the *Belle Epoque* are always a great hit.

In sum, the first-year history course can be seen as an essential and important grounding for the entire "Civilisation" programme.

FOOTNOTES

1. HOFFMANN, S., 'Paris vu par un nouvel Huron', *French Politics and Society*, 7, (September 1984).

2. *PARTI SOCIALISTE, Projet socialiste pour la France des années 80* (1980), pp.159-170.

3. Mitterrand's speech to the Socialist Party Congress in Metz in 1979.

4. For details on all of these battles, plus an overview of the changing role of history in French society, see RIOUX, J.P, 'Twentieth-century historiography: Clio in a Phrygian bonnet' in HOWORTH, J. and ROSS, G., eds., *Contemporary France: A review of interdisciplinary studies*, (Frances Pinter, 1987), pp.195-212.

5. The success of historical best-sellers like Pierre-Jakez Hélias's *Le Cheval d'Orgueil* or Emmanuel Leroy Ladurie's *Montaillou* suggests that French readers are looking for a "good human interest" story rather than for an explanation of the universe.

6. The 16-volume *Nouvelle Histoire de la France contemporaine*, is published by Seuil. COBBAN, A., *A History of Modern France* (Pelican books, 1961) (first edition). BROGAN, D., *The Development of Modern France, 1870-1939*

(Hamish Hamilton, 1940), new edition, 1967. WRIGHT, G., *France in Modern Times* (Chicago, Rand McNally, 1960) new edition, 1974. MAGRAW, R., *France 1815-1914: the bourgeois century*, (Fontana, 1983). MCMILLAN, J.F., *Dreyfus to De Gaulle. Politics and Society in France, 1898-1969*, (Arnold, 1985).

DISCUSSION ON JOLYON HOWORTH PAPER

Nicholas Wahl commented that the History lecturer in the United States tended to limit subject coverage to those parts of French history he or she thought important so that the undergraduate course in History could not be counted on as a source of information in the way **Jolyon Howorth** put it, to provide an essential overview of the main developments leading to the world of to-day, and especially the France of to-day. There was no possibility of this. So the question arose as to where students got their information. It seemed to him that among the most important aims of the History component was to lay out the chronological sequence and to give some information on which further study could be based. Secondly, he thought it excellent if the History professor could produce concepts, approaches and methods of a broad range of the Social Sciences. However, in his experience in the States, relatively few professors had had the benefit of a term or a year at the Ecole des Hautes Etudes where they could learn the *Annales* methods. Most of them were still trained, if they were historians of France, in the traditional kinds of History, where certainly research did not bring them into too much contact with the Social Sciences. Generally historians had not caught on to the *Annales* school; they were now doing so. Now that the school was dying out in France they were relearning its methods in Kansas and elsewhere, and they were the most fervent *Annales* historians, i.e. social historians with a Social Science background. In fact, they were recreating the *Annales* school in America. He thought in any case that relatively few American undergraduates got much out of history in respect of such concepts.

As far as periodisation was concerned, he was not certain that 1789 was the right date, he thought that Eric Cahm had already mentioned, like others, the end of the Ancien Régime. He thought it was very difficult to teach the Revolution without going into the *contentieux* of the end of the Ancien Régime: 1750, 1787, the Enlightenment. Finally, he found it a little cavalier to jump over the period 1815-1870. He thought it was not slow motion but actually a pretty fast motion sometimes, a replay of the various stages of the Revolution. If one wanted to look at it that way, one might think that it revealed naughty things about the Revolution. The more important reasons to look closely at this period were connected with economic history, since this was a very important period in French economic history. You could not understand what happened otherwise under Napoleon III or Louis-Philippe: there would be a lot about France you would not understand. The same was true of History of Ideas: the beginning of socialism, Marxism, liberalism... How could one understand neo-liberalism without it ?

Jolyon Howorth agreed that it was necessary to deal with the History of Ideas and said that he had been trying to suggest that that period of French history was a slow-motion action replay of the very fast action of the Revolution. He felt that to portray it in that way helped students to rehearse and remind themselves of the stages of the Revolution and the problems that had come out in it. That was the point he had been making and he did not underrate the important of any of the points that **Nicholas Vahl** had raised. **Nicholas Vahl** stressed that the most important point related to information. Where was the undergraduate to get information about France if he did not get it from the History course ? Basically, if the History course became too conceptual, where would he get the information from about the Restoration, the July Monarchy and so on ?

Jolyon Howorth replied that this information should come from lectures of course and also from the background reading, from such books as that by Cobban. This might not necessarily be the best information they could go for, but information was not lacking.

Laurence Wylie felt disturbed about the need for information, agreed that it was necessary but had noticed that in many of the bibliographies reproduced for the seminar John Ardagh's book was included. He wondered how appropriate it was at this level. There was, however, another kind of history which he thought was very necessary at least for American students, and perhaps for British students - he tried to get all his students to read very carefully Lavisse's little primary school history of France and told them that they would never be able to understand the French mentality, French thinking, French conversation even unless they learnt the myths that other generations of the French had grown up on. In fact, when he heard that one of the students was going to take Stanley Hoffmann's course, he would say : "By the way you have to go out and get the history book which Stanley Hoffmann used when he was in *lycée*". If you learnt that you would, in baseball terminology, start off with three balls, you would really be ahead. He thought that a lot could be learnt from textbooks children used in other countries and that really people did not pay any attention to this point. **Eric Cahm** confirmed that when he recently had to teach a course in France on English history, the first book he read was a school textbook and he found this an absolutely essential starting point.

Laurence Wylie added that he could not see how the students could understand the French Revolution without learning where the idea of it had been born, i.e., under Guizot and the people between 1815 and 1848. They would never catch on to the whole concept of a revolution, or a new bourgeois régime, unless they realised Guizot really invented them in the 1820s. **Christopher Pinet** asked Jolyon Howorth whether it was right to confront the fiction of history, because it seemed to him that a lot of students came to the history course in particular with the idea that there was objective and factual information in history, whereas one of the things he had been trying to show his students through the teaching of Natalie Davison's book, *The Return of Martin Guerre* and the comparison of it with the film, is that the historian is in fact very often writing fiction or that there were gaps that the historian could not account for in his thesis. **Jolyon Howorth** said that he was quite provocative in that respect as well, and consequently drummed home the fact that there was no such thing as historical truth. There were not a lot of opportunities to analyse this but he did use one example, the Paris Commune, which after all existed essentially as myth in French history. For **Christopher Pinet** this meant that if one read Gordon Wright's book, one had the varieties of history so that students could be confronted in that kind of way with different interpretations.

THE SOCIAL SCIENCES AND FRENCH STUDIES

by Neville Vaites, University of Reading

Social science disciplines in recent years have become more specialised and technical as a result of developing their subject areas by producing rigorously formulated and testable hypotheses. For Departments and individuals the advancement of research and teaching requires the adoption of strategies favouring specialisation and depth. There is no longer room for generalists within disciplines or across disciplines. France, as a society and culture, offers case studies and theorists of importance to Social Sciences. But, in seeking to promote and invigorate the study of French society, research projects or teaching programmes must take increasing specialisation into account by providing adequate skills and resources.

The more progressive French Departments in British institutions for higher education have offered their students for many years a varied menu of Language, Literature, History and Philosophy. Some of their teachers of French philosophy and history have achieved eminence in their respective disciplines. Moreover they have built an institutional platform for their research and teaching by establishing combined-subject degree courses drawn from two Departments such as French and History or Philosophy.

It is only in recent years that French Departments have given serious attention to the more specialised social sciences, signalling their academic interest in France as a living society by normally adopting the "Studies" label and creating new combined subject-degree courses. But in many cases, the substance behind the label in the degree courses was expected to come mainly from departments such as Politics, Economics and Sociology, for it was there that those researching and teaching in French aspects of those disciplines had traditionally made their homes. Nevertheless, such academic marriages between French Studies and Social Science Departments could be considered sound and healthy so long as the traditional importance of French language and culture persisted within the British education system. It provided a setting within which social scientists could assume at least a reading knowledge of French among their students, and a familiarity with major French issues, events and personalities. At the same time, French specialists could assume that considerable attention would be given to France within Social Science departments.

The contention to be developed in this paper, however, is that traditional academic marriages between French Studies and Social Science departments are no longer viable due to important changes in recent years. It will be argued that new strategies and structures are needed in order to take these changes into account, and that initiatives will have to come from French Studies rather than from Social Science departments. A wider perspective reveals similar changes affecting the study of other foreign languages and societies. The new strategies and structures proposed here may therefore be transferable. They may indeed be strengthened by co-ordinating the policies and activities of all the foreign language Departments. But the case is discussed here in terms of French Studies for the specific purposes of the Portsmouth seminar and the ensuing publication.

The first important change in recent years is that, whatever the international recognition of French political and economic achievements since World War Two, there has been a serious decline in the study of the French language. For various complex reasons that have been widely discussed there has been in recent years a sharp decline in the number of students in British higher education either specialising in French Studies or using French subject matter and materials in the study of other subjects such as Social Sciences. Where they are used, English translations have tended to become the accepted norm, and a vicious circle increasingly devalues the specific qualities of French language and culture. This is sometimes attributed to the tremendous impact of American language and culture since 1941, increased by rapid technological developments in the mass media in recent years. All Foreign Language studies have been adversely affected by this. To some extent the phenomenon is beyond control, but many language specialists believe that its harmful effects could be offset by a supportive change in official values and financial priorities in favour of Foreign Language studies (1).

A second development reducing the importance attached to French Studies is that theSocial Sciences have become more theoretical and less concerned with comprehensive coverage of national case studies for their own sake. France is only given particular attention if she provides theorists and experiences of obvious importance and relevance to a theoretical analysis.

This may simply be a natural consequence of progress in the Social Sciences. It may also reflect another kind of American influence, on thought as well as language, towards an emphasis on abstractions and theoretical constructs. The result is the Social Science departments are tending to pay less attention to France for her own sake, and there is a decline in the numbers of their teaching staff and research students willing and able to study French. Moreover social scientists must take account of the growth in size and complexity of world society within which the French component is relatively diminishing.

The third problem discouraging French Studies in Britain is due to the French themselves. Their emphasis on the particularity of French society and culture has sometimes led them to organise and publish official information and statistics in forms that do not relate readily to international data such as that issued by bodies such as the OECD (2). Moreover their normal view, according to which anyone in the world wishing to investigate French theorists or case studies should take the trouble to learn the French language, severely restricts world attention paid to French experience. Although France is admirably supportive towards academic research and publications in general, she could further promote their interests by devoting some resources towards publications of translations, especially of works by younger French social scientists. Reliance on market forces, according to which a publisher will wait until a large number of people have read a French text and clamour for a translation before he will consider commissioning one, results in long delays before French works win a world-wide readership and influence. The rapid pace of research and publications in the Social Sciences today makes such long delays a serious inhibiting factor affecting French cultural influence in the world. Some long-established French social scientists have succeeded in penetrating the international market in their different fields and have had some works translated, for example men like Aron, Duroselle, Grosser or Michelat, who consequently appear in all respectable bibliographies. But what about the many younger social scientists in France whose powers of research and analysis are just as great but whose influence is largely confined to France for purely linguistic reasons ? The French government could reduce this problem by subsidising translations of works it considers worthy of international attention. This kind of action might well increase the world-wide use of French texts that have not been translated, as foreign readers follow up such publications written or referred to by social scientists who catch international attention initially through translation. People will learn and use French if given an adequate incentive. The argument could be tested by a statistical investigation into whether the untranslated works of the world-famous men referred to above were exported in greater numbers after a translation of one of their books had been published.

A fourth discouragement to French studies is also due to the French themselves. Authors are often guilty of writing exclusively for the French market and not giving serious attention to relevant case studies and theorists in other countries. This sometimes renders their approaches eccentric and difficult to relate to others. Moreover, their technical presentation is often haphazard. One is fortunate to find a French social science book with source references, bibliography and index matching up to conventional international standards. Perhaps the CNRS should enforce standards on authors and publishers in this respect. All four of these problems illustrate the special linguistic and technical characteristics of French Social Sciences that require the time and resources that only French Studies departments can provide for effective study, as will be shown even more clearly by considering each of the main social sciences in turn.

Economics

As a discipline, Economics now gives increasing emphasis to analytical theories and mathematical approaches, treating national case studies at a secondary level of importance, especially those coming from a middle-sized economy such as the French. Recent financial pressures on higher education institutions in Britain have made it less likely that the primary interests of newly-recruited staff and research students will be directed towards France. Coincidental influences such as secondary interests and a reading knowledge of French tend to determine whether or not French case studies form part of an Economics syllabus. They are more likely to appear in option courses that have a lower status than courses on economic analysis. The problem is exacerbated by the paucity of French economic theorists using similar approaches to those of their British and American counterparts and proving suitable for inclusion in economic analysis courses (3).

In spite of these difficulties, there is plenty of scope for study of French economic experience in important spheres such as European Community practice and policy, international finance in the European Monetary System and development economics in West Africa. French business organisations and strategies have often been novel and successful, and can be studied through the work of analysts such as Michelat. If these studies are neglected by Economics departments it will be the responsibility of French Studies departments to promote them. There is some governmental encouragement for Economics and its vocational affiliates such as Business or Management Studies, and it is important that French departments should not restrict their horizons to merely providing Business French language components in Combined Degree courses, but that they should take the opportunity to promote a comprehensive and purposeful academic study of French policy and practice. A year of study by British students in a French firm or business school or university is of course essential, but that experience should be integrated into related studies in their British degree syllabus.

Politics and International Relations

Politics Departments have traditionally concentrated their interests on studies of governmental systems. Conventional practice is to categorise systems into presidential, based on the American model, parliamentary, based on the British model, and totalitarian, based on the Soviet model. If a parliamentary multi-party system is studied (usually for pejorative purposes) the Italian model is most convenient. The French case is peculiar and hard to use as a model. This is due to the hybrid Fifth Republic constitution, conventionally allowing for presidential predominance until 1986, but also allowing the prime minister, his government and the National Assembly to assert their powers as shown by the recent experience of *cohabitation*. Moreover the French multi-party traditions have been considerably reshaped into a bipolar mould under the Fifth Republic. This is perhaps also why recent French political analysts such as Borella, Hamon and Schwartzenberg have not achieved as much international attention, as measured by inclusion in bibliographies or by translations, as that given to the older generation of analysts such as Duverger and Goguel.

Traditional interests in government have recently been overtaken by a rapid expansion of International Relations studies, including defence and security. In this field, there is an emphasis on theoretical analysis using American approaches; and empirical study of world politics since World War Two often emphasises bipolar structures which naturally focus attention on the United States. Nevertheless, Gaullism and an independent nuclear force have attracted considerable international attention to the French case; and so has the wider French influence within the European Community. It is significant, however, that the French IR analysts who have attracted most attention in Britain and the United States have been critics of Gaullism such as Aron, Grosser and de Rose. This situation is now improving as energy and finance are poured into IR and defence studies. The development of IFRI's international contacts and the proliferation of French IR periodicals have provided a respectful world audience for newer analysts such as Artaud, Lellouche, Moisi and Smouts (4). A clear indication of international recognition of French expertise was the recent appointment of Heisbourg as director of the IISS in London.

It remains true, however, that their intellectual formation and linguistic limitations lead to a preference for American sources and methods in British Politics Departments and a corresponding neglect of their French counterparts. It is the responsibility of French Studies departments to ensure adequate attention to French case studies and theorists in Politics and IR syllabuses, especially in combined degree courses, and to ensure adequate library collections of French books and periodicals (5).

Sociology

Sociology Departments have traditionally shown great interest in France, whether in theorists from Comte to Crozier or in case studies of social phenomena. The rapid change from rural to urban predominance since World War Two, the tensions between individuals, groups and the highly centralised state bureaucracy, the experience of educational, religious and racial conflicts, all attract international interest towards French society, especially when problems erupt into violence as in farmers' demonstrations or in "events" such as May 1968. Sociology, while geared to theoretical analysis, encourages eclectic studies of various aspects of social structures and behaviour. Optional courses and case studies therefore tend to be given considerable importance, probably more than in the Social Science disciplines discussed above (6). The combination of theoretical and empirical interest in France has created an international audience for French sociologists such as Aron, Bourdieu, Crozier, Mallet and Meynaud.

It nevertheless depends on accidental influences on the composition of staff and research students as to whether or not a Sociology Department has a French specialist, and in recent years it has been more difficult for such a person to find students able and willing to use French sources.

French Studies Departments therefore have a responsibility on both linguistic and intellectual levels to ensure adequate study of the varied experience and characteristics of French society.

History

History Departments continue to give considerable attention to France because of her traditional importance as a great power during the modern era, and because of her seminal influence on European political and cultural developments. But there are three causes for anxiety about the study of France in British History Departments. Firstly, their syllabuses are geared to Europe, and therefore stress comparative rather than national history. Just as American institutions like Stanford University agonised over replacing retiring national specialists like Gordon Wright and Gordon Craig with comparativists, so one fears that British counterparts like Cobban, Hampson and Johnson may be a declining breed of historians of France. Secondly, a related problem is that fewer students are able and willing to use the French language. Many Departments, including those at prestigious Oxford colleges, have to provide students with documentary and secondary materials in English translation. Thirdly, the fame of the *Annales* schools of historiography created by Bloch and Febvre has focussed British attention on the strengths of French research into social history as seen in the works of Braudel, Duby and Le Roy Ladurie. But the reorganisation of French archives in recent years, and the introduction of a "thirty year rule", have given rise to a new generation of contemporary historians specialising in French and international politics. They owe nothing to the *Annales* school, whose influence is consequently in decline. Yet the works of historians like Artaud, Bariéty, Girault, Pédroncini and Vaïsse are as yet hardly known in Britain and have not been translated. It is the responsibility of departments of French Studies to undertake the study of French history using French sources, and to ensure that all major aspects of French experience are given due attention. New developments in research and the French historiographical debate need to be taken into account through regular use of French publications.

Conclusions

This analysis indicates the various reasons why Social Science departments have tended in recent years to reduce their commitments to French Studies. Staff specialising in France and linguistically competent in French have become more scarce, and the uncertain coincidence of their presence in certain departments tends to determine whether or not French theorists, case studies and experience form a component of a Social Science syllabus. A saving grace is that some Departments have staff with a strong secondary interest in French Studies who are capable of including them in general survey courses. But serious specialised study of France, using French sources, now increasingly depends on the imagination, ambition and resources of French Studies or combined Language departments if it is to receive effective treatment in British institutions of higher education. Social Science departments often regret their declining competence in French Studies and wish their staff and students could use the French language as a tool. They are therefore willing to support French Department activities, especially if benefits are shared.

The appropriate philosophy and related strategy for fulfilment or responsibilities now shouldered by departments of French Studies should take the following lines. First of all, it is important to get away from the second-rate, ramshackle philosophy of a "finishing school" merely producing generalists who know the French language. Courses in French "Civilisation" are inadequate and do not earn the respect of Social Science departments. In their drive to increase student numbers and financial resources, French Departments should maintain and develop a coherent academic philosophy and purpose, geared to producing specialists in certain aspects of French Studies, if necessary accepting a division of skills and labour according to which institutions are recognisably strong in some fields but not in others (7).

Each Department could achieve coherence and respect in both French Studies and Social Sciences by keeping to the following strategic principles. Firstly, to pursue ambitions related to the ideal aim of providing facilities for specialised teaching and learning of the Politics, Economics and Sociology as well as the History and Philosophy of France. No existing department has staff numerous or skilled enough to achieve that aim on its own. One solution to this problem may be to negotiate support from staff in Social Science departments where French expertise exists. If it does not exist, funds should be created to pay for outside help in the form of lectures, seminars and examination questions provided either by staff from other educational institutions in Britain or France, or by suitable specialists based in the civil service, commerce or industry. They could be attracted by offering research finance and resources in departments of

French Studies. The acquisition of such expertise could bring important spin-off benefits to a department and to an institution of higher education as a whole.

Secondly, degree courses linking French and Social Sciences should be carefully structured to create an even balance in the numbers of examination papers, avoiding a major-minor relationship on principle. The component courses within a degree programme should provide adequate scope and rewards for case studies, such as those on France, perhaps by using a mechanism such as double-weighting for essays and dissertations categorised as case studies. This would be further justified if French case studies written in English were accompanied by summaries in French and *vice versa* as a matter of principle. This arrangement would counteract the strong current tendency of Social Science departments to privilege courses in theoretical analysis that give advantages to students reading single-subject degree courses over those with one foot in other departments such as French Studies.

A third strategic principle derived from that above is for French Studies departments to avoid links with other departments based entirely on Language teaching, whatever the financial temptations. To avoid becoming mere service departments, which is a considerable danger in the current proliferation of more vocational degree courses combining French with Business or Management studies, French Departments should only undertake links guaranteeing a coherent academic combination of intellectual as well as linguistic disciplines to which the French contribution is approximately 50% in both quantity and quality. This could involve, for example, courses on the economic, social and political context within which French Business and Management operate. It should also involve a year of relevant study in France.

A fourth principle is to ensure that students have a lengthy period of study and experience, preferably one year, of life in French society. This is increasingly important to counteract the relative decline in French intellectual and linguistic influence on British society in recent years. Moreover it is an essential means to improve the active command of the French language developed by British students. And it is particularly important for those linking French with Social Sciences to carry out study and fieldwork in France itself. While they are based at their British institution, it is of course important that students undertake much of their learning in French. But the emphasiss of Combined Subject students should be on the acquisition of intellectual as well as linguistic skills to compare and compete with those of counterparts in other Departments such as Social Sciences. This may require reading and discussion in specialised parts of a French Studies syllabus to be devoted to works in English by theorists such as Talcott Parsons, Friedman, Keynes or Samuelson; and case students of French experience published by British and American scholars such as Hampson, Johnson, Hoffmann and Wylie should not be ignored because they are in the English language. Specialists in France recognise their value, and so should specialists in French Studies based in Britain.

A fifth and final strategic principle is to ensure that there are adequate arrangements to bring French Studies and Social Science specialists, both staff and research students, together regularly to enable them to co-ordinate the promotion and defence of their overlapping interests. This would not only generate sympathy and co-operation but would also facilitate the search for financial support to fulfil the responsibilities requiring new resources discussed above. To some extent, these purposes can be served by inter-disciplinary institutions such as Graduate Schools or Faculty Boards. But undergraduate programmes and resources create special problems that require handling by a special Liaison Committee or Board of Studies comprising representatives from Language and Social Science departments. Problems of research staffing, student admission, syllabus, library resources, year abroad and examinations could be tackled much more efficiently by the regular action of such a committee.

Hitherto, many Language departments have not managed to appoint more than one Social Science specialist on their staff. Several such people are needed to cope with responsibilities for specialised research, teaching and administration that are generated by their commitment to promote Social Sciences within the field of French or other Language studies. In their uphill struggle they have received valuable physical and psychological support from outside their Departments and institutions through the energetic activities of new professional organisations, such as the Association for the Study of Modern and Contemporary France. Publications supporting research and teaching, and short conferences bringing together staff from universities, polytechnics and schools, help to reduce the sense of beleaguered isolation. But the intensification of academic and financial pressures on the time and energy of Social Science specialists in Language departments has made it essential that they strengthen their position within their respective institutions. They need to formulate clear strategies within the departments and to create appropriate mechanisms between departments in order to ensure that they get sufficient resources to meet the increasingly rigorous demands of educational institutions and the society they serve.

FOOTNOTES

1. When this paper was read in its original form at the seminar, Nicholas Wahl spoke about currently encouraging signs in the United States that increases in funding have brought a reversal of the earlier decline in foreign language studies. This should lead educational authorities in Britain to increase their financial support for Foreign Languages.

2. This was a point emphasised by my colleague M.-P. Allum, when this subject was discussed at a research seminar at Reading University in October 1987.

3. After many years of difficulty in organising a year of relevant studies at a French university for Reading students combining French with Economics, they are now sent normally to Paris X-Nanterre, where the Economics syllabus and staff relate very well to British and American approaches.

4. On recent developments in International Relations research and organisation see SMOUTS, M.-C., 'The Study of International Relations in France', in *The Journal of International Studies*, Vol.16, No.2 (Summer 1987), pp.281-6. The Institut Français des Relations Internationales (IFRI) was founded in Paris in the mid-1970s.

5. An important issue is how to divide or combine responsibilities for library collections. Should French Studies departments only undertake to order and finance publications in French, leaving relevant publications in English to the Social Science departments, or should they be given responsibility and resources to acquire all important publications about France in whatever language they happen to be? At Reading University, for example, the Librarians ascribed responsibility for all Social Science periodicals to Social Science Departments which then met their recent requirements for 9% financial cuts by axing five French language periodicals essential to the work of the French Studies Department.

6. The Sociology Department at Reading University encourages specialised empirical study by giving a double weighting to the dissertation among Finals Papers.

7. The French Studies Department at Reading University could apply this principle, for example, by adopting a specific label to indicate its specialised strengths in French History and Politics, while Departments at other Universities and Polytechnics might signal their particular strengths which might be similar or might include alternative specialisations such as Philosophy, Economics or Sociology. The enriching effect of including the wealth of specialised French thought and writing from these fields in a French Studies syllabus, rather than limiting it to survey or dabbling courses associated with the "Civilisation" label, was emphasised by my colleague Dr. Bridget Jones, a specialist in contemporary French drama and society including the Francophone "Third World", when this subject was discussed at a Reading University research seminar in October 1987. This issue had generated debate at the Portsmouth seminar where some participants claimed to be producing generalists in French "Civilisation" and to be proud of it.

TEACHING METHODS, MATERIALS AND PROBLEMS

AN INTRODUCTION TO CONTEMPORARY FRANCE
by Claire Duchen, Oxford Polytechnic

In this paper, I want to think about the specific problems of a course
introducing contemporary France and the study of contemporary France to
First-Year undergraduates, and propose an approach that might contribute to
overcoming the problems (1).

The First Year is often considered to be less significant, less important,
than the more advanced stage of the degree course. This is a mistake, as
the First Year can make or break it: studying patterns, motivation and
interest in the topic, indeed the whole educational experience of the
student, can be set in the First Year.

In designing a course for First-Year students, the starting point must be
to consider the aims and objectives of such a course, and for this we need
to look both backwards and forwards: we must look first at the "raw
material" - that is, the students who enter. Most have done the literary
A-level and have little if any idea about France itself; nor do they have
any experience of studying Politics and Society: moreover, particularly in
the case of the young women who make up the majority of students of
Languages, they are resistant to the notion of "politics"; and finally,
they have varied linguistic ability - and in any case have forgotten all
their French over the summer holidays).

For our academic purposes, the First Year is a transition in both content
of study and in methods of teaching and studying, between the ingestion of
information that is carefully reproduced for A-level, and the ability to
work independently that we try to encourage at later stages of the degree
programme.

We should also look at the end-product: at the careers of our graduates. In
spite of the students' own perception, we are not primarily involved in

vocational training - students may use their languages, but then again, they may not. Depending on the structure of their degree course, the graduates of Contemporary Studies degrees go into careers similar to those of other Arts, Humanities or Social Science graduates. Our long-term aims must therefore be concerned with the student's general educational development, with furthering the acquisition of the skills outlined by the UGC.

In the long term, we want students to develop sensitivity to the world they live in; to develop their critical and analytical skills; and of course to develop their linguistic competence. In a more immediate sense, the First Year is groundwork for the whole degree - it prepares students for later in-depth study and for the year that most students of French spend in France.

At the end of the First Year, then, there is a certain amount of "baggage" we want the students to acquire. In terms of content, we want them to grasp certain essential socio-political and historical concepts and gain an idea of the broad chronological sweep of French history. For instance, of central importance are the Republic, the questions of Left and Right, of political change, social class, gender, geography as determining/affecting life-cycle/attitudes of individuals/the nation, questions of economic development and of interaction between individual and group, family and society.

On a more prosaic level, we want students to acquire certain study skills: how to organise their thinking; how to read critically; how to develop arguments and put them in writing in a coherent fashion (and put them in French); how to familiarise themselves with listening, responding and discussing questions in French; how to read texts in French; how to grasp the different nature of different texts/documents, of different registers and styles.

Such is the vastly ambitious nature of a three-term course, in planning at Oxford Polytechnic, taught three hours a week in a combination of lecture and seminar (2). How can it possibly be achieved ?

The primary concern for first-year students is unquestionably motivation. France and the study of France (or even the study of anything) is relatively alien to the First-Year undergraduate, who is, at the same time, leaving home probably for the first time with the euphoria (or rather the shock) that this entails. The students are doing a number of courses (at Oxford Polytechnic, these are called modules) at the same time, with all lecturers assuming that their own is the most important. With the students already sufficiently alienated, we need to find a way to teach socio-political structures and trends in a historical framework that students find "relevant" to their own experience (either as contrast or comparison); that they will find interesting in a subjective as well as objective way; that they will grasp and understand and even, possibly, remember.

Personalising history is one way to do this, giving them something to latch on to, identify with. This is why I propose that a First-Year course might focus on the *"récit de vie"* - the life of an individual.

Starting from the premise that everybody loves a story, the *récit de vie* - sometimes called *"approche biographique"* or *"ethnobiographie"* - provides a basis for the kind of historical and socio-political introductory survey that I have in mind. Teaching history through life-stories personalises, individualises study in a way that statistics and textbooks cannot.

Without wishing either to turn French history into a giant soap opera, and without wishing to trivialise and infantilise the study of France, I believe that the personal life story/history, in a careful context, can highlight factors of change, social structure and the impact of political life on the individual etc. It can provide a pivot for perception of the interaction between family and society; of different social milieux and social relations; of gender roles, evolution and so on.

For the purposes of my First-Year course, the *récit de vie* would be used as raw material around which to build a thematic study of France, which will indicate the complexity and diversity of experience. The *récit* would be **one central, but not exclusive, component of a course which has many others.**

The main problem is over the texts to choose. We would have to choose the life of individuals whose experience tells us something specific - either someone who lived close to the heart of events we wish to describe - Charles de Gaulle, Léon Blum, Georges Séguy, Simone de Beauvoir, Benoîte and Flora Groult, Lucie Aubrac - or it could be someone whose life illustrates a particular theme we wish to explore (for instance the *"exode rural"*) or the experience of immigrants).

What therefore has to be decided first of all is the theme or unifying feature of the term. I would suggest one broad theme per term, centred on two *récits de vie* and supported by a number of authentic documents and secondary sources. In my view, possible themes would be social structures of France (Term 1) in which a picture of France at (for instance) the turn of the century could be built up;   the Republican tradition (Term 2) in which the more complex ideas connected with the 1789 revolution and the gradual implantation of the Republic and parliamentary democracy in France could be introduced;   and France since 1945 (Term 3) in which discussion could focus on social and political change in the post-war era.

One could, for instance, use extracts from *Le Cheval d'Orgueil* or another peasant *récit* as the core of the first dossier.   The next task is to identify questions to ask/themes to consider, supported by documents taken from J. Ozouf (*Nous, les maîtres d'école*, from *Le Tour de la France par deux enfants*), M. Segalen (*Mari et femme dans la société paysanne*), E. Weber(*Peasants into Frenchmen*), L. Wylie for the present day.   Complementing the written texts could be films (for instance the film of *Le Cheval d'Orgueil*, or another film describing rural life such as Olmi's *The Tree of Wooden Clogs*).   Maps and graphs could be used and students could also be introduced to the use of tables and statistics (as in Colin Dyer's useful book *Population and society in twentieth-century France*).   The lecturer would guide students through.

The guiding questions for a first term could be: who lived in the countryside on the eve of the First World War ?   what kind of work was done ?   what was the relative place of agriculture in the French economy ? what characterised rural life in terms of relationships within families and in the village, and in terms of the village and the nation ?   how did children learn about France ?   and what was the influence of the Church/Republic at local level etc. ?   In this way, the broader framework of the structure of the French population and the economy would be introduced, as would certain questions about how attitudes are formed and how different stances towards society emerge.

The seminar would initially focus on the *récit*, with the lecturer making the links between the individual and the social and political context.   There would then be progressive integration of *récit de vie* and contextualising material through the year.

The same approach could be adapted to the question of class structure. Again, a personal account might make the student more aware of the variety of experience, and prevent the taking of certain values and attitudes as given – an optimistic view might suggest that such an approach would encourage sensitivity to the experience of others.   The *récit de vie* (working class or bourgeois – for instance, use Simone de Beauvoir's memoirs) would serve as a springboard, allowing discussion of a number of issues and problems relative to the issue of class, while taking students through the inter-war period (or whichever period is chosen).

A second term might focus more specifically on political questions. I would suggest the Republican tradition as essential, but have not as yet found a life-history on which to base an approach to the Republic. It could be done through an examination of one person's experience of the Dreyfus Affair or maybe of the Vichy regime, crises which highlight attitudes both for and against the Republic. Focussing on the Dreyfus Affair, for instance, one could look at the life of a young Dreyfusard (Léon Blum ? Charles Péguy ?) supported by texts from *La France radicale* (collection Archives), from Eric Cahm's invaluable book, by documents such as Zola's *J'accuse ...!*, articles from the newspapers of the time, extracts from the memoirs of others whose lives were affected by the Affair. If Vichy provided the focus, it would possibly be easier to find texts of different kinds. An examination of the Republic would have to include notions of Left and Right, the challenges to the Republic, the significance of the Revolution, insofar as it informs the experience of the individuals in the text.

A third term could bring the background knowledge acquired in the first two up to date by studying France today. Again, there is a wide choice of texts, interviews, memoirs, at least partly due to the recent growth of Sociology as a discipline, to the interest in social history and use of oral history and in the tales of the previously silent/silenced sectors of society.

The lecturer would have to put together a course of this kind with care and attention, watch the levels of linguistic and other difficulty, and offer guidance to the students. Students will tend to generalise from the particular, so the specificity as well as the representativity of the *récit* must be stressed at all times.

The lecturer would have to watch carefully over the coherence of the course, and not take on too much or it would be too busy, too bitty. One would have to select certain themes and explore, provide a basis, a springboard, from which to continue, and not an all-encompassing account of France in the 20th century.

We are not interested in the life story for its own sake, but for the relationship to the world that it illustrates. We are concerned about how the narrator perceived him/herself and his or her world; we need to take into account the problems of interpreting what is said, maybe the conditions of production and the reasons behind the writing of the particular text.

The *récit* provides pleasure in reading, in discovering a world other than one's own. A life history is more readable than sociological or political treatises, and for students who have mainly studied literary texts at school, it would provide an accessible route into the "harder" texts that they will be expected to deal with later on. The student can compare his or her own culture/experience with the object/subject of study and find an invaluable peg on which to hang a hat.

The seminars would be infinitely flexible according to the lecturer's preference and students' needs - (a blend of linguistic and comprehension exercises, *explication de texte*, vocabulary-building, discussion of events described and short presentations on themes (e.g. women and men's work in the peasant family, how the Second World War affected *un tel*, girls' education), combining the experience recounted in the text and information provided in other texts.

A course based on thematic *dossiers de textes* hingeing on the experience of one individual would therefore be more authentic, more personal and more memorable, expose the student to history, social and political change in a digestible (but not trivial) fashion, exposing them also to a variety of texts. It is not necessarily pandering to the students' lack of "vital spark" but is based on a realistic appraisal of how people learn and on a broader interpretation of the text and how to exploit the text. The flexibility built into a course of this kind allows the lecturer to walk the fine line between challenging the student and providing guidance and indeed the spoon can be withdrawn for some, maintained for others.

FOOTNOTES

1. For my purposes, "Civilisation" or "Contemporary France" will be defined, as for most participants of this seminar, as social, historical and political culture, specifically excluding Literature and Literary Criticism as objects of study.

2. I am aware that not many institutions offer the luxury of so much time, and the course I propose is not appropriate to the needs of all.

STUDYING MATERIALS FOR LANGUAGE AND CONTENT:
AN INTEGRATED APPROACH
by Linda Hantrais, Aston University

The place of "Civilisation" courses in British higher education

Many different approaches are adopted in the teaching of "Civilisation" in
British universities and polytechnics. The information contained in the
CRAC Degree Course Guides to French Studies in higher education in Britain,
published every two years, gives a fairly comprehensive picture of the
structure of degree courses in a large number of institutions. The Guides
show how the "Civilisation" component is increasingly gaining ground, and
this trend is confirmed by the results of the survey conducted by Hare and
Roach of "Civilisation" teaching in British universities, reported elsewhere
in this publication. The current growth in the importance of "Civilisation"
teaching in higher education can be interpreted primarily as a response to
changing demand amongst undergraduates.

The type of materials required to support a French "Civilisation" course
will depend primarily on the level of language proficiency of the students,
the importance attributed to the subject within the teaching programme and
the background and training of the staff involved. In Britain, a reasonable
A-level standard is a normal prerequisite for a first degree in Languages,
although clearly this is not the case in the United States, Australia and
New Zealand. The choice of materials will further be determined by the way
the course is taught and in which language, whether it is optional or aimed
at a wide unspecialised audience. Access to supporting documents may be
constrained by financial or geographical factors.

Categorising "Civilisation" courses in higher education in Britain

The many types of courses described in the CRAC Guides and in other
literature about French "Civilisation" teaching in Britain can be grouped
into several broad categories, for which different sets of material will be
appropriate. At one extreme are the institutions where "learning about the
country" is seen as part of the canvas against which French literature, the

dominant course component, must be situated: for example Flaubert's *L'Education sentimentale* can only be fully appreciated by an undergraduate student who knows the social history of the period. If students on these courses are expected to spend a period of residence in France during which they will "learn to speak the language", they must also need information of a more contemporary nature about the country in preparation for residence abroad. Hare and Roach show that in more than half the course units on French "Civilisation", there is no form of assessment at Final Honours level, which would seem to illustrate their low status in the degree programme. On these courses, language study as well as knowledge about the society tend to play a subordinate or instrumental role. Language testing has traditionally been confined to literary translation, prose composition and the general essay, and as Tony Lodge (1984) demonstrates in an unpublished report, this situation is still far from being unusual in British universities today.

At the opposite extreme from the traditional literary courses are those where the study of the language is eclipsed by the analysis of institutional structures or the theory of Area Studies disciplines, which arguably may not belong in a Languages department.

In between these two extremes are the courses where the study of "Civilisation" is one of many possible approaches to understanding the context in which the language is used. The content may serve primarily as the subject matter for linguistic analysis and text manipulation, or Language and content may be given equal or similar weighting and attention. This is the case for some of the courses – still relatively few in number – where the decision has been taken to make Literature into a subsidiary or minor element and to promote the study of the country's social, economic and political institutions as the main thrust of the programme, but without losing sight of the importance of language study. The objective is to produce graduates who are fully conversant with the workings of the foreign society, while being able to operate effectively in the language in communication with their French counterparts. It is this middle block of courses which would seem to be of most relevance for the development of new programmes, although the institutional conditions may not always be very conducive to such an approach.

Teaching the different categories of "Civilisation" courses

In cases where "Civilisation" is a minor or functional component of a programme, the teaching is often done by a French *lecteur* in "conversation classes" - this may be the only part of the programme taught in French - or by an academic who has acquired the relevant background knowledge. He or she may have "converted", albeit often reluctantly but of necessity, to "Civilisation" studies. The status of the activity is generally low, and it is not given much academic recognition. In some institutions "Civilisation" may be taught by a Language centre rather than a French department. Where the disciplinary study of French Politics, Economics or Sociology is the main purpose of the degree programme, the specialists teaching it are unlikely to be linguists. Courses are generally taught in English and addressed to students who are not necessarily linguists.

Courses in the middle band have to face the problem of how to recruit suitably trained and qualified staff to a Languages department in order to teach about the country when most lecturers in French have received their training in the traditional mould, i.e. French Language and Literature. As a result of this difficulty, or for reasons of principle, many of these courses are taught in English, as has traditionally been the case for Literature: the subject specialist is generally "bought in", and it is very rare to find academics who are able to teach their specialism in French. The question then is how to bridge the gap between language and content, and what status to attribute to the language teacher. The linguist is assigned the task of making the link for the students, using "contemporary" published and recorded materials. The native speaker with a Social Science qualification is normally not interested in the language teaching aspect or qualified to handle it. In most cases, the native speakers in Languages departments will have been trained in France in English Language and Literature, but they have the advantage of being able to draw on their own experience and of being able to keep abreast of contemporary developments through the media.

For the purposes of this paper, despite the difficulties described, it is assumed that there are linguists with Social Science training, or social scientists with expertise in the language, and that in both cases their research interests underpin their teaching, so that the teaching activity is intellectually demanding and satisfying, as befits an academic course. Although most of the degree courses in Britain teaching French "Civilisation" still make a clear distinction between language and content,

161

it is also assumed that the preference is for approaches which seek to contextualise language and which view content, in its broadest sense, as an integral part of language acquisition, so that language is not understandable divorced from knowledge of context, and content cannot be understood in isolation from language. The current interest in communicative competence in language learning is evidence that the emphasis is increasingly on the acquisition of language in such a way as to allow the learner to operate effectively in the foreign society in a wide range of professional, administrative and social contexts.

Relating materials to approaches

In some institutions, the cultural aspect of French "Civilisation" implies the traditional study of Literature, albeit with emphasis on its historical, political or social dimensions. This may be supplemented or replaced by film. In looking at the sorts of materials which can be used to support the teaching of Area Studies, no reference is made to materials for studying French literature, since they are assumed to be unproblematic in that they have long been available and exploited, and they would seem to fall outside the scope of this paper.

Many of the references to source materials added to the course descriptions from the institutions represented at the seminar are to works in English, analysing various aspects of French history, the economy, social or political life. There obviously are some useful books in English, but if students are to maximise exposure to the language, they should be encouraged to read as much material as possible in French, and reference is made here almost exclusively to publications in French. The different categories of materials can be related to the types of courses which have been identified.

Textbooks

Courses which are designed to give students a taste of (and hopefully) for French "Civilisation" may be compared to those Literature courses, encapsulated by Lagarde and Michard in the 1960s, and in other surveys of French masterpieces, where, by studying key extracts from the work of the nation's main literary figures, students feel they know what the main trends are and can speak fairly authoritatively about them, using relevant quotations to illustrate their points.

In some institutions French "Civilisation" is approached in the same way through the study of a few selected texts on topics ranging from the educational to the electoral systems, generally accompanied by language exercises intended to familiarise students with the relevant vocabulary, the more common syntactical structures of popular journalism or the relevant administrative text. The books which adopt this approach, such as *Le Français en Faculté* (1980) or the more recent *Travaux Pratiques*(1987), following in the tradition established by Blanc(1964), Biggs, Chicken and Leeson (1971), or Nott and Trickey (1971) in the 1960s and early 1970s, are usually self-contained and self-explanatory and do not therefore need any further elucidation. The Scottish universities have devoted particular attention to developing this type of course book, which is often organised in conjunction with audio materials, and they have also sold well elsewhere in the United Kingdom and throughout the Anglo-Saxon world. There are now video courses, such as *Lyon à la une*, again a product of the Scottish universities, which are based on similar objectives and the same teaching context. They are designed for use by the language teacher, with little or no specialised knowledge of the range of topics covered, their main objective being "the acquisition and improvement of practical linguistic skills which will be relevant to students' future needs" (according to the publicity sheet for *Travaux Pratiques*). Since the emphasis is generally on language rather than content, these textbooks are suitable for courses structured around language acquisition and may be particularly appropriate in the Scottish or American contexts, where First-Year students are not necessarily already language specialists. In English higher education, few academics, as opposed to language teachers, are keen to adopt ready-made courses and to use a single textbook as their main teaching tool.

Surveys in French of the contemporary scene

For the more adventurous lecturer or student, wanting to extend knowledge of the subject "tasted", or for the undergraduate preparing a seminar paper or essay, materials will be needed which set out the main issues and provide supporting information, and there are many useful publications in French which fulfil this purpose.

Longer extracts of texts are provided by the Hatier *Profils*, and a more analytical overview is given in regularly updated publications such as *Francoscopie*, *L'Etat de la France* or *Faits et Chiffres*, which can be dipped into and used as reference tools, compendia or a "potted France" in French. Reviews, such as *Les Cahiers Français* and *Après-demain*, which treat different themes in each issue, provide fuller coverage on selected topics from a wider range of source materials, with authoritative specialist

163

articles in a popularised and usually very readable form. These are all valuable for updating information or for finding a ready-made summary of the main points and arguments. *Donnees Sociales* is an extremely informative publication, based primarily on quantitative data, but with some useful analytical articles, presented objectively.

All these materials are for courses requiring more than language acquisition exercises, but they can provide a means of extending vocabulary and appropriate phraseology, for example in the presentation of statistical information (for the analysis of socio-economic statistics, a useful guide is Levy, Ewenczk and Jammes, 1981). They are invaluable sources for preparing seminars and essays, but since they are not written specifically with the foreign language learner in mind, students who use them need to have a sound command of the language.

Integrated language and content texts

In response to the increasing number of courses which aim to ensure that students acquire a high level of proficiency in the language at the same time as in-depth knowledge of the country's institutions and structures, a series of Contemporary Language Studies was launched by Macmillan in the early 1980s, with the object of presenting an introduction to and analysis of French social, economic and political institutions and structures, illustrated by texts and leading on to linguistic exercises, further specialised reading and essay writing. Eric Cahm's *Politics and Society in Contemporary France (1789-1971)* (1972) provides an early prototype for the historical overview, supported by documentary materials in French, but without the linguistic applications.

Most "Civilisation" courses include a historical dimension or core, but the contemporary orientation generally implies the study of current affairs and events. The problem with most commercial publications in Britain is that the scope for constant updating is very limited, and students tend to feel they are not being kept abreast of the contemporary scene unless they are provided with the latest information. To maximise use of publications in this category, the illustrative texts and linguistic exercises can best be used as examples which elucidate trends and ways of approaching the study of texts. The lecturer needs to update materials and to apply the analytical framework to recent events. The suggestions for further reading also offer a starting point rather than a comprehensive bibliography.

Ephemeral publications

The survey texts referred to above are ephemera and as such are fairly regularly revised and updated. Not much of a distinction needs to be made between them and the wide range of magazines, government fact sheets, advertising and electioneering materials, with which radio and television broadcasts can be included. In Britain it is relatively easy to obtain up-to-date materials, and there are a number of publications which are supplied free of charge. Micro-films, on-line information retrieval systems and satellite television are useful complements or alternatives, but they can be expensive to access. Where it is possible to subscribe to newspapers and magazines, choices have to be made from a very wide range of periodicals. What to select depends again upon the type of course, its aims and the people involved in the teaching, although it is always advisable to try to familiarise students with a variety of viewpoints and intellectual levels within journalism, while also exposing them to more official publications, so that they are presented with as many different approaches as possible. The linguistic interest of analysing texts from a range of language varieties or of comparing texts from different registers which treat the same theme is not to be underestimated.

Scholarly or research works

Exclusive use of the press for supporting materials is not to be recommended (and this includes broadcasting), for it undermines the academic nature of the activity. Even if different viewpoints are confronted, this is no substitute for the publications which are based on academic research. The list of possible reference works in French, which provide serious and detailed coverage of the range of topics included in civilisation courses, is voluminous. Where provision is made for postgraduate study and specialist options, and where French-speaking staff teach the French "Civilisation" course themselves, the latter are obviously essential reading. Useful materials can be found in specialised journals, such as *Sociologie du Travail, Revue Française des Affaires Sociales, Population* and *Revue Française de Science Politique*. The publications from research centres, for example the *Cahiers* of the Centre d'Etudes de l'Emploi, are invaluable for information on current research findings, and the ASMCF review, *Modern and Contemporary France* is an important sourced for details about the most recent publications in France.

Reading for language and content

Whatever the nature of the text and whether it is written or oral, students should be encouraged to read for both language and content. This approach implies that they are learning to manipulate texts and are not simply absorbing information passively. There are several key questions which can be asked about a text in order to alert students to its contentual and linguistic features: students will need to inform themselves about the source of the texts, the event which inspired it and the medium through which it is presented to the reader or listener; they will want to find out who the author is and who the intended readers are; they will need to be able to identify the author's motives, his or her starting point and conclusions; the tone, form and structure of the text are also important for an understanding of the interactive process between author and reader; finally students can seek to extend their own productive skills by analysing and imitating the linguistic tools and procedures exploited by the author both to convey a message and to ensure that it is received by the readers or listeners in the way intended.

Through careful analysis of the content and language of authentic texts from a wide range of oral and written sources, students can be introduced to the many facets of French society and can learn how to apply the knowledge acquired to real life situations, whether they be professional or social.

REFERENCES AND SAMPLE RECOMMENDED TEXTS

(* indicates items referred to in the text)

General

* LODGE, A., *The teaching and assessment of French language skills at final honours level* (unpublished report, 1984).

* LEVY, M.L., EWENCZK, S. and JAMMES, R., *Comprendre l'information économique et sociale. Guide méthodologique* (Hatier, 1981) Collection J. Brémond.

* TOWNSEND, G., *CRAC Degree Course Guide 1984/5: French in UK Universities, Polytechnics and Colleges* (CRAC, 1984).

Textbooks

* ADAMSON , R. et al., *Le Français en faculté: cours de base* (Hodder and Stoughton, 1980).

* BIGGS, P., CHICKEN, P. and LEESON, R., *La France: aspects sociaux, politiques et économiques* (Longman, 1971).

* BLANC, M., *Visages de la France contemporaine* (Harrap, 1964).
* CAHM, E., *Politics and Society in Contemporary France (1789-1971): A Documentary History* (Harrap, 1972).
* HARTLEY, D., ed., *Travaux pratiques*, (Hodder and Stoughton, 1987).
* NOTT, D.O. and TRICKEY, J.E., *Actualités françaises: A Complete Course for Advanced Students*, (The English Universities Press, 1971).

PAOLETTI, M. and STEELE, R., *Civilisation française quotidienne*, (Hatier, 1981).

Surveys in French of the contemporary scene

Regular publications: general overviews

* *Faits et chiffres. Aide-mémoire de la vie économique* (Les Editions SGB, 1987).
* INSEE, *Données Sociales* (INSEE, 1987), triennial.

INSEE, *Tableaux de l'économie française 1987*, (INSEE, 1987).

* MERMET, G., *Francoscopie. Les Français: Qui sont-ils ?* (Larousse, 1986).

Quid 1988 (Robert Laffont, 1987).

SOFRES, *Opinion publique 1986* (Gallimard, 1986).

SOFRES, *L'Etat de l'opinion: clés pour 1987* (Le Seuil, 1987).

* VERDIE, M., ed., *L'Etat de la France et de des habitants*, (La Découverte, 1987).

Specialised overviews

ARNAUD, R., *Panorama de l'économie française* (Dunod, 1986).

CHAPSAL, J., *La Vie politique sous la Ve République* (PUF, 1984) (2nd ed.)

FOURNIER, J. et QUESTIAUX, N., *Traité du social: situations, luttes, politiques, institutions* (Dalloz, 1984) (4th ed.).

PARODI, M., *L'Economie et la société française depuis 1945* (Armand Colin, 1981).

REYNAUD, J.-D., et GRAFMEYER, Y.,eds., *Français qui êtes-vous ? Des essais et des chiffres* (La Documentation Française, 1981).

Hatier

* *Profil Actualité* series

04500 *L'Etat et la politique économique en France depuis 1945*

04501 *La Population de la France des années 80*

Profil Dossiers

04513 *La Décentralisation*

04511 *La Presse écrite*

04535 *La Publicité*

Profil Formation

04330 *500 fautes de français à éviter*

04327 *Améliorez votre style 1*

04328 *Améliorez votre style 2*

04324 *Conduire une réunion*

04333 *Du plan à la dissertation*

04331 *Ecrire avec logique et clarté*

04320 *Explorez le journal*

04326 *Le Français sans faute*

04334 *Lexique des faux amis*

04322 *Prendre la parole*

04332 *Le Résumé de texte*

04333 *Travailler en groupe*

04321 *Trouver le mot juste*

Journals

ǂ *Après-demain*

Autrement

ǂ *Les Cahiers Francais*

Problèmes politiques et sociaux

Problèmes économiques

Regards sur l'actualité

Integrated language and content texts

ǂ Macmillan Contemporary Language Studies Series:

HANTRAIS, L., *Contemporary French Society* (1982)

HOLMES, G. and FAWCETT, P., *The Contemporary French Economy* (1983).

SLATER, M., *Contemporary French Politics* (1985).

Ephemeral publications

Newsletters and factsheets

CHAMBRE DE COMMERCE ET D'INDUSTRIE DE PARIS, *Lettre mensuelle de conjoncture*

CONFEDERATION FRANÇAISE ENCADREMENT, *Les Dossiers de l'Avenir.*

DELEGATION A L'AMENAGEMENT DU TERRITOIRE ET A L'ACTION REGIONALE *Lettre de la DATAR*

INSEE, *Ecoflash*

MINISTERE DE LA CULTURE ET DE LA COMMUNICATION, *Développement Culturel*

SERVICE D'INFORMATION ET DE DIFFUSION DU PREMIER MINISTRE, *Lettre de Matignon*

Daily Press

Le Figaro, L'Humanité, Libération, Le Monde (Le Monde: Dossiers et documents, *Le Monde de l'Education*, *Le Monde Diplomatique*)

News magazines

L'Expansion, *L'Express*, *Le Nouvel Observateur*, *Le Point*

Specialised journals

Economie et Statistique, *Futuribles*, *Population*, *Population et Sociétés*, **Pouvoirs*, *Revue Française des Affaires Sociales*, **Revue Française de Science Politique*, **Sociologie du Travail*, *Travail et Emploi*.

THE YEAR ABROAD

by Joe Coutts, Buckinghamshire College of Higher Education

For the benefit of our American guests, I should begin by explaining what a
College of Higher Education is, and what sort of courses it offers. There
is a wide diversity in the work of the Colleges of Higher Education, if
only because they have grown out of widely differing institutions. The
Buckinghamshire College was the product of a combination of a teacher-
training college and a college of technology and art. Subsequently, the
teacher training was diversified into courses in the Humanities and Social
Sciences, while courses in Technology, Design, Management, Business Studies
and Languages developed at graduate and postgraduate levels. The School of
Management Studies and Languages is a department with entirely advanced
work, at the same level as the polytechnics. French is taught on a range
of courses up to postgraduate level, with a bias towards economic,
commercial and financial aspects of French-speaking countries.

The paper which follows is based on two research projects, one for the
CNAA, the other for the Central Bureau for Educational Visits and Exchanges.
Both projects are intended as reponses to questions which are being asked
as to how institutions can justify the additional resources needed for a
four-year degree course. The Central Bureau project is a more direct
response, attempting to identify the quantifiable benefits of work and study
abroad, whereas the CNAA project is primarily an investigation into forms
of assessment of the work placement abroad, and the means whereby this
assessment may be incorporated into the final degree classification.

Since the scope of the research extends beyond the area of interest to this
seminar, I shall confine my paper to considerations of the professional
placement, insofar as it affects the development of linguistic skills and
the appreciation of the socio-cultural context of the work environment.
These seem to be the areas most related to French "Civilisation" teaching.

The research methods used have been a series of questionnaires, addressed
to students, institutions, potential employers and recruitment consultants,
and a number of semi-structured interviews with students, recruitment

consultants and placement employers (the latter in France, Germany and Spain). The question of assessment has also been discussed with partner institutions in Clermont-Ferrand, Osnabrück and San Sebastián.

The findings which follow relate mainly to the CNAA research project, although some of the comments from British employers are equally applicable to the Central Bureau project.

The questionnaire to students was addressed to 112 graduates from the BA (Honours) European Business Studies course at the Buckinghamshire College, a four-year sandwich course in which the study of one Foreign Language (French, German, Spanish and, latterly, Italian) forms an integral part. Responses were received from 69 graduates who had completed the course over the five-year period 1983-87.

The number of students taking French as the foreign language totalled 28, of whom 27 spent a year in France, and 1 in Belgium. The other figures are Germany 31, Spain 10. No figures are yet available for Italy, as the option has only recently been offered.

The results of the questionnaire have been analysed on an Apricot computer using the SNAP programme (Survey and Numerical Analysis Package). I shall concentrate on the results of interest to this seminar viz. Question 5 (factors influencing the student's choice of course), Question 9 (financial problems), Question 10 (disadvantages of undertaking a work placement), Question 11 (how far the work placement satisfied the stated objectives), Question 12 (foreign language proficiency), Question 13 (personal benefits of work placement), and comments from students on their experience during the year in France.

Students were asked (Q.5) how important the following were in their choice of undergraduate course : a) their aptitude for languages at school, b) peer group influence, c) the chance to develop job-related skills in a foreign language, d) the opportunity to work abroad, and e) career outlets from this course. They were invited to reply on a 1 to 4 scale, ranging from 1 - "very important" to 4 - "not at all important". Results (69 responses) were:

	1 V. IMPT	2	3	4 NT AT ALL	TOTAL
a) Aptitude at school	25	32	8	4	69
b) Peer group influence	0	4	10	55	69
c) Job-related skills	31	27	9	2	69
d) Work abroad opportunity	35	28	5	1	69
e) Career outlets	38	22	7	2	69

171

It will be seen that career outlets from the course (e) scored the highest with (d), (c) and (a) ranking as important, but peer group influence (b) as not important. Students were concerned with the end result of the course, taking advantage of what it could offer, but not influenced by what schoolfriends were doing.

The question of financial problems often arises with work placements abroad. In Question 9, students were asked to what extent they had financial problems during their placement, with possible replies on a 1 to 4 scale, from "very serious" to "no problems".

Responses according to country were:

	1	2	3	4	TOTAL
	V. SER		NO PROB.		
France	1	7	12	7	27
Germany	5	7	13	6	31
Spain	1	2	5	2	10
Belgium		1			1

Over 10% (7) encountered very serious problems, mostly in Germany; almost 25% (17) encountered some serious problems. Less than 22% (15) could say they had no problems.

Possible drawbacks of undertaking a work placement were presented to students (Q.10), who were asked to what extent certain disadvantages had arisen as a result of the work placement abroad. Students were asked for replies, ranging from 1 - "a great deal" to 4 - "negligible".

The results showed that two main problems emerged. The first related to lack of stimulus in work undertaken whilst on placement. Overall, responses were:

	1	2	3	4	TOTAL
	GT DEAL		NEGL.		
Lack of stimulation in work undertaken on placements	13	23	20	13	69

Analysed according to country, the responses were:

	1	2	3	4	TOTAL
	GT DEAL		NEGL.		
France	4	9	8	6	27
Germany	9	9	8	5	31
Spain	0	4	4	2	10
Belgium		1			1

Many students also experienced difficulty in returning to academic study after the work placement:

	1	2	3	4	TOTAL
	GT DEAL			NEGL.	
Difficulties in returning to academic study after work placement	9	30	16	14	69

The other questions referring to the disruption of social contacts, difficulties in integrating socially while abroad, prolongation of course study, and the need to produce a piece of written work while abroad produced mainly negative responses, except for the question on the financial burden of a year abroad, which revealed that some students had residual financial problems.

In Question 11, students were asked to reconsider the stated objectives of the work placement abroad, and judge to what extent these had been fulfilled, although very few students felt they could apply their college studies in the real world, and on their return to college many found it difficult to see the links between the work experience and college work. They felt a high measure of success in the acquisition of language skills and exposure to the foreign industrial environment which had encouraged them to apply successfully for employment in international business organisations. Responses are on a scale 1 - "most emphatically" to 4 - "not at all". Q.11: To what extent did the work placement abroad enable you to:

	1	2	3	4	TOTAL
	M. EMPH		NT AT ALL		
a) Apply your college-based studies in the context of practical experience abroad	3	10	34	22	69
b) Operate successfully abroad through exercise of the appropriate language skills	43	24	2	0	69

(cont. on next page)

	1	2	3	4	TOTAL
	M. EMPH			NT AT ALL	

c) Operate successfully
   abroad through
   exposure to the
   foreign industrial

environment	19	32	12	6	69

d) Gain a sound basis
   in work experience so
   so that full benefit
   might be derived from

the rest of the course	7	21	31	10	69

e) Acquire the confidence
   to apply successfully
   for employment in
   international business

organisations	22	31	11	5	69

The response to Question 12 should be of particular interest in the context of the seminar.   Respondents were asked to rate their ability in the foreign language in respect of a) reading proficiency, b) written proficiency, c) oral proficiency and d) listening comprehension, before the placement, immediately after, and currently, with an indication of the years intervening.

Results 1 = excellent 4 = weak were : for all languages (for French)

	1	2	3	4	TOTAL
	EXCELL.			WEAK	
Before					
a) reading p.	10(6)	43(15)	15(7)	1(0)	69(28)
b) written p.	1(1)	26(12)	31(11)	11(4)	69(28)
c) oral p.	4(1)	30(13)	29(12)	6(2)	69(28)
d) listening c.	8(3)	31(13)	27(10)	3(2)	69(28)
Immediately after					
a) reading p.	33(17)	35(11)	1(0)	0(0)	69(28)
b) written p.	9(5)	40(18)	13(4)	7(1)	69(28)
c) oral p.	39(16)	28(11)	2(1)	0(0)	69(28)
d) listening c.	47(19)	21(8)	1(1)	0(0)	69(28)

174

	1 EXCELL.	2	3	4 WEAK	TOTAL

Current

	1 EXCELL.	2	3	4 WEAK	TOTAL
a) reading p.	17	41	10	1	69
b) written p.	4	26	30	9	69
c) oral p.	9	37	22	1	69
d) listening c.	14	43	11	1	69

Regrettably, figures are not available for French in the last table.

It can be seen that students consider that a) their reading ability was improved by the placement, and has not regressed too seriously, b) their written ability improved but has almost returned to the pre-placement level, c) their oral ability made a substantial improvement, but has since regressed, whilst d) their listening comprehension made considerable progress, and has not been so badly affected by the passage of time.

Question 13 asked about the personal benefits derived from the work experience abroad. The responses to this series of questions were predominantly positive. The only striking negative result was that students did not feel any increased motivation in their academic studies. Otherwise, increased self-reliance, benefits of exposure to a wider cross-section of the community and the development of inter-personal communication skills were rated highly. The sections of the question relating to the understanding of the foreign culture were answered (for students of French) as follows: 1 - most emphatically, 4 - not at all.

	1 M. EMPH	2	3	4 NT AT ALL	Total
Greater awareness of the cultural/artistic life of the foreign country	11	12	3	1	27
(Belgium)			1		1
Increased understanding of political/economic life of the foreign country	5	18	4	0	27
(Belgium)			1		1

It is perhaps this appreciation of cultural differences which is the most important end-product of international courses. Our American guests are probably familiar with the writings of Edward T. Hall who has spent his entire life studying intercultural communication. Dr. Hall has a theory about monochronic and polychronic cultures. I quote from John Ritchhart of *Stern* magazine, in an article adapted from a speech given in Brussels in 1980: "The Germans are what Dr. Hall, author of *Hidden Differences*, calls monochronic, one thing at a time. the French are polychronic, many things at once... if the German's schedule does not allow enough timne for a comfortable meal, and that is usually the case, then he eats all the more quickly, in less quantity, or not at all. When the alternatives are *mousse au chocolat* or the daily agenda, the agenda always wins. This is hard for the French to understand. Time is there for the individual. A business conversation cannot be precisely scheduled in advance. There has to be enough time for all the unexpected eventualities. To do business, you have to get to know your business partner on a personal level, and that takes time".

Graduates who completed the questionnaire were also invited to give their comments in an open-ended section. Some of the more salient remarks follow:

Male graduate A: College life too restricted - difficult to return to academic work.

Improved on what he had learned in computing and learned about work relations.

Began to appreciate the formality within a company.

Computing, logistics and production used on placement and these were more interesting to him in the subsequent coursework because of the interest aroused then.

The different attitudes to socialising in France - one of the most striking discoveries about the year abroad.

Female graduate B: Hard going back to academic work, but she was able to apply what she had done on placement.

It appealed to her to do a fourth year.

But by this time she had lost contact with friends from home.

The firm was helpful to her in providing material for placement report.

Language always her weakest subject and it improved.

Still making good use of the experience from abroad and from the course.

Has the confidence to apply for a job abroad but not internationally oriented.

Learned to cope - flat burgled, did not have enough money to phone home.

Communication skills helped by relaxed atmosphere of a family
company - informalilty.

Female graduate C: On placement she was at Vichy and she felt the

employers were unsure of what they could expect her to do. After two
months she asked for more work. She would be willing to go and work
in France if the opportunity arose.

When applying for her first job she was aware of a bias against
coming from a college rather than a polytechnic or university. Feels
this prejudice may have lessened by now. It would be useful to keep a
second language going as well.

Male graduate D: The placement was vital for language development and

this was seen as the most significant contribution to the course as a
whole.The academic semester was excellent - being treated as a French
student and doing the same examinations. It looks good on a c.v. now.
He does not at present use French in his job, but hopes to do so. A
second language would be useful - he is in banking. all banks are
looking for salesmen. Japanese speakers are at a premium.

Lack of stimulus on placement - at BNP doing basic administrative
work.

The year abroad was of great value and was the major reason for doing
the course. It is a vital part of the course, but he did not feel it
brought any specific skills apart from linguist ones.

He mentioned the bias towards university graduates for getting the
first job, but after that first break it is experience which counts
more than the institution you attended.

The questionnaire to employers was addressed to 92 firms selected from the
companies listed in ROGET (Register of Graduate Employment and Training)
on the basis of their likely interest in recruits who had either a foreign
language or an international training background. Positive replies were
received from 41 employers in the United Kingdom: two felt they could not
supply answers to the questionnaire; the others failed to respond but one
agreed to be interviewed as he felt the questionnaire was not appropriate
in his case.

The replies of interest to the seminar are those to Question 7 (the need
for competence in foreign languages), Question 14 (advantage for the

employer of recruiting a graduate who has studied or worked abroad) and Question 18 (the personal skills of importance in graduate personnel). This last question sought to establish the ranking which employers would give to skills which they themselves had indicated as desirable in advertisements for staff.

Employers were asked (Q.7) to state how competent graduate recruits needed to be in foreign languages on a simplified scale: very, fairly, not at all. Replies were:

	VERY	FAIRLY	NOT AT ALL	NIL RESPONSE	TOTAL
oral/aural	18	12	10	1	41
written	15	15	9	2	41

It is interesting to note that written competence is almost as important as oral/aural skills, perhaps calling in question the widely-held belief that business firms require graduates who have highly-developed oral skills rather than the ability to write the foreign language.

Replies to Question 14 were on a yes/no basis, as follows:

Is there any discernible advantage for you, the employer, if the candidate has spent some time studying abroad?

YES	- 27	
NO	- 12	
NIL RESPONSE -	2	TOTAL 41

- working abroad?

YES	- 35	
NO	- 6	TOTAL 41

These replies clearly indicate that employers value the additional training provided by a work placement abroad.

In reply to Question 18, asking employers to tick the personal skills (up to 6) of paramount importance in their graduate personnel, the most frequently mentioned were, in rank order:

	TIMES MENTIONED
Communication skills	32
Literacy	29
Self-motivation	26
Ability to handle pressure	25
Numeracy	25
Enthusiasm	22
Teamwork skills	21

Last in order of frequency was sensitivity, mentioned 4 times.

It is worth reiterating that these were all qualities which had been specifically mentioned by companies in job advertisements.

It was felt that it would be worth approaching recruitment consultants for their views, since this is a growing sector of the employment arena and they are in contact with both employers and recruits.

The recruitment consultancies were selected on the following basis:

1) An entry in *Executive Grapevine*, which indicated they had special interest in recruiting recent graduates, business studies graduates with a foreign language skill from any disciplines. Some companies with European affiliates were also approached.

2) Some were already in contact with the Buckinghamshire College of Higher Education or known personally to the researchers.

3) Some had advertised for candidates with a language qualification in the national press during the first half of 1987.

The response rate was encouraging: 20 replies (19 companies and 1 secretarial agency) to 32 questionnaires sent.

The recruitment consultants were asked if they had considered that a candidate for a post would be at an advantage if he/she had worked abroad over another similarly qualified candidate without work experience abroad. Replies were YES - 17, NO - 2 (NIL - 1).

They were then asked to list any practical benefits they saw for a Business Studies student spending time on a work placement abroad. Replies were:

a) for the student:

> Experience of other national systems - the workplace, legislation, procedures, attitudes
>
> Language ability
>
> Technical knowledge
>
> Understanding the country and more especially its customs
>
> Complex business negotiations - which are often different in different countries
>
> Work experience useful in finding employment after course
>
> Broadening and maturing experience
>
> Self development
>
> Helps him/her appreciate different methods of working and how business methods and solutions are in vogue in other countries
>
> EEC experience
>
> If you are not permitted to speak English at any time, you quickly learn to live, eat, sleep, work and (the real test) to dream in

the language you wish to master, giving lifetime instant reaction in every situation. Ultimately you need to feel happy to negotiate (i.e. sell) in the language.

Broadening of culture

Language becomes alive - i.e. not concerned with translation into English but solving the problem in the language concerned as do their compatriots in other European educational systems

b) for a potential employer

Language ability

Knowledge of other systems

Persistence, adaptability and tolerance of individual

Look to 1992

Knowing that the student had experience in foreign lands, more especially a tolerance of their ways. The expression is "knowing they can hack it".

Employees with work experience abroad could be seen as more likely to have a realistic and mature appreciation of relevant areas of business and the work envvironment

Hopefully on a *stage* in Business development, the student will have gained a) understanding of the social behaviour in the country, b) ability to arrange, coordinate and double check in the language which is current in business, c) ability to convince and motivate others in the language, using logic, politeness and charm, d) some grounding in the industry/commerce/service where he is being trained.

A more rounded individual, probably more fluent in the overseas language than an academic student.

There is no substitute for first-hand experience in a foreign country - employers appreciate this.

Someone who can apply language and who understands the business mores of the country

Can apply lateral thinking to further societies having experienced a parallel one

An invaluable asset.

At three subsequent interviews with recruitment consultants, these points were reinforced. A period abroad was seen as essential for anyone hoping for fluency in the foreign language and the point was strongly made that learning a language is a cumulative skill. It cannot be done quickly if it is to be effective. A period of three months was seen as a minimum that could be of any lasting value.

Interviews with French employers echoed these comments: most felt that a *stage* should be at least six months in length, and they expected students to have a level of proficiency in French which would enable them to be fully integrated into the workforce. By extension, students were observed to become fully integrated in the cultural environment. The only drawback for students who achieved this level of integration was that they had difficulty in re-adjusting to the British environment on their return for the final semesters of the course. The problems of acculturation training for international managers appear to be replicated on a smaller scale among undergraduates following a work placement on a European business course.

TEACHING CIVILISATION: SOME PRELIMINARY CONSIDERATIONS
by Edward C. Knox, Middlebury College

Hereafter, some questions I think any teachers of Civilisation would do well
to consider, as would those who are to train them. This list was drawn up
before the conference, but read as the penultimate paper. It has only been
slightly amended in light of other presentations.

Seen from outside

Definition: are we talking about civilisation or Civilisation*,
everyday culture or high culture?

In France and the US this debate has pretty well been resolved in favour of
"small c" culture, at least to the point of granting it (grudging)
legitimacy. I get the sense that in Great Britain History, Politics,
Economics and the History of Ideas (= French Studies in the US) are
included; in the US, the literary professionals still set the official
language-teaching priorities, with attendant problems of status for
Civilisation.

It will probably be obvious in what follows that I belong to the "small c"
crowd, and it may well be that this preference skews somewhat my
problematic. On the other hand, we presumably have a pretty good idea
already how to train French historians, political scientists, etc. What I
am most interested in is that part of culture that falls at present to the
language teacher: culture that is everyday, as it affects individuals or
groups of individuals, and as it manifests itself through verbal or other
mediations.

Time frame: is it current or historical Civilisation? Both clearly
have legitimacy, but one cannot do everything at once. Moreover, students
- at least young people in the US - clearly prefer to learn about things
contemporary (and their peers) ahead of the historical. Effectively, this
amounts also to a preference for everyday culture over cultural monuments.
One may quarrel with it, but it does appear to be a fact of life.

*In this publication Civilisation has been capitalised for
typographical reasons only.

French Civilisation or francophonie ?   In the US at least there is more and more pressure from publishers to include *la francophonie* in textbooks; somewhat the equivalent in France, I expect, is *l'interculturel*, about which we have heard so much in the last three or four years.   US language teachers are generally at sea with respect to their knowledge of French culture other than literature and something of the historical context that surrounds it: most would find **la francophonie** totally opaque.

Taught explicitly or implicitly ?   This is again somewhat the same split between everyday and high culture, and between Language courses and "content" courses.   One can of course - indeed many textbooks do - talk about *le roi Soleil* in the middle of a section on past tenses.   Conversely, a course in French Civilisation can focus primarily on "small c" civilisation rather than the high achievements of French cultural history.   Which is more desirable? To what extent must one choose, and to what end?

Who teaches? More specifically, who is competent to teach Civilisation, and how did he/she get that way ?   This is of course, the topic I am supposed to be addressing, so I will substitute instead an anecdote.   When in 1984 Middlebury College advertised a "tenure track" appointment in French - extremely unusual if not unique: most announcements call for a combination like civilisation and medieval French, and most are not tenure track - we received over 100 responses (to be expected) only five of which could legitimately be considered to correspond to the job description. A very large share of the others started their letters with a sentence like "I have always been interested in French civilisation...".   The person we hired was an undergraduate history major at Brown and did his doctoral thesis at Yale on *Les paysans de Balzac*.

What are the institutions that offer a PhD in French Civilisation or French Studies?   (A question we never did ask at the seminar: how were our British colleagues trained originally ?)   What kind of research does one pursue and publish as a *civilisationniste* ? Most broadly, in what climate (professional, institutional, national) is the teaching and research to be carried out?   It was my distinct impression at the seminar that the American contingent was uniformly impressed by the teaching and research being done in Great Britain, the more so that the state of British higher education appeared so precarious to us all.

For what audience ?

    a. what is their level of French? Again, language vs. content, but perhaps more profoundly: do they learn something simply because we insert it, and do we insert it because it is demonstrably important or for our own professional sense of worth?

b. what is their age ? From an early teenager to a young adult to a student who has been out of school for a few years, aptitudes, interests and experience vary widely: how and to what extent is this taken into account?

c. what is the relationship between teacher and learner: what difference in age and sex, but also in culture? What is the teacher's responsibility as cultural "model" (cf. linguistic model in the case of language)?

To what end ? Is the goal of the teaching of Civilisation linguistic, intellectual, utilitarian, cross-cultural, etc.? Who decides?

Seen from inside

Does one teach in French or English? On what does the choice depend: personal comfort? the subject matter? the discipline? the goal of the curriculum? Are a course on contemporary French Politics taught in English in the political science department and a similar but presumably simpler course in French taught by one with less official qualifications equally Civilisation courses? Why and so what ?

How to characterise the content of civilisation? I mentioned above my own gravitation toward that which is individual, everyday and semiotically mediated. One could better cite Debyser's seminal division into anthropological, sociological and semiotic (in Béacco/Lieutaud, *Moeurs et mythes*). Both suppose one kind of definition of civilisation. The point is, how do you teach it if you cannot describe and define it ?

How to distribute and categorise it ? Here we encounter the attempts, from Nelson Brooks and Howard Nostrand 25 years ago through Seeley's *Teaching Culture* to the recent ACTFL proficiency guidelines, to identify the areas and domains of what we call Civilisation. Personally, I regret that ACTFL elected to withdraw the culture guidelines (in the face of the inherent difficulty of the task and the copious criticism their first efforts inspired). In any case, it is not clear (to me) just who will do the inventory of *faits de civilisation*. Two major problems, by the way, that the ACTFL entreprise highlighted nicely if somewhat unwittingly, are the difficulty of taking intracultural variations into account, and the problem of culture as knowing vs. culture as doing. One might consult here Porcher, *La civilisation*.

E.D. Hirsch, a well-known critic of English literature and literary theoretician, has received a great deal of publicity recently for his book on *Cultural Literacy: What Every American Needs to Know*. His definition of culture is broad, but where does trivial pursuit leave off and significant research begin?

According to what order, what progression, shall we teach ?

    a. is a progression possible or desirable? most would agree on an order when teaching language: is there any similarity with Civilisation? what by the way is the relationship between Civilisation and communicative competence: inclusion., overlap, interpenetration?

    b. shall we proceed by sector ? by theme ? by "interest" ? by specific competence ? Here one might look at Lieutaud and Beacco's *Tours de France* as the most fully worked out scheme.

From what and on what do we work: a synthesis or an isolated (or integrated) *fait culturel* ? in a textbook or in authentic materials? through oral, written, visual, mediation? What is the difference ?

How does the student work ? To what extent is his/her foreignness to be acknowledged and/or exploited ? What are desirable exercises for Civilisation ? How does the student go from passive ingestor to independent investigator ? The most recent useful remarks along these lines are in Zarate, *Enseigner une culture étrangère*. One could also consult my bibliographies on the teaching of French Civilisation in *French Review* 1985 and 1987.

What is the role of study abroad? When should it occur and for how long, with what kind(s) of preparation, what kind(s) of experience (academic/professional/experiential) are most desirable, with what kind(s) of reintegrations, etc.?

How do we evaluate ? In particular, how do we go beyond the simple checking of facts? In general, just what is cultural competence ?

POST-GRADUATE TRAINING IN FRENCH CIVILISATION
THE "BUILDING-BLOCKS" APPROACH
by Nicholas Wahl, New York University

Civilisation training beyond the BA degree in American French departments
falls roughly into three categories. First, as a distinctly minor subject
in an essentially literary doctorate; second, as a minor subject in a
Master's degree programme intended for secondary school teachers of French;
third, as an accompaniment to specialised language training (i.e. business
French) taken along with graduate training in Business Administration and,
in a few cases, leading to a joint Master's degree in Business and French.
Although there are some exceptions, most institutions offering these kinds
of training have developed graduate Civilisation courses that are simply
advanced versions of the undergraduate courses in Civilisation: they are
"synthetic" courses that juxtapose different disciplinary materials in order
to teach a subject that is of specialised interest to the instructor. The
latter is often a teacher of Language or Literature who has an area of
competence which overlaps a non-traditional French department field such as
the Arts, Cinema, Music, Architecture, Social History, Political Ideas,
Current Affairs, Popular Culture or French Cultural History in the broadest
sense.

Cognate courses in French Politics, History or other disciplines in which
French data are used may be given "credit" toward the degree. Often Social
Science specialists on France are invited to give lectures in courses or,
indeed, offer courses of their own on a visiting basis. But in most cases
the courses taken in Social Science departments or offered in the
civilisation programme by outside social scientists are chosen on an
elective basis and are either very specialised (as a course on France in a
Social Science would usually be) or, on the contrary, are very general and
synthetic since they are designed specially for Civilisation students by a
Social Science teacher who has little confidence in their background in the
subject. In short, most existing graduate programmes in Civilisation are
unable, for a variety of compelling reasons, to provide a basic grounding in

those subjects which form the basis for an understanding of contemporary French culture and society: History (including the History of Ideas), Politics (including Foreign Policy), Sociology, and some notions of the economy and of contemporary mores, beliefs and family life - that is, some elements of Social Anthropology. This means that the student who specialises in civilisation, either for teaching or other vocational purposes, while introduced to a broad if thin panorama of contemporary French Culture and Society, is probably obliged to "thicken" his or her knowledge of History, Politics, Sociology, etc. through individual reading, usually without the supervision of specialists in those disciplines.

An alternate approach consists of constructing the overall programme of study with successively more specialised "blocks" of information offered in courses that are unambiguously disciplinary and "analytic" - e.g. French politics in the Fifth Republic, 19th-century French history, French political and social thought, contemporary French literature, problems of the French economy, etc.. Rather than synthesise History, Politics, Sociology, Culture and Ideas in a single or a series of courses on, say, France since World War Two, the building-blocks approach to that topic would begin with basic offerings of a disciplinary nature in the above subjects. Then, in a second stage, more specialised courses would be offered, still with clear disciplinary identities, building upon the basic courses. For example, a course on religion or on education, a course on politics and Literature since the war, a course on Public Administration or Public Law or a course on France's relations with its former African dependencies - all of which would assume some earlier disciplinary knowledge of History, Politics, Society and Culture.

The advantage of this approach is in the flexibility it offers students in preparing for the often very different kinds of careers in the civilisation area. At the same time it builds confidence by giving at least a minimum mastery of the basic blocks of information that can later be combined in different ways to meet changing vocational needs. Obviously, in the above schema, students will not have a grounding in all aspects of French society and culture since World War Two. In practice, students working under the block approach will have to decide rather early in their graduate training whether their primary interest is society or culture - the two *versants* of the Civilisation field in the USA. After sampling the basic blocks in both *versants*, they will proceed to more specialised work on either societal subjects (mainly social science courses) or cultural subjects (mainly humanistic courses) but in both cases they will gain intensive knowledge of discrete, disciplinary-linked subjects, including elements of bibliographical information, a basic acquaintance with reference materials and even some knowledge of the research being conducted in the field of their specialisation. Moreover, having concentrated on either the society or the cultural *versants* they will, thanks to the disciplinary orientation of the courses, have acquired at least the fundamentals of either social or cultural analysis - that is, to be able to grapple with societal problems as do social scientists or to deal with cultural data as do humanists or, perhaps, even a bit of both. Experience has shown at New York University that in one semester of intensive post-graduate study, students with literary backgrounds can master social analysis as can those with social science backgrounds learn to deal with cultural concepts.

Since the building-block approach, when successful, encourages progressive confidence in the mastery of the basics, students trained in this approach can compete more effectively with those whose training is principally in one or another of the component disciplines. The emphasis here should be on the word "more" for clearly they will have to pursue on their own further specialised training if they are to work in, say, political journalism or in a bank that deals with French business. But they at least will have had some training in specialised subjects and will be able to carry on with them either by self-tuition or in further formal education. For the future teacher of Civilisation the building-block approach provides the essential analytic information and the bibliographical tools with which they can devise their own synthetic courses for undergraduates - whether the courses are societal, cultural or, again, a bit of both.

Even before they take up full-time teaching, their block training may equip them better for the choice of a thesis topic and with the research tools needed to deal with subjects that are peculiarly civilisational - falling as they often do in the interstices between social studies and humanistic concerns, yet requiring modes of analysis borrowed from both areas. For the civilisation PhD student it is usually a mistake to choose a principally literary subject for which the traditional PhD in French is intended. To pick a clearly civilisational topic such as, say, the visual arts under Vichy or nationalism and literature in the Dreyfus period is to lead from strength and only in-depth training in Political Theory, History, Art History in addition to Literature can ensure that such civilisational topics become fully successful dissertations.

For the MA candidate who looks to employment in business, government or other non-profit occupations, the building-block approach provides a range of information which can be combined in a variety of ways according to the requirements of successive jobs. For those on the society side of the training, a solid grounding in History, Human Geography, the political economy in France and its current politics provides the basis for success in the on-the-job training programmes of commercial banks or on the entrance examinations of government agencies in the US. Moving from a bank to, say, a foundation would require perhaps drawing upon their additional knowledge of French education or of problems of French society which are often the subject of academic research in the policy-oriented disciplines. Similarly for those on the culture side of block training, the essentials learned in courses on French Thought, Literature and Society, the Arts, as well as History and Politics provides the grounding for a career in the cultural services of government, then moving to a foundation or perhaps working in international public relations, cultural journalism or teaching French and French civilisation in a secondary school.

There are, of course, obvious problems with the building-block approach. The most important is that it requires either large budgetary resources to hire outside teachers of the social science subjects or - equally daunting - it requires the co-operation of other disciplinary departments which, naturally, also has real budgetary implications. A second problem is that students with an undergraduate degree in French often have difficulty with graduate courses in the Social Sciences unless some transitional and remedial *recyclage* is made available. Third, the integration of different blocks of information cannot be done by the students alone but requires guidance from the faculty and, especially, a more substantial amount of essay writing (and essay correction by the faculty!) than is possible in short MA programmes. Finally, the approach presupposes a good knowledge of the language and at least some direct experience of French society and culture, both important in helping students to integrate the blocks of information from the start of their postgraduate training. It should also be noted that the kind of training implied by the block approach requires an amount of reading and essay writing that calls for important library and periodical resources which also impose financial strains on a department.

Yet the existing employment opportunities for MAs and PhDs in French civilisation suggest that the building-block approach might well serve them best. The experience of NYU's Institute of French Studies since 1978 has shown that there is, at least in the States, a slowly growing need for entry-level personnel in business who have the language and who know coentemporary France. This is especially true in companies involved in either France's efforts to penetrate the American market or in American firms competing in Europe and in countries where the vehicle language and elite culture is that of France. The career patterns in these businesses require adapting and increasing one's knowledge of France while working and for this the more in-depth training of the block approach has advantages because it has left the student with the tools and the confidence to pursue such knowledge independently.

As for teachers of French Civilisation in higher education, although their training in America is still lodged principally in traditional French departments for whom Civilisation remains - if it exists at all - a very poor cousin, there are persistent indications of changes which students of the block approach may usefully exploit. First, a substantial number of undergraduates today want to learn French mainly to understand contemporary French society and culture and not simply to study literature in the original language. Those French departments which have met this demand by creating "Civilisation tracks" in the undergraduate programeme have been obliged to accept "cognate" work done in Social Science departments (including History) because their own faculty have neither the interest nor the experience in teaching courses on contemporary French society. Even "cognate" work done in other Humanities departments must be accepted for credit because of the narrowly literary concentration of their own faculty. If the demand for the "Civilisation track" continues and if undergraduate enrolments remain buoyant and if there is the massive renewal of faculties in the 1990s as expected, then French departments will be increasingly attracted to "purpose-trained" Civilisation teachers - those who can provide "in-house" the non-literary courses that are now often taught by faculty from other departments or taught inadequately by members of French departments whose real interests are elsewhere.

Second, the continuing popularity of undergraduate interdisciplinary programmes such as women's studies and international studies offer French departments an opportunity to parrticipate fully only if they have faculty who are credibly trained in the materials and the approaches of the non-literary disciplines. Third, as the wage bill of higher education continues to rise steeply in the US, four-year colleges especially may seek economies by hiring junior faculty who have the competence to teach in more than one department. A PhD in French Civilisation, trained under the block approach, may well have advantages not available to the traditional French PhD, no matter how many minor courses the latter took in non-literary subjects within the department for such courses necessarily do not have clear disciplinary identities outside of literature and do not give evidence of training and some research in Political Science, History, etc.

To be sure, the proof of this pudding is in an "eating" that, for the moment, is only a nibble. But leaving aside the specific employment opportunities for those trained under the building-block approach, one can say that, when successful, the system can offer, at the very least, a superior sense of mastery over raw data, a broader knowledge of the disciplinary subjects that inform our understanding of French society and culture, and a more comprehensive view of the ways higher education can serve to train students for various careers in which advanced knowledge of contemporary France is required.

CONCLUSION AND AFTERTHOUGHTS
by Eric Cahm, Université de Tours

Relativising our view of France

The first lesson to be drawn from a multi-national seminar of this kind
is that France may seem surprisingly different when looked at from
different places, and through different cultural spectacles. To a lecturer
in Southern California, and still more to her students, France is indeed a
distant prospect: the students may begin their initiation with no solid
information at all, only a mass of stereotypes. Seen from Canberra, too,
France is not the France we in Portsmouth feel is just beyond the horizon
of the Solent, a mere boozy day-trip away. New Caledonia looms large to
an Australian eye in a way inconceivable in Europe, while a visit to France
must remain a very momentous and rare prospect to Australian students.
Whether the teacher is remote or near geographically or culturally however,
there is much to be said, at the beginning of any course on France, for a
dusting and clear-out of students' stereotypes about the country: Theda
Shapiro's exercise of asking incoming students to write down the first
names and words they think of when they think of France is always
revealing. It could be followed by an actual First-Year course, in which
the real place, in to-day's France, of peasants, of wine and food production,
of gastronomy, of Paris, of fashion, perfume, and *l'amour*, could be
explained. This must be an excellent way-in to "small c" culture.
Furthermore, we need, both as teachers and students, to be kept continually
aware of the results of our own cultural conditioning in the way we look at
France, in order to relativise those parts of our view which we know not to
be shared by others. *"D'où parles-tu de la France ?"* must be our constant
question to ourselves. The danger for British lecturers is that France
may be taken too much for granted, precisely because of its proximity and
familiarity: in America, distance has no doubt led to a greater awareness of
the *interculturel*. But the whole area of cultural difference needs to be
explored further by all those teaching French. Peter Findlay has
suggested we incorporate it explicitly into our syllabuses.

Beyond cultural awareness, however, the seminar discussions have shown that the study of France raises fascinating questions of identity. There seemed to be general agreement that it is difficult, undesirable even, to aim to give our students a wholly French identity: for Christopher Pinet, identity is an individual matter which will be influenced by experience of France. But in the end an American remains an American, and in any case there is no single model of French identity to aim at. What perhaps worried Alice Kaplan about her student who gave a perfect mimic of a *polytechnicienne* in defending her dissertation was the artificiality in this performance - like that of the American whose Oxford accent was more Oxford than that of Oxfordians. What was wrong here was this element of artificiality, even of pose. There would be nothing wrong even with playing a role, if the result aimed at was simply to give the best possible academic performance: we all play roles and adopt different personae in different situations, and as I said, if the academic performance was outstanding, so much the better. What must be avoided is mere mimickry, the adoption of French speech and manners simply for effect. Jolyon Howorth rightly said that the aim is rather to enable the student to function effectively in a French context. This involves effective communication skills and also the development of sympathy and understanding of the French way of life. It does not, on the other hand, involve jettisoning what is valuable in the home culture in favour of a mere show of Frenchness or an uncritical *engouement* leading to the 100% adoption of French ways. What is needed is a balanced approach, in which taking up the French way of life is tempered by the critical detachment of the foreigner, who can make his own contribution in terms of the positive features of his own culture. To attempt to make our students 100% French would be to adopt in effect an absurd French nationalist stance, and to perpetuate an exclusionist mentality based on a mythical and impossible national homogeneity. Culturally, what is needed to-day is not exclusion and the perpetuation of mental frontiers, but a tolerant attitude towards cultural difference, which can welcome cultural diversity and regard mutual interchange between peoples as normal and healthy. In a word, we want the best of France and the best of home. Now that the media and communications satellites are turning the whole world increasingly into a global cultural village, in which French TV ads are becoming indistinguishable from American ones, this synthesis of the best individual features of each culture offers a better hope than a homogenisation based on the lowest common denominator.

193

What is French Civilisation ?

The second lesson of the seminar is that if there is a good deal of questioning and of divergence of view about what we mean by Civilisation, there is at the same time a conviction that it is what our students are asking for, and a determination to develop it as a subject, as **the** way we want to teach about France. To Americans, the concept of Civilisation is more familiar, though the fact of the Knox-Carduner survey still suggests a questioning attitude. The American respondents seem to lean, like Edward Knox himself, towards a definition based on "small c culture", and related to an anthropology of everyday life. To the British participants in the seminar, who are all deeply engaged in teaching about France, the word Civilisation itself is still unfamiliar and appears in quotation marks, or even with a query: is **this** the Civilisation you are talking about ? But most of the British participants are just as convinced as their American colleagues that, whatever it is, it is the key to their teaching work. And in practice there is a good deal of consensus: all are agreed that to teach French Civilisation is to teach not, or not only, about French Literature, but to teach about the French way of life, to-day and yesterday. Frequently, too, on both sides of the Atlantic, Civilisation is seen as an essential means to a proper understanding of the French language to-day.

In Britain, the shift towards Civilisation has already taken whole degree courses in many cases much further from Literature than is the norm in the US. They have moved towards the study of France through a collaboration between History and the Social Sciences. This has gone so far in many cases as to exclude Literature altogether. British definitions talk of "Societal Studies", to use an ugly phrase. Teaching practice in the US therefore remains more firmly based on Literary Studies, with a strong extension from traditional approaches towards a broader socio-critical stance, which has produced papers at the seminar on high and popular culture: it was characteristic that these should have come from the American side. The "new universities" in Britain are closer to American practice: as I pointed out in my historical sketch, they were influenced at their inception towards a model based on a multidisciplinary, mainly cultural history, which derived from the *cours de civilisation* of the French themselves. There has been more recently a general development of Contemporary Cultural Studies in Britain, as Adrian Rifkin told the seminar, and this, in turn, has had its impact on the more adventurous universities or polytechnics. However,the development of new approaches to teaching about France in the technological sector has been predominantly based on the History-plus-Social Sciences model, without but sometimes with Literature. And the Hare and Roach survey shows that across all the universities covered, of whatever type, Government, Society, History and the Economy in that order are far ahead of the rest of the competition as components in French Civilisation teaching. So that an understanding is growing up in Britain that the History-plus-Social Sciences model (or the reverse) is what Civilisation is most probably about, even if room for questioning and dispute remains.

The principal area of dispute on this side of the Atlantic is whether to eliminate or maintain a Literature strand: while the Hare and Roach paper calls for an integrated "Language-Civilisation-Literature course", a number of speakers have taken it for granted, as do many of the courses in the technological universities and polytechnics, that Civilisation has nothing to do with Literature.

Apart from this, the main issue seems to be for and against a generalist approach. Neville Waites argues that Civilisation is too broad and superficial a concept to offer solid academic guarantees, and seems to imply that, as at Reading, Surrey or elsewhere, the study of France must be tied to one other main Social Science discipline, or to History, on a Joint Honours pattern. This is the bi-disciplinary approach commended by Jean Carduner and Nicholas Wahl in the US, and it may indeed claim solid academic credentials. Linda Hantrais, for her part, is inclined to see wholly Civilisation-based courses, like Literature courses, as moving too far from a central concern with Language.

Civilisation itself does not anywhere in these analyses, however, emerge as a central concern of the degree programme: in many cases it remains instrumental to Language work, just as in the old framework it was as instrumental to Literature. In Joint Degree schemes, the weighting of the main discipline, as well as that of Language where two languages are involved, means that France can only be a principal vector of the work: time will not allow it to be the central theme of the programme. It is only, however, when Civilisation becomes, with Language, the central concern of a single-subject degree in French that it can fairly be judged. And for that, the whole degree scheme must necessarily be devoted to France: the richness of French Civilisation is such that this is hardly too much time. It seems to me, too, that Literature is a part of Civilisation, and that to explore French Civilisation to the full, a collaboration between Language,

History, the Social Sciences, **and** Cultural Studies is in fact needed, in the
context of a constant concern with the anthropology of everyay life.   Only
in that way can students be enabled to acquire a knowledge of the "*total
way of life of the French people*" (my italics), to borrow Laurence Wylie's
definition.   And this is precisely what Geoffrey Hare and John Roach call
for in their conclusion.   It is, in fact, if I may be permitted to say so,
also what the Portsmouth French Studies degree has been attempting to
approximate to since its inception.   It is what was attempted on the
French degree at North East London Polytechnic.   I should like to add
that this approach in no sense implies sacrificing Language to Civilisation:
maximising the role of Civilisation must mean at the same time maximising
contact with that Civilisation and this necessarily, by the same token,
involves maximising the role of Language in the degree (without spurning
the use of classics in English just because they are in English - the
golden rule must remain: the best of both worlds.)

Hare and Roach are surely right in thinking that this is the inevitable
direction of the movement towards Civilisation: i.e. towards a collaboration
between Contemporary History, the Social Sciences **and** Literature, or rather
French Culture past and present.

A broad approach to teaching Civilisation

In regard to this broad History-plus-Social Sciences-plus Culture (large
and small c) approach I am suggesting, it may now be useful to review some
of the problems raised in the seminar in regard to teaching about the
French way of life through the various disciplines, as well as about
progression and the problems of articulating one discipline with another.

History,   As regards the historical starting-point of our studies of
France, I believe there might be a good deal of agreement with the view I
share with Nicholas Wahl that the natural beginning of our studies is the
end of the Ancien Régime, since it is impossible to understand contemporary
France adequately without a grasp of the 1789 Revolution and the nature of
its quarrel with the state and society which preceded it.   In the History
course, the subsequent development of French political culture, with its
anti-state mentality, its centralising tendency, and its propensity to
revolution and street demonstration, should not be neglected.   French
history, too, has an economic and social as well as a political dimension,
not to mention the history of political, economic and social ideas and the

history of philosophy and culture.   So that even here, without looking any
further, there is the material for a very substantial course.

The Social Sciences.   As to the Social Sciences, a full diet would
include not only the Politics, Economics and Sociology of France, but also
her Demography and Social Anthropology, and of course her Geography.   The
students' task now, not to mention that of the teachers, begins to seem
daunting in size, since each of these disciplines has its own battery of
theories, methods and concepts, which it considers essential for handling
its findings, and each concerns itself with the world at large and not only
with France.   Most of the Social Science specialists, in Britain at any
rate, are not French-speaking, and, as Neville Waites indicated, are
becoming less willing to give special attention to France and use its
language in teaching.

Clearly however, it is necessary to introduce students of French
Civilisation to the theoretical, conceptual and methodological foundations
of these disciplines.   This has suggested, in Portsmouth at least, that
Foundation Courses should be provided in both History and the Social
Sciences.   But over the years, there has been a realisation that the
disciplinary framework provided can and must be reduced strictly to
essentials, to what is *actually* relevant to an understanding of
contemporary France.   This is a good deal less than what the average
social scientist thinks necessary to offer his own First-Year students !
Such a paring-down and adaptation, however, can do much to lighten the
Civilisation student's load.

In Economics, whole tracts of theory can be dispensed with, notably micro-
economic theory, as long as the basic *circuits* of the economy and its
international context are presented, together with such concepts as growth,
crisis, inflation, and *niveau de vie*, and as long as the outlines of French
economic history and the history of economic doctrines in France have been
adequately presented in the History course.   It will then be possible to
give an empirical account of the French economy in the present.

In Politics likewise, much abstract theory can also be jettisoned, provided
the nature of the state, of the three branches of government, of Right and
Left, of political parties and of democratic representation is simply and
clearly presented, as well as political developments over, say, the decade
leading up to the present, as a prelude to the empirical picture of current
French political institutions.   (The latter should, by the way, include the
actual mechanisms of the electoral system, which seem to be neglected in

many textbooks.) Much of the groundwork for the study of French politics will have been laid in the History course, in respect of the growth of French governmental institutions, and of the administration, national and local, as well as the history of political ideas and of party ideologies, and of French political culture in general.

In regard to the Sociology of France, the essential concepts are those of social class and of *catégories socio-professionnelles*, and those of elites and social mobility. As has been suggested, the study of French society cannot, either, be divorced from Population Studies and so involves an introduction to the main concepts of demography, and a presentation of the development of the French population. Laurence Wylie reminded the seminar of the crucial importance of child-rearing, the family and education in determining the behaviour of the French in society, and we should also therefore resolve to devote a substantial part of our course on French society to these areas, as always in their historical context. I may add that the recent revival of public interest in French individualism, and in the range of anti-society reactions which remain endemic in French life, should encourage us to ensure no course on France does not deal with the relations, past and present, between the **individual** and society. Once again in the area of Sociology, the theoretical and conceptual framework can be limited to familiarising the students with the basic concepts mentioned above, in the context of an account of French social history, before embarking on the treatment of the current state of French society and of welfare provision.

Teaching French Civilisation through History and the Social Sciences is possible, therefore, subject to two conditions: each discipline must be handled very selectively, so that it becomes not Politics, but **Politics as applied to France,** which gives the discipline a somewhat different and narrower profile, as it is skewed towards the specifics of France, rather than towards the world, or what is worse and all too common, very largely towards the home-country. Attention to France must be maximised throughout, and here one cannot help agreeing with Homer Sutton and Linda Hantrais that, throughout, teaching should be carried on as far as is reasonable in French and through French-language texts.

There is always a case for comparative approaches: History, and still more the Social Sciences, have a universalist bent, which may relativise or even exclude France. Introductory courses in the Social Sciences taught in English and which do not even refer to France are not, alas ! unknown.

Our task is, while seeing that context and comparisons are not neglected, to try to ensure that France and French remain at the centre of all the courses taught. This is less difficult in History, where a course on France alone seems perfectly acceptable to historians although all historians would expect a study of French history to be placed in its European framework. It is enough in History, in my view, to bring in such of the European or international context and trends as are actually of importance for France. The History of Ideas in France, in particular, may call for the treatment of Locke or Marx. In the Social Sciences, there may be a good deal of geographical concentration and adaptation to be done, for if here, too, European and world phenomena of importance to France, e.g. economic crisis, must be dealt with, comparisons can be limited to those which directly concern France, such as those between the French and the US presidential systems. Other matters traditionally dealt with in Comparative Government, but which have no application to France, can on the other hand be dropped.

Literature. What then of Literature ? What seems to me to emerge from the seminar is that in the British institutions where the History-Social Sciences approach has been developed most fully, the reaction against Literature has gone too far, and there is a danger that the baby may have been thrown out with the bath-water. Literature will in fact not go away. For French Civilisation cannot be conceived without its literary and indeed its broad cultural dimension. These have always been and still remain an integral part of France's total way of life. Here the contributions from Alice Kaplan and Christopher Pinet make it clear in the first place that modern socio-critical approaches may breathe new life into teaching Literature through a study of the formation of the literary canon, and that popular culture is a powerful teaching tool. Tony Callen and Peter Findlay, with whom I have worked for many years at Portsmouth, have I hope convinced you as they long ago convinced me that Literature is an essential part of Civilisation. The history and society of France cannot be fully understood without reference to her literature and her culture at large. There is no better way to understand the *Zeitgeist* than to confront literary creations with contemporary political, social and economic ideas and trends. And there are decisive advantage here **for the study of Literature** itself. Works and aesthetic schools can be seen in their proper overall context, instead of being looked at at best in the light of

199

odd scraps of undigested data from History, the Social Sciences or wherever.

Cultural Studies and Cultural History. And this is not simply a matter of Literature. To complete his or her picture of France, the student needs to be aware of the whole field revealed by the Cultural Studies revolution. This covers not only Literature but also Art and Architecture, Music and Cinema, high and popular culture. It involves, too, as Peter Findlay and Adrian Rifkin pointed out, an inter-disciplinary collaboration between the aesthetic study of these arts and the *regard* at least of sociologists and historians. There is no faster growing area in Contemporary French History than that of Cultural History, which includes, side by side with the history of artistic creation, the study of ideas, beliefs and feelings as expressed in a community, and their manifestations in terms of practises (e.g. concert or church-going, or political activity), ideas and practises which serve in part to define that community as a community. This more anthropological approach to culture involves further a study of the ideological content of the media, education, religion and of politics itself. Though in some ways Cultural History so conceived overlaps with the traditional histories of Literature and Ideas, or even with "straight" Religious or Political History, its greater concern with ideas, beliefs and feelings as expressed by the broad mass of a community relativises somewhat the creative work of the exceptional individuals who are the providers of works of high culture, and the role of religious or political leaders. It is also concerned as much with cultural consumption as with cultural production. Cultural History thus brings us back to the concern of Christopher Pinet and American colleagues with French popular culture, in the past as well as the present, and points to the need, as a part of the study of French Civilisation, to look at the whole historical development of popular culture in France over the contemporary period, before the television age. There are some striking parallels in fact between the content of 19th-century popular novels and that of to-day's TV and press: the concern with star personalities, sensationalism and crime go back a very long way. A further whole strand of French Civilisation thus emerges here, which involves a study of the overall history of French culture from the beginning of our period, followed by an examination of the state of French culture to-day, both in terms of cultural production, high and popular, and of cultural consumption, or *pratiques culturelles*, plus of course *la politique culturelle de l'Etat*. The whole cultural field is still in process of being defined, but it is a growth-point in French history to-day, has recently been consecrated by its appearance in the programme of the *agrégation d'histoire*, and it is safe to say that it will play a growing part in the teaching of French Civilisation in the future. There are few textbooks so far, except Maurice Crubellier's seminal *Histoire culturelle de la France XIXe et XXe siécle* (Colin, 1974), but the publication of one on 20th-century France by Michéle Cointet is imminent.

What comes out of the preceding survey of how History, the Social Sciences and a study of French Culture can be combined in an overall teaching pattern on French Civilisation is in the end quite a clear and simple ideal four-strand course model, along the following lines:

> CONTEMPORARY FRENCH POLITICAL HISTORY leading into
> INTRODUCTION TO POLITICS; FRENCH POLITICS TO-DAY

> CONTEMPORARY FRENCH ECONOMIC HISTORY leading into
> INTRODUCTION TO ECONOMICS; THE FRENCH ECONOMY TO-DAY

> CONTEMPORARY FRENCH SOCIAL HISTORY leading into
> INTRODUCTION TO DEMOGRAPHY, SOCIOLOGY AND SOCIAL
> ANTHROPOLOGY; FRENCH SOCIETY TO-DAY

> CONTEMPORARY FRENCH CULTURAL HISTORY leading into
> INTRODUCTION TO CULTURAL STUDIES; FRENCH CULTURE TO-DAY

If French historical Geography and the Geography of France are added, this would make a fifth strand.

The France of everyday life. Of course such a discipline-bound approach may still not cover all the ground, and it is clearly true to say that there is a mass of facts about France essential to an understanding of French Civilisation which escapes through the meshes of even such a broad array of disciplines. This is, to my mind, one way a British observer may tend to look at what American teachers of French Civilisation have called the everyday-anthropological. There is a need to cover some of these everyday facts from an early stage of the course, for example in the context of language work, but they first need to be defined. But as Edward Knox remarks, who is to do the inventory of Civilisation ? A look at some published elementary texts such as Michaud and Torrés's *Nouveau*

Guide France (Hachette) will suggest such areas as types of wine and food, details of currency and banks, the legal system (which deserves an academic study to itself !), the PTT, hospitals, the Sécurité Sociale and other areas of French life which have their own language and conventions. British students have told me, too, how badly they need guidance about general social conventions and forms of *politesse* in France if they are to avoid social gaffes when they arrive. One scene I shall always remember is some poor benighted foreign tourist in a Paris restaurant being lectured by the waiter as to what courses properly constituted a meal, and in what order. He clearly did not **know**... I myself still feel the French have a grasp of the complexities of cheap deals on the SNCF of which I feel envious, and an innate ability to know how to end a letter which escapes me, as does the correct way to eat cheese (with a knife and fork ?). These points may begin to sound trivial, but if, as Vaughan Rogers says, it is a myth still fostered by French Literature lecturers that French Civilisation is **wholly** made up of facts about which there can be no discussion, there are an immense number of small facts about everyday life which go with the weighty matters which can be dealt with through disciplines, and they too play a part in Laurence Wylie's "total way of life of the French people." Some of them are to do with survival, and it is perfectly obvious that practical survival kits for everyday situations should in no way be despised as a part of the training we give in Civilisation.

It will be clear from this and what I have said above that I, for one, do not wish to choose between the History-plus-Social Sciences approach being developed in Britain and the everyday-anthropological favoured in the US: both seem to form an essential part of a *total* study of the French way of life, and my overall conclusion from the seminar will be seen to be that what is needed is a marriage across the Atlantic of both kinds of approach. The seminar will have been a success to my mind if it can lead in this direction. The answer to our endless questioning about just what French Civilisation consists of must surely lie in a comprehensive definition of our subject integrating the contributions of both approaches. Civilisation is everything we think it is, and more...

Progression

The seminar, having thus helped hopefully to define the ground covered by a French civilisation course, has also raised, particularly in Nicholas Wahl's paper, as in Edward Knox's, the question of progression within such a course. Nicholas Wahl's "building-blocks" approach addresses the problem primarily as it relates to post-graduate courses, and proposes the combination within discrete course units of blocks of both information and disciplinary initiation. This approach will certainly be of practical value in the planning of undergraduate courses too, where so often teaching hours for Civilisation are severely restricted.

Ultimately, however, as has already been suggested above, French Civilisation is so considerable an academic field that it cries out to occupy the whole of a degree programme in French. Only then can the full range of disciplines be deployed and all the relevant *faits de civilisation* adequately treated. And it is only then that the problems of progression and of the articulation between the contributory disciplines can be perceived clearly enough to be properly dealt with.

Experience in Portsmouth has shown that there are here a whole range of course-planning problems which are quite new and deserve increasing attention, as French Civilisation teaching develops.

As far as progression goes, despite Jolyon Howorth's (not quite serious ?) suggestion that History should come at the end of the Civilisation course, most of us will feel that a basic chronological pattern is essential, for each component of the course, since a grasp of historical origins is crucial for understanding all aspects of France to-day. That is not to say, of course, that the historical presentation of Napoleon I's centralisation should not refer forward to centralisation in the 20th-century administration. But it seems essential furthermore that the Civilisation course as a whole should be chronologically structured, so that the treatment of political, social, economic and cultural trends and events proceeds *pari passu* and that those which are contemporary with each other are treated at the same point in the course. In this way, the total pattern of each decade or period will emerge, and each phenomenon, whether political, social, economic or cultural, will be seen in the context of all the others with which it coincides in time, and as a part of a total *moment*. This is to take to its logical conclusion the principle embodied in the inter-disciplinary studies of one year mentioned by Christopher Pinet, and to make it into the fundamental structural principle of the whole History course. It involves the careful elaboration by a team of an overall chronological *grille* into which all the teaching of the History course is fitted, and the abandonment of disciplinary slots which go their own way regardless.

It seems to me that, as part of a similar *démarche*, it is essential, too, not to introduce the Social Sciences until the historical coverage in the course has reached the 20th century, since they primarily concern themelves with the present.   In this way, the Social Sciences can be brought to bear essentially on the period with which they are most concerned: such aspects as the history of political ideas and of party ideologies fit naturally into their appropriate place in the historical part of the course.   It is essential too, in my opinion, not to overburden the first introduction of the Social Science disciplines with the most elaborate parts of their respective theories and concepts, as tends to happen too often: if the latter really are applicable to France, their presentation should be delayed until the end of the course: there is much to be said in any case for beginning with a more empirically-based approach to the Social Sciences, and for not putting the theoretical cart before the empirical horse in an aprioristic and authoritarian way.

Naturally, the general principles of progression that apply to any academic course apply equally here: notably progression from the broad and general to the more narrow and specialised.   This suggests that a broader chronological sweep, covering a longer time-span, is appropriate to the earlier units of the course covering the first part of the period from the mid-18th century, whereas at the end of the course, much shorter time-spans leading up to the present are appropriate.

Finally, there should be a progression from firmly discipline-based course units at the beginning of the course to inter-disciplinary problem-based course units in the Final Year. This is essential if the disciplinary collaboration is in the end actually to take place, and not to be limited to a mere juxtaposition of discipline-based views of France which remain on parallel lines but never meet.

The way forward

All this may sound impossibly remote and utopian, in the context, on both sides of the Atlantic, of lack of time, lack of qualified colleagues who are French-speaking, and of constant pressure from the Literature lobby and politicians anxious to cut education budgets.   I would contend however that unless some such adequate pedagogic model for the disciplinary and other content and for the structural framework for French Civilisation teaching can be worked out, the subject will remain ill-defined and open to the criticisms of the Literature lobby and other rivals in the power-struggles which are the staple of our working lives. It is essential, in order to impose the subject of French Civilisation in the long run, to give it an adequate academic backbone.

The academic and political climate as it emerged at length at the seminar discussions may seem depressingly hostile, both in the US and Britain, but nothing but good can come of the attempt to define the aims and methods of our activity more clearly. Even in the short term, French Civilisation courses on a small scale can only gain from the experience gained in full-scale operations, and it is to be hoped that the present publication may be a step towards further understanding.

But undoubtedly concerted action will also be necessary, and if the seminar can also lead to such action at an international level, French Civilisation teaching can again only be strengthened thereby. Further meetings will obviously be needed, if only because the matters raised at the seminar would be enough to occupy several conferences. I conclude on this point by commending Edward Knox's paper, with its very full agenda of items for future discussion, some of which I have tried to address here. He also reminded British colleagues once again that they need to relativise their view of their current discontents as well as their view of France: US colleagues at the seminar regarded the institutional position attained by French Civilisation teaching in British higher education as enviable... So perhaps we should not look upon the Portsmouth week-end only as a discussion of French Civilisation and its discontents, the title for this book suggested by Siân Reynolds, but carry on trying to think constructively about teaching the subject, despite the hardness of the times.

"Or voilà un peu ce que j'aurais dit", as Péguy said of his failure to get a word in edgeways at Sorel's Thursdays - that is if I had had the time and the wit to do so at the seminar itself. The book has been for all the participants an occasion for afterthoughts, and I crave the reader's indulgence for mine.

Postscript

If I may add one more personal note, I can report in July 1988 that I hope to be able actually to put some of the theory I have adumbrated above into practice on the spot in France within the framework of a three-year degree course in French Language and Civilisation for foreigners at the University of Tours, to which students on year abroad or junior year abroad programmes may also be admitted in Year 1 or Year 2 to study side-by-side with those aiming at enrolment for the three years.   (For details of the programme, which is under active consideration by the University of Tours at the time of writing, with hopes of a 1989 start, *see* the Appendix below.)

EXTRACT FROM PROPOSAL FOR A THREE-YEAR STUDY PROGRAMME IN FRENCH
LANGUAGE AND CIVILISATION FOR FOREIGN STUDENTS AT THE UNIVERSITY OF
TOURS LEADING TO A DIPLOMA OF THE UNIVERSITY

CREATION D'UN DIPLOME D'UNIVERSITE DE LANGUE ET DE CIVILISATION FRANÇAISES
POUR ETUDIANTS ETRANGERS

PROJET PEDAGOGIQUE

Justificatif: un pas décisif vers l'Europe et le monde

Le projet présent vise à créer à l'Université de Tours un centre universitaire pour l'étude de la langue et de la civilisation françaises contemporaines, afin d'offrir à des étudiants étrangers une formation menant à la délivrance d'un diplôme d'université à bac + 2 et bac + 3. Le titre du diplôme sera DIPLOME DE LANGUE ET DE CIVILISATION FRANÇAISES. Cette filière préparera à des carrières à l'étranger dans l'enseignement supérieur ou secondaire, dans les services, notamment la fonction publique, ainsi que dans le commerce et l'industrie.

Plus de deux ans passés à Tours, puis trois mois passés à Paris, apporteront à l'étudiant une vision équilibrée de la France et le contact non seulement avec l'Université de Tours et avec la Touraine, mais aussi avec la capitale et toutes ses ressources intellectuelles et culturelles.

Il va sans dire que dans le cas d'une formation basée sur la langue et la civilisation françaises contemporaines, les possibilités offertes par un enseignement dispensé sur place seront légion: contact quotidien avec la langue dans son cadre naturel; contact avec des enseignants francophones intégrés normalement dans la société et non vivant à l'étranger; contact direct et régulier avec les medias et avec tous les phénomènes politiques, économiques, sociaux et culturels du temps; possibilité d'utilisation des bibliothèques françaises; possibilité de mini-stages et de visites commentées dans les entreprises, les administrations, les mairies, les tribunaux, à la Bourse, à l'Assemblée Nationale, etc.

Cette formation inter-disciplinaire de type langue et civilisation répondra en outre à une forte demande de la part des étudiants étrangers qui se détournent des études de français exclusivement basées sur la littérature et, dans leur pays comme lors de leur séjour en France, souhaitent de plus en plus étudier le français dans le contexte de la civilisation française, en suivant des programmes pluridisciplinaires.

... il sera possible d'accueillir pour un an des stagiaires étrangers, par exemple dans le cadre du programme Erasmus. Ces étudiants s'inscriront seulement en première ou en deuxième année, **mais ils suivront les mêmes cours que ceux qui sont inscrits pour le diplôme.**

Les universités étrangères apprécieront la possibilité qui leur sera ainsi offerte d'envoyer leurs étudiants pour un an à l'Université de Tours poursuivre un programme structuré où ceux-ci seront bien encadrés et auront la possibilité de passer les mêmes examens que des étudiants inscrits pour le diplôme. Le fait que les études des stagiaires se dérouleront en présence d'etudiants préparant le diplôme sera une garantie supplémentaire de sérieux.

Programme d'études

Le programme d'études pour le diplôme, centré sur la France contemporaine, sera cohérent, intégrant la langue française, l'histoire, l'histoire des idées, les sciences sociales, l'histoire littéraire, l'histoire de l'art et de l'architecture, la haute culture et la culture populaire.

L'étude de la langue, en première et deuxième année, sera conçue en fonction de l'apprentissage des pratiques essentielles pour répondre aux besoins spécifiques des étudiants à court et à long terme: compréhension écrite et orale, expression écrite et orale, à la fois dans le contexte universitaire de l'étude de la civilisation, et dans celui de la vie courante et professionnelle. Tout l'enseignement de la civilisation sera, en outre, dès le départ, dispensé en français. Les étudiants seront logés, à Tours comme à Paris, autant que possible chez l'habitant, et non pas en résidence, Chaque étudiant s'engagera, comme le font les étudiants de Middlebury College aux Etats-Unis, à ne parler que français au centre. Au bout de deux ans passés en France dans un tel bain linguistique, on peut estimer que le niveau atteint en français permettra à l'enseignement de la langue en troisième année de prendre la forme d'un cours portant moins sur des structures linguistiques que sur les techniques de rédaction et d'exposé oral, cours qui ressemblera plutôt à une "conférence de méthode" type Sciences Po'.

L'étude de la civilisation française suivra chronologiquement l'évolution de la France depuis la fin de l'Ancien Régime, en insistant de plus en plus sur la période la plus récente. A chaque stade cependant, les diverses disciplines devront collaborer pour éclairer simultanément telle période, tel problème dans l'histoire de la France; les années 1870, par exemple, sont celles de l'Impressionisme, mais aussi celles où s'établit le système moderne de gouvernement local en France.

En première année, il s'agira de faire appel aux disciplines qui sont le plus tournées vers la France du passé, en leur demandant un large panorama intégré de tout ce qui, dans le passé de la France, compte encore dans son présent. L'histoire, mais aussi l'histoire des idées (y compris celle des idées politiques et économiques) et la géographie apporteront toutes les données sur le passé qui sont nécessaires pour comprendre la vie politique économique et sociale du présent; l'histoire de la littérature, celle de l'art et de l'architecture, l'histoire de la haute culture, mais aussi celle de la culture populaire, éclaireront la culture d'aujourd'hui.

Dès la deuxième année seront introduites les sciences sociales proprement dites, qui sont plus axées sur les réalités présentes, et cela dans le contexte d'une présentation historique de la France depuis 1945.

La troisième année sera surtout celle de l'étude inter-disciplinaire des problèmes de la France du présent.

Les périodes traitées chaque année seront de plus en plus courtes, de plus en plus rapprochées du temps présent; ainsi, le niveau d'étude s'approfondira progressivement, et la spécialisation, en troisième année, portera sur la France d'aujourd'hui, mais dans le contexte d'une bonne base générale de culture contemporaine, et en histoire et en sciences sociales.

Pour permettre notamment le recrutement en première et en deuxième année d'un contingent d'étudiants qui ne s'inscriront en stage que pour une seule année - dans le cadre d'échanges type Erasmus, ou simplement au titre de year abroad ou de Junior year abroad lorsqu'il s'agit d'étudiants britanniques ou américains - il est prévu que le programme de chaque année d'études formera une entité indépendante. Cela permettra un recrutement supplémentaire de stagiaires. Les études suivies à Tours pourront être intégrées aux programmes de l'université-mère, ou simplement offrir un complément de civilisation à des programmes de licence monodisciplinaires, à dominante littéraire ou autre, suivis dans les universités étrangères.

Une première année portant sur la période qui s'étend de 1760 à nos jours; une deuxième année consacrée à la période depuis 1945, traitant de façon différente et approfondie l'histoire récente et les matières déjà effleurées à la fin de la première année, tout en offrant une solide initiation aux sciences sociales pour préparer la troisième année; une troisième année axée sur la France du présent et qui permettra de profiter de toutes les ressources de Paris: un tel programme conviendra à la fois à des étudiants inscrits pour le diplôme ou en première ou en deuxième année seulement.